The Singer's Repertoire

Singer's Repertoire

Part II
Mezzo Soprano
and Contralto

Second Edition

by

Berton Coffin

The Scarecrow Press, Inc.
New York   1960

Copyright 1960 by

Berton Coffin

L. C. Card No. 60-7265

To my daughter

Martha

in loving appreciation

Foreword

"The Singer's Repertoire" in its second edition has
been divided into four parts. Part I includes songs for Coloratura Soprano, Lyric Soprano and Dramatic Soprano.
Part II includes songs for Mezzo Soprano and Contralto.
Part III includes songs for Lyric Tenor and Dramatic Tenor
and Part IV includes songs for Baritone and Bass. This
has been thought to be a service to the individual singer who
is primarily interested only in that material which is suitable for his particular voice.

Several of the song lists have been augmented and du-
ets, trios, songs of limited range and chamber operas for
two, three or four voices have been added. Intentionally no
lists have been made of "easy" songs since this has been
felt to be a misnomer. That which is easy for one is not
necessarily easy for another. Young singers may have short
ranges but they frequently have very fine tastes, possibly
some language background and even fairly good musicianship
due to previous instrumental study. Hence, instead of a
list of "easy" songs, the compiler has listed a broad spec-
trum of songs with limited range.

"The Singer's Repertoire" is an effort to aid all
singers and teachers of singing in their repertoire problems.
The singer at no stage in his career is free from this problem. In the beginning he has to select the suitable songs
for his vocal powers and development. As he becomes a
successful amateur singer he secures various engagements
which are always presenting new song needs. Should he become a professional singer the needs will be multiplied
many times with a changing repertoire required season after
season. Should he become a teacher of singing or a vocal
coach he will have hundreds of potential singers, each one
with different needs. Therefore, no matter with what
phase of vocal work one is concerned, the repertoire problem is always present and one's storehouse is always
changing, always being added to.

"The Singer's Repertoire" has profited in its growth
and development by the advice, counsel and criticism of
many experienced singers and many noted teachers of singing.

From these discussions, four repertoire aids appear to be paramount:

1. Aids for program building (for this problem the guide lists recital songs in the various languages; songs for opening and closing recitals; and songs by classification.

2. Aids for training repertoire (this problem has been approached by indexing technical characteristics of songs).

3. Aids for specific or seasonal occasions (see Christmas, Easter, Wedding and Patriotic lists).

4. Aids in sacred repertoire (hundreds of songs have been studied and those appropriate are listed).

The above aids are based on contemporarily performed songs and arias as programmed in countless recitals, in recordings and in the media of radio and television. This mass of material has been interpolated into appropriate listings. The compiler has not assumed the position of musical analyst except for the sacred listing and in augmenting the smaller lists. Questions have not been asked as to why certain songs are sung or not sung; if the song has been found in the above mentioned sources, it is listed, otherwise it is not included in this volume. This book is based on the preselection of songs sung by noteworthy or accepted singers, and is not a compendium of all vocal repertoire which would surely approximate 100,000 song titles. It is merely a distribution of some 8,000 songs into 818 lists for the nine voice classifications rather than an annotated bibliography of songs. For each voice classification there are 71 - 92 lists whereby the characteristics of various songs are shown. It is well known to all teachers that a matching of song traits to the strengths and limitations of any singing personality will assure the individual's best success. This is a very difficult thing to do and it is hoped the problem will be made easier by the multiple listings of this work.

Due to the large number of programs examined, all voices should be represented in proportion to their natural distribution. The largest segments will be the lyric soprano and baritone, because there are more of those voices; the smallest segments will be the coloratura soprano, dramatic tenor and bass since these voices occur less frequently. The compiler has made no attempt to classify voices in this study but has merely listed the songs according to the voice classification stated on the programs.

A work of this kind can never be complete in contemporary song (although publication in this field is lamentably limited) since new songs are appearing and others are falling into disuse. However, the classic, romantic and impressionistic repertoire is now relatively stable. These songs comprise the living repertoire of today.

Boulder, Colorado

Table of Contents

Repertoire for the Mezzo Soprano Voice

American, British, French, German, Italian, Misc.

Repertoire for the Contralto Voice

American, British, French, German, Italian, Misc.

Publisher Code

† - Published by more than one company

A

ABC - ABC Music Corp.
AHC - Asherberg, Hopwood and Crew
AMI - Amici
AMM - American Music
AMP - Associated Music Publishers
ARR - Arrow Music Press
ASB - Ashbrook
ASC - Arthur P. Schmidt
ASH - Ashdown
AUG - Augener
AXE - Axelrod

B

BAF - Bayley and Ferguson
BAR - Barenreiter
BER - Berlin
BES - Bessel
BIR - Birchard
BLO - C. A. Blodgett
BMI - Broadcast Music, Inc.
BOH - Boosey and Hawkes
BOO - Boosey
BON - Bongiovani
BOS - Boston
BOT - Bote and Bock
BRA - Brandus and Cie
BRE - Bregeman
BRH - Breitkof and Haertel
BRM - Barton and Mead
BRO - Broude
BVC - Bregman, Vocco and Conn

C

CAR - C Cardilli
CFI - Carl Fischer
CHA - Chappel
CHE - Chester
CHM - Champagne
CHO - Choudens
CMC - Composers Music Corp.
CMP - Composers Press
CNN - Conn
CRA - Cramer
CRF - Crawford
CRZ - Cranz
CSC - Cos Cob
CST - Costallet
CUR - Curwen

D

DBH - Desylvia, Brown and Henderson
DES - DeSantis
DIT - Ditson
DRE - Dreiklang
DUR - Durand

E

ECS - E. C. Schirmer
ELK - Elkin
ELV - Elkan-Vogel
ENO - Enoch
ESC - Eschig

F

FAM - Famous
FEI - Feist
FLA - Flammer
FOE - Foetisch
FOX - Fox
FRA - Frank
FRL - Forlivesi
FRS - Forster
FST - Forsyth
FTZ - FitzSimmons

G

GAL - Galaxy
GAM - Gamble Hinged (GAH)
GER - Gershwin
GLO - Glocken Verlag
GOL - Goldsea
GOT - Goodwin and Tabb
GRA - H. W. Gray
GSC - G. Schirmer

H

HAC - Hachette
HAM - Hamelle
HAN - Hansen
HAR - Harms
HEU - Heugel
HHE - Hinds, Haydn and
       Eldredge
HNR - Heinrichofen
HNZ - Hunzinger
HOM - Homeyer
HRM - Harmonia (HMP)
HSC - Hans Schneider

I

INT - International

J

JCH - John Church
JFI - J. Fischer
JOB - Jobert
JUR - Jurgenson

JWI - J. Williams

K

KAL - Kalmus
KIS - Kistner
KSS - Kustner and Siegel

L

LAC - Lacour
LED - Leduc
LEE - Leeds
LEM - Lemoine

M

MAR - Marks
MAT - Mathot
MCG - MacGimsey
MCR - McLaughlin, Reilly
MER - Mercury
MET - Methuen
MLR - Miller
MLS - Mills
MOR - Morris, E. H.
MOV - Movietone
MUP - Music Press

N

NAG - Nagel Verlag
NEM - New Music
NOR - Norsky Verlag
NOV - Novello

O

OCT - Octava Music Co.
OXF - Oxford

P

PAR - Paragon
PEE - Peer
PET - Peters
PON - William Pont
PRE - Presser
PRM - Paramount

PRO - Prowse
PTR - Paterson

R

RBR - Riker, Brown and
      Wellington
REM - Remick
RIC - Ricordi
ROB - Robbins
ROG - Winthrop Rogers
ROM - Roma
ROU - Rouart, Lerolle
ROW - Row

S

SAL - Salabert
SC - Schott
SCH - Schlesinger
SEN - Senart
SHA - Shapiro
SHU - Schuberth
SIM - Simroch
SIR - Sirene
SON - Sonzogno
SOU - Southern Music Co.
SPA - Spada
STB - Stainer Bell
SUM - Summy

T

TEM - Templeton
TRA - Transcontinental

U

UME - Union Musical
      Española
UNI - Universal

V

VIC - Victoria
VLP - Valley Press

W

WEI - Weinberger
WHB - Whitney Blake
WHI - White Smith
WIL - Williamson
WIT - Witmark
WLL - Willis
WOO - Wood
WOR - Words and Music
WTR - Weintraub

Z

ZER - Zerboni

Directions for Use

All songs are listed alphabetically by composer with the song listings alphabetized under each composer. The lists are to be read in the following manner: first, the composer's name is given, then the title, then the opera, operetta, cantata, oratorio, if it is an aria. In cases where a solo instrument accompanies the voice and piano that instrument has been indicated.

Next are shown the keys HML. The last letter of the key is important: should it be L - the low range is shown; if the last is M, the medium range is shown; and if it is H - the high. BF-EF indicates a range of B flat to E flat (CS-FS would indicate C sharp to F sharp). The three letters at the extreme right of page are a code for the publisher (code at front of book, i.e. GSC indicates G. Schirmer; SC indicates Schott). Where a dagger (†) appears the song is published by more than one firm.

The Miscellaneous listings are total lists including songs other than those found in the American, British, French, German and Italian listings. However, if there is a void in any of these lists (American, British, French, German, Italian), those songs will be included in the Miscellaneous list. Latin songs always appear in the Miscellaneous lists as do the Portuguese, Hungarian, Hebrew, etc.

This book does not include popular music as such but does have a separate listing of the lighter numbers which are frequently needed. These songs are found under the heading - Songs of Popular Appeal.

The Handel Songs are found in the British, German and Italian lists; Wagner in the German and French; and Mozart in the Italian, German and French. American compositions are found in the American lists regardless of whether French, German or Italian texts are used. Likewise English composers are in the English lists.

The classical Italian arias are listed under song rather than opera because the works are no longer staged and they are thought of as song literature.

Part II

Mezzo Soprano

American Recital Songs

Mezzo Soprano

Alberti	My lady sleeps	M	DS-FS	AMP
Bacon	Is there such a thing as day?			
-----	Let down the bars			
-----	Lonesome grove	HM	C-E	CFI
Barber	A nun takes the veil	MH	C-G	GSC
-----	Dover Beach	M	BF-F	GSC
	String quartet			
-----	I hear an army	LH	D-AF	GSC
-----	Monks and raisons	M	DF-E	GSC
-----	Nocturne	HM	CS-FS	GSC
-----	Rain has fallen	HM	D-E	GSC
-----	Sleep now	MH	EF-AF	GSC
-----	Sure on this shining night	MH	D-G	GSC
-----	The daisies	M	C-F	GSC
-----	The Queen's face on the	L	C-E	GSC
	summery coin			
Barnett	Music, when soft voices die	M	C-E	GSC
Bartholomew	When we are parted	M	CS-E	GAL
Beach	Ah, love but a day			ASC
-----	Wouldn't that be queer?	HM		ASC
Bernstein	Afterthought			
Bibb	A rondel of spring	HL	BF-D	GSC
Bone and Fenton	Blue water	MH	DF-AF	CFI
Bowles	Heavenly grass	ML	B-E	GSC
-----	Letter to Freddy	M	EF-EF	GSC
-----	On a quiet conscience	M	C-F	MUP
-----	Sugar in the cane	M	D-FS	GSC
Braine	Dawn awakes	HML	A-D	ASC
Branscombe	Across the blue Aegean	M	G-G	GAL
-----	At the postern gate	MH	DF-AF	ASC
Browning	Phoenix			
Campbell-Tipton	A spirit flower	LHM	B-G	GSC

(Campbell-Tipton)	After sunset	HM	DS-A	GSC
-----	Invocation	L	C-FS	GSC
-----	The crying of water	LH	FS-GS	GSC
Carpenter	Berceuse de guerre	M	C-G	GSC
-----	Dansons la gigue	M	B-E	GSC
-----	Don't ceare	M	C-D	GSC
-----	Go, lovely rose	M	DF-EF	GSC
-----	I am like a remnant of a cloud of autumn	L	BF-F	GSC
-----	If	M	D-E	GSC
-----	Light, my light	M	C-G	GSC
-----	May the maiden			DIT
-----	On the seashore of endless worlds	M	C-FS	GSC
-----	Serenade	LH	CS-A	GSC
-----	Slumber song	ML	BF-F	GSC
-----	The cock shall crow	M	B-E	GSC
-----	The day is no more	M	GS-DS	GSC
-----	The green river	M	B-E	GSC
-----	The Lawd is smilin' through the do'	L	B-E	GSC
-----	The player Queen	M	BF-EF	GSC
-----	The pools of peace	M	D-F	GSC
-----	The sleep that flits on baby's eyes	M	B-FS	GSC
-----	To a young gentleman	M	C-F	GSC
-----	To one unknown	M	A-DS	GSC
-----	When I bring to you colour'd toys	LM	CS-FS	GSC
Carter	Dust of snow	M	D-E	AMP
Castelnuovo-Tedesco	Springtime	M		CHE
-----	The daffodils	M	BF-F	GAL
Chadwick	Allah	LH	CS-GS	ASC
Chanler	The doves	M	C-F	AMP
-----	Wind			GSC
Charles	Clouds	HML	C-EF	GSC
-----	Song of exaltation	M		GSC
-----	Sweet song of long ago	HML	A-D	GSC
-----	The white swan	HL	C-F	GSC
-----	When I have sung my songs	HM	BF-EF	GSC
Clough-Leighter	My lover he comes on the skee	HM	D-F	BOS
-----	Who knows?	M		GSC
Cowell	St. Agnes morning	M	C-G	MER
-----	The donkey	M	D-F	MER

24

Creston	Joy			
-----	Out of the dusk			
Crist	Into a ship dreaming	LMH	EF-GS	CFI
-----	Love's offering			
-----	Nina Bobo	HL		CFI
-----	O come hither	HM	B-GS	CFI
Davis	Nancy Hanks	H	D-G	GAL
Dello Joio	Mill doors	M	D-E	CFI
-----	New born	M	C-D	CFI
-----	The assassination			CFI
-----	There is a lady sweet and kind	M	C-F	CFI
Diamond	Let nothing disturb thee	M	C-F	AMP
-----	The shepherd boy	M		SOU
Dobson	Yasmin	M		GSC
Dougherty	Declaration of independence	L	C-C	GSC
-----	Love in the dictionary	M	C-G	GSC
-----	Loveliest of trees	HM	C-E	BOH
-----	Serenader			
-----	Song for autumn			
-----	The K' e	M	D-F	GSC
-----	The taxi			
Duke	Evening			
-----	I can't be talkin' of love	H	CS-G	GSC
-----	I've dreamed of sunsets	M	C-G	GSC
-----	Loveliest of trees	L	C-D	GSC
-----	Luke Havergal	M	BF-F	CFI
-----	On a March day	M	B-GF	BOH
-----	To Karen, singing	M	CS-G	ELV
-----	XXth century	M		VLP
-----	Viennese waltz	H	C-GF	ROW
-----	Voices	H	FS-A	BOH
-----	White in the moon the long road lies	M		VLP
Dukelsky	The ladies of St. James			
Edmunds	Billy boy	ML	BF-EF	ROW
-----	Fare you well	MH	F-AF	ROW
-----	Milk maids	M	DF-F	MER
Edwards	Awake beloved	ML	C-F	GSC
-----	Little shepherd's song			MLS
-----	Sometimes at close of day	HML	C-E	GSC
Elwell	Music I heard	M		AMP
-----	Renoucement	M	G-G	GSC
-----	The road not taken	M	B-FS	GSC
Engel	A decade	M	F-F	GSC
-----	A sprig of rosemary	M	EF-F	GSC
-----	Sea shell	M	EF-EF	GSC
Fairchild	A memory			BOS

25

Foote	On the way to Kew			ASC
Gaines	My heart hath a mind			
Ganz	A memory	HM	B-D	GSC
Giannini	Be still my heart			ELV
-----	Tell me, o blue, blue sky	H		RIC
Gilberte	Two roses	LMH	CS-G	CFI
Golde	Calls	HL	BF-EF	GSC
-----	O beauty, passing beauty	MH	CS-GS	GSC
-----	Sudden light	HL		RIC
-----	Who knows	HM	BF-F	GSC
Griffes	By a lonely forest pathway	HML	A-EF	GSC
-----	Night on ways unknown has fallen	L	GS-F	GSC
-----	O'er the Tarn's unruffled mirror	HL	G-E	GSC
-----	Sorrow of Mydath	M		GSC
-----	The dreamy lake	H	GS-GS	GSC
-----	The lament of Ian the proud	MH	DS-AS	GSC
-----	We'll to the woods and gather May	M	D-F	GSC
Hadley	Make me a song	H	C-AF	GSC
-----	My shadow			ASC
-----	The time of parting	HLM	E-G	CFI
Hageman	Animal crackers	HL	C-D	GSC
-----	At the well	LH	EF-AF	GSC
-----	Charity	LMH	DF-AF	GSC
-----	Do not go, my love	HL	B-EF	GSC
-----	Evening	HL		RIC
-----	Miranda	HL		GAL
-----	Music I heard with you	MH	E-A	GAL
-----	Voices			
Harris	Agatha Morley	M	C-D	CFI
-----	Someone came knocking at my door	M		GAL
-----	Fog	M	D-F	CFI
-----	Vanished summer	M	C-E	GAL
Hindemith	Echo	H	D-FS	AMP
-----	Envoy	M	EF-F	AMP
-----	The wildflower's song	MH	E-G	AMP
Hopkinson	Beneath a weeping willow's shade	H	D-G	†
-----	Give me thy heart			
-----	My days have been so wondrous free	LH	EF-G	†
Horsman	In the yellow dusk	MH	FS-A	GSC
Hovaness	How I adore thee	M		WHB
Howe	Berceuse	HM	EF-F	GSC
Kagen	Upstream	H	CS-F	WTR

Kingsford	Command	HLM	EF-G	GSC
-----	Courage	M	C-F	GSC
-----	Wallpaper for a little girl's room	M	BF-F	GSC
Kramer	Allah			
-----	For a dream's sake	HL		JFI
-----	Our lives together	HL	D-E	GAL
-----	Swans	HL		RIC
La Forge	To a messenger	HLM	CF-G	GSC
Lamont	Music			
Levitzki	Ah, thou beloved one	H	EF-AF	GSC
Lockwood	O, lady, let the sad tears fall	M		MER
MacDowell	The swan bent low	LH		ELK
Mana-Zucca	Rachem Trumpet	HML		CHA
-----	Speak to me			
Manning	Chinoise			
Metcalf	At nightfall	HML	C-DF	ASC
Mopper	Men	M	D-FS	BOS
Naginski	Look down, fair moon			
-----	Night song at Amalfi	M	D-EF	GSC
-----	The pasture	M	BF-EF	GSC
Nevin	One spring morning	MH	DS-F	BOS
Nordoff	Serenade	H	CS-FS	AMP
-----	There shall be more joy	M	CS-FS	AMP
-----	This is the shape of the leaf	M	B-E	SC
-----	Willow River	H	D-G	AMP
Olmstead	Thy sweet singing	HL	BF-EF	GSC
Ormond	Pierrot	HM		RIC
Parker	The lark now leaves her watery nest	LH	D-BF	JCH
Porter, Q.	Music, when soft voices die	HM	D-C	MUP
Protheroe	Ah love, but a day	LMH	F-AF	GAM
Rawls	The balloon man	L	A-FS	AMP
Rogers	Requiem			
-----	The last song	MLH	E-AF	GSC
-----	Time for making songs	HM	CS-F	DIT
-----	Wind song	LM	C-G	GSC
Rorem	The lordly Hudson	M	DF-G	MER
Rummel	Ecstasy	LMH	GF-AF	GSC
Sacco	Jabberwock from through the looking glass			
-----	Mexican serenade	HL	D-EF	BOS
-----	Rapunzel	MH	FS-BF	GSC
-----	The ragpicker	MH	C-AF	GSC
Saint Leger	April			
Salter	The cry of Rachel	LH	C-AF	GSC

Sargent	File for future reference	M	CS-E	DIT
-----	Manhattan joy ride	M	D-F	GSC
-----	Twentieth Century	H	EF-GS	LEE
Schuman	Holiday song	M	C-F	GSC
-----	Orpheus with his lute	M	C-FS	GSC
Silberta	You shall have your red rose			
Smith	An ocean idyl			
Spencer	For whom the bell tolls	MH	F-AF	BOS
Spross	Will o' the wisp			JCH
Stein	The puffin	M		CFI
Still	If you should go			LEE
Swanson	Joy	M	BF-EF	LEE
-----	The valley	L	BF-DF	LEE
Taylor	As love a sleeping lay			
Thompson	Velvet shoes	M	C-E	ECS
Thomson	Dirge	M	D-F	GSC
-----	Preciosilla	H	EF-A	GSC
Tureman	A winter sunset	L	BF-E	GSC
Tyson	Noon and night	LH	F-AF	GSC
-----	Sea moods	LH	E-AF	GSC
Wagenaar	I stood in dreams of darkness	M	CS-FS	GSC
-----	Look, Edwin!	M	C-F	GSC
Ware	This day is mine	MH	EF-AF	BOS
Warner	Hurdy gurdy	M	D-F	CFI
Warren	Snow towards evening	LH	EF-AF	GSC
-----	We two	LH	E-A	GSC
-----	When you walk through woods			
Watts	Green branches	HM		DIT
-----	Joy	HL	D-F	GSC
-----	Like music on the waters	H		GSC
-----	Transformation	ML	AS-DS	GSC
-----	Wild tears	L	A-F	GSC
Weaver	A book of verses	H	D-AF	GAL
Weill	In autumn			
Worth	Midsummer	LM	E-A	GSC

British Recital Songs

Mezzo Soprano

Arne, T.	Come away, death	M	C-AF	AUG
-----	In infancy			NOV
-----	Where the bee sucks	HM		†
-----	Why so pale and wan?			GSC
Bainton	Ring out, wild bells	M	C-EF	OXF
Bantock	A feast of lanterns	HM	D-F	GAL
-----	Evening song			

(Bantock)	Hymn to Aphrodite			
-----	I loved thee once, Atthis			
-----	Silent strings	MH	F-G	BOO
-----	The celestial weaver			
-----	Yung Yang	MH	E-G	GAL
Bax	A lullaby			
-----	Cradle song			CHA
Benjamin	Calm sea and mist			CUR
-----	Hedgerow			CUR
Besley	Time, you old gipsy man!	L	A-E	BOO
Brewer	The fairy pipers	HML		BOH
Bridge	All things that we clasp	HL		BOS
-----	Love went a-riding	HL		BOS
-----	Mantle of blue	H	D-F	ROG
-----	O that it were so	LMH	D-G	CHA
Butterworth	Loveliest of trees			AUG
-----	When I was one and twenty			AUG
Clarke	Eight o'clock			ROG
-----	Shy one	HL	BF-G	BOH
-----	The seal man	M		BOH
Coleridge- Taylor	Big lady moon			BOO
-----	Life and death	HML		ASC
-----	She rested by the broken brook	HL		DIT
Delius	Love's philosophy			†
-----	Twilight fancies	M	D-FS	CFI
Dowland	Come again! sweet love	M	D-E	STB
-----	Come away			BOO
-----	Deare, if you change			BOO
-----	Flow, my tears	M	D-E	STB
-----	Sorrow, sorrow stay	M	D-D	BOS
Dunhill	The cloths of Heaven	LM	EF-G	STB
Edmunds	I know my love	HL	BF-EF	ROW
-----	The faucon	M	D-F	MER
Elgar	Like to the damask rose			FOX
-----	Pleading	HML		NOV
-----	Shepherd's song			AHC
-----	The swimmer			BOO
-----	Where corals lie	HL		BOO
German	Charming Chloe	HML		NOV
Gibbs	Five eyes	HL	D-D	BOS
Goossens	Melancholy	M		CHE
Green	My lips shall speak the praise	M	E-F	OXF
-----	Salvation belongeth unto the Lord	M	F-EF	OXF
Gurney	Under the greenwood tree			ROG
Handel	Pack clouds away			PAT

29

Harty	Across the door			NOV
Head	A piper	HL		BOO
-----	Sweet chance that led my steps abroad	LM	C-F	BOH
-----	The ships of Arcady	ML	BF-EF	BOH
-----	Why have you stolen my delight?	LH		BOH
Henschel	Morning-hymn	MH	DS-GS	†
Holst	Creation			GSC
-----	Indra (God of storm and battle)	M	B-F	CHE
-----	The heart worships	ML	BF-D	STB
-----	Weep ye no more	M		STB
Horn	Cherry ripe	M	D-G	†
-----	I've been roaming	L	B-E	†
Ireland	Bed in summer			CUR
Johnson	Dear, do not your fair beauty wrong			DIT
Milford	So sweet love seemed Cello	HL	D-D	GRA
Morley	It was a lover and his lass	HM		DIT
Murray	The wandering player	M	C-F	CFI
Peterkin	A curse on a closed gate Voice and viola	M	D-E	OXF
-----	The garden of bamboos	M	EF-F	OXF
Pilkington	Rest, sweet nymphs			STB
Purcell	Ah, how pleasant 'tis to love			AUG
-----	Hark! how all things with one sound rejoice			NOV
-----	If music be the food of love	M	D-G	BOO
-----	Man is for woman made			
-----	Not all my torments			NOV
-----	There's not a swain on the plain	M	B-G	BAF
Quilter	Blow, blow thou winter wind	HL	C-E	BOO
-----	Dream valley	H	EF-GF	ROG
-----	Drink to me only	LMH	GF-GF	BOH
-----	Fairy lullaby			
-----	Music and moonlight	L	C-EF	CUR
-----	O mistress mine	HML		BOO
-----	The fuchsia tree			BOO
Ronald	Love, I have won you	HML	EF-EF	ENO
-----	Southern song			ENO
-----	The dove			ENO
Rosseter	When Laura smiles	LM	D-E	STB
Sanderson	Jewels			
-----	Quiet	ML	AF-EF	BOH

30

Scott	Lullaby	MML	BF-DF	GAL
-----	The unforeseen	HML		GAL
Sharp	My mother did so before me			MEU
-----	Whistle daughter, whistle			DIT
Shaw	Song of the Palanquin bearers	LH	E-F	CUR
Somervell	A song of sleep			
Stephenson	Love is a sickness	HML	C-D	BOO
-----	Ships that pass in the night	HML	DF-DF	BOO
Sullivan	Orpheus with his lute			BOO
Vaughn Williams	A piper			OXF
-----	Bright is the ring of words	L		BOH
-----	How can the tree but wither			OXF
-----	Linden-Lea	HML	C-D	BOS
-----	Silent noon			GSC
-----	The call	M	D-F	STB
-----	The twilight people	L	BF-EF	OXF
-----	The water mill	L	C-D	OXF
Walton	Lay of the silver Persian			
Warlock	Sleep			OXF
Wilson	Phillis has such charming graces	ML	CS-EF	BOO

French Recital Songs

Mezzo Soprano

Anon	Lamentation napolitaine			
Aubert	Le vaincu			DUR
-----	Le visage penché			DUR
-----	Vieille chanson espagnole			DUR
Bemberg	Chant hindou	HML	A-EF	†
Berlioz	La captive	HL		GSC
-----	Le spectre de la rose			CST
-----	L'isle inconnue			CST
-----	Villanelle	H	E-FS	†
Berton	Hymne d'amour	HM	B-DS	LRO
Bizet	Adieu de l'hôtesse arabe	H	BF-G	†
-----	Eglogue			
-----	Pastorale	H	C-FS	GSC
Chabrier	Les cigales	HML		†
-----	Romance de l'étoile			ENO
-----	Villanelle des petits canards	HML	B-E	†
Chaminade	Chant slave			GSC
-----	The silver ring	HM	BF-F	GSC

31

Charpentier	Les yeux de Berthe			HEU
Chausson	Chanson perpétuelle	H	CS-GS	ROU
-----	Dans la forêt	HL		INT
-----	Le charme	HM	BF-EF	HAM
-----	Le colibri	M	F-GF	BOS
-----	Le temps des lilas	MH	D-GS	†
-----	Les papillons	M	C-F	GSC
Cocquard	Hai luli			GSC
Debussy	Ballade des femmes de Paris			DUR
-----	Ballade que fait Villon à requeste de sa mère			DUR
-----	Beau soir	LH	C-FS	†
-----	C'est l'extase	LH	CS-A	†
-----	Chevaux de bois	H	C-G	†
-----	Cinq poèmes de Baudelaire			DUR
-----	Colloque sentimental			DUR
-----	De grève	HL		†
-----	De soir	HL		†
-----	En sourdine	M	C-FS	†
-----	Fantoches	H	D-A	JOB
-----	Il pleure dans mon coeur	LH	CS-GS	†
-----	Je tremble en voyant ton visage			DUR
-----	L'échelonnement des haïes			HAM
-----	L'ombre des arbres			†
-----	La chevelure	M	CF-FS	†
-----	La flûte de Pan		B-B	†
-----	La grotte			DUR
-----	La mer est plus belle	HL		INT
-----	La mort des amants			†
-----	Le faune			DUR
-----	Le son du cor	HL		†
-----	Le temps a laissié son manteau			DUR
-----	Le tombeau des Naïades			JOB
-----	Les ingénus			DUR
-----	Mandoline	HM	BF-F	†
-----	Noël des enfants qui n'ont plus de maisons			DUR
-----	Placet futile			DUR
-----	Recueillement			DUR
Delibes	Le rossignol	M		GSC
-----	Passepied	LH	DS-CS	GSC
Duparc	Au pays où se fait la guerre			SAL
-----	Chanson triste	MH	FS-AF	†
-----	La vague et la cloche	HL		ROU
-----	La vie antérieure	HL		†
-----	Lamento	ML	EF-EF	†
-----	Le manoir de Rosamunde	HL	B-F	BOS

(Duparc)	L'invitation au voyage	HM	E-F	†
-----	Phidylé	MH	EF-AF	BOS
-----	Testament	HL		INT
Dupont	Cendrillon	M		
Fauré	Adieu	MH	F-F	†
-----	Après un rêve	HM	C-F	GSC
-----	Arpège	MH	E-FS	HAM
-----	Au cimetière	LH	D-F	†
-----	Automne	MH	D-FS	GSC
-----	C'est l'extase	HL	C-FF	GSC
-----	Clair de lune	MH	C-G	†
-----	Dans les ruines d'une abbaye	M	E-FS	†
-----	En prière	H	F-F	†
-----	La fée aux chansons	LH	F-F	†
-----	Le parfum impérissable	LH	GF-GF	
-----	Le secret	LH	F-G	†
-----	Les berceaux	LMH	BF-G	†
-----	Mandoline	HL	F-E	†
-----	Nocturne	H	F-A	MAR
-----	Notre amour	H	DS-B	†
-----	Prison	LH		†
-----	Rencontre	H	EF-AF	†
-----	Serenade Toscane	MH	G-AF	HAM
-----	Soir	LH	D-GS	†
-----	Spleen	H	E-FS	MAR
-----	Toujours	LH	F-AF	†
Ferrari	Le miroir	M	E-F	GSC
Février	L'intruse	M	B-DF	HEU
Fourdrain	Alger le soir	M		RIC
-----	Carnaval	M	C-F	RIC
-----	Il neige des fleurs			
Franck	Le mariage des roses	M	E-FS	BOS
-----	Lied	LH	FS-FS	†
-----	Nocturne	LH		†
Garat	Dans le printemps de mes années	M		DUR
Georges	Hymne au soleil	LH	E-A	HOM
-----	La pluie	HL		INT
Godard	Florian's song	LMH	D-FS	GSC
Gounod	Adore and be still	HL		GSC
-----	Au printemps	LMH	DF-AF	GSC
-----	Au rossignol	LMH	D-G	CHO
-----	Vénise	HL		INT
Hahn	A Chloris	H	DS-FS	HEU
-----	D'une prison	L	BF-EF	HEU
-----	L'heure exquise	M	DF-F	†
-----	Les cygnes			HEU
-----	Offrande	M	D-D	†

(Hahn)	Paysage	MH	EF-G	HEU
-----	Si mes vers avaient des ailes	HLM	B-FS	†
Honegger	Chanson (Ronsard)			SEN
-----	Les cloches			SEN
-----	Psalm 130 (Mimaamaquim)			SAL
Hue	Berceuse triste			
-----	J'ai pleuré en rêve	HL	D-E	BOS
-----	Sur l'eau			HEU
Indy	Lied maritime	LH	B-G	†
Koechlin	L'hiver	H	E-G	†
-----	La lune	M	C-F	ROU
Lalo	Chant breton	M	E-E	HAM
Leguerney	L'adieu	M	B-FS	DUR
Lenormand	Quelle souffrance	HM	AF-F	HAM
Liszt	Jeanne d'Arc au Bucher			
Lully	Au clair de la lune	H	E-D	CFI
Martini	Plaisir d'amour	M	BF-EF	GSC
Massenet	Crépuscule	M	D-E	GSC
-----	Marquise			
Messiaen	Le sourire	H		DUR
-----	Pourquoi	H		DUR
Milhaud	Chansons de négresse			SAL
-----	La tourterelle	M	B-G	DUR
Paladilhe	Lamento provinçal	M	CS-FS	HOM
-----	Les trois prières			
-----	Psyché	HM	BF-F	GSC
Paulin	Que deviennent les roses			
Pessard	L'adieu du matin	ML	BF-D	GSC
Pierné	Ils étaient trois petits chats blancs			MAR
-----	Le moulin	ML	C-E	BOS
Poldowski	Colombine	H	D-GF	CHE
-----	Dansons la gigue	M	EF-G	MAR
-----	Spleen	M	D-F	CHE
Poulenc	A sa guitare	M	D-FS	DUR
-----	Air grave			ROU
-----	Air vif	H	C-AF	ROU
-----	Amoureuse	M	BS-F	DUR
-----	Avant le cinéma	M		ROU
-----	Fleurs	M	DF-F	ROU
-----	Hôtel			AMP
-----	Miroirs brulants			DEI
-----	Rodeuse au front de verre	M	BF-F	DUR
-----	Violon			ROU
-----	Voyage à Paris			AMP
Ravel	Asie	M	BF-G	DUR
-----	Chanson francaise			
-----	D'Anne qui me jecta	HM	CS-FS	GSC

(Ravel)	Kaddisch	H	C-G	DUR
-----	La flûte enchantée	M	DS-FS	DUR
-----	La pintade			DUR
-----	Le martin-pêcheur			DUR
-----	Le paon	M	C-F	DUR
-----	Manteau de fleurs	H		INT
-----	Nicolette	L	B-FS	ELK
-----	Sainte	M	C-G	ELV
-----	Sur l'herbe	MH	C-G	DUR
-----	Tout gai!	MH	EF-F	
-----	Trois beaux oiseaux du paradis			DUR
-----	Vocalise en forme de habanera	MH	BF-G	MAR
Rhené-Baton	Berceuse			DUR
-----	Sérénade mélancolique			
Rousseau	Arpèges			
Roussel	A un jeune gentilhomme			
-----	Le jardin mouillé	M	C-FS	ROU
Saint-Saëns	Aimons-nous			DUR
-----	L'attente			DUR
-----	La cloche	LH	DF-AF	†
-----	Le lever de la lune			DUR
-----	Mai	H	G-FS	DUR
-----	Tristesse			
-----	Tournoiement			DUR
Satie	Daphénéo			ROU
-----	Je te veux			SAL
-----	La statue de bronze			ROU
-----	Le chapelier			ROU
Severac	Chanson de Blaisine			
-----	Chanson pour le petit cheval			ROU
-----	Ma poupée chérie			ROU
Tremisot	Novembre			ENO
-----	Nuit d'été			
Widor	Contemplation	HL	BF-AF	
-----	Je ne veux pas autre chose	HL	C-EF	HAM
-----	Non credo			DUR

German Recital Songs

Mezzo Soprano

Ahle	Bruenstiges Verlangen	M	E-E	GSC
Bach, J.S.	Bist du bei mir	HML	A-EF	†
-----	Come Christians greet this day	L	BF-F	CFI

35

(Bach, J.S.)	Dir, Dir Jehovah			†
-----	Komm suesser Tod	MH	C-G	†
-----	Liebster Herr Jesu			BRH
-----	O Jesulein suess			
Bach, W.F.	No blade of grass can flourish			DIT
Beethoven	An die Geliebte	M	E-E	†
-----	Andenken			†
-----	Busslied			†
-----	Das Geheimnis			
-----	Die Ehre Gottes	HL	AF-EF	†
-----	Die Trommel geruehret			†
-----	Faithfu' Johnie			
-----	Ich liebe dich	HL	BF-DF	†
-----	Mignon (Kennst du das land)	M	E-FS	AUG
-----	Vom Tode	L	A-EF	GSC
-----	Wonne der Wehmut			†
Brahms	Ach, wende diesen Blick			†
-----	Alte Liebe	HL	C-F	†
-----	Am Sonntag Morgen	L	CS-FS	†
-----	An eine Aeolsharfe	H	EF-AF	†
-----	Auf dem Kirchhofe	HL	BF-EF	CFI
-----	Auf dem See	HL	D-F	†
-----	Bei dir sind meine Gedanken	MH	E-FS	†
-----	Blinde Kuh			†
-----	Botschaft	HL	D-F	†
-----	Das Maedchen spricht	H	E-FS	†
-----	Dein blaues Auge	MH	BF-G	†
-----	Der Jaeger	HL		†
-----	Der Kranz			†
-----	Der Schmied	HL	EF-EF	†
-----	Der Tod, das ist die kuehle Nacht	L	AF-F	†
-----	Die Mainacht	HL	BF-FF	†
-----	Dort in den Weiden	LH	A-A	†
-----	Es traeumte mir			†
-----	Feldeinsamkeit	HL	C-EF	†
-----	Fruehlingstrost	LH	E-A	†
-----	Gestillte Sehnsucht Viola and piano			†
-----	Immer leiser wird mein Schlummer	LH	DF-A	†
-----	In Waldeseinsamkeit	H	ES-G	†
-----	Klage	LH	FS-FS	†
-----	Lerchengesang	LH	FS-GS	†
-----	Liebestreu	ML	C-F	†
-----	Maedchenlied	HL		†

(Brahms)	Meine Liebe ist gruen	MLH	ES-A	†
-----	Mit vierzig Jahren	HL	FS-D	CFI
-----	Mondenschein	LH	D-GF	†
-----	Muss es eine Trennung geben?	LH	FS-FS	†
-----	Nachtigall	MHL	BF-FS	†
-----	Nicht mehr zu dir zu gehen			†
-----	O komm holde Sommernacht			†
-----	O kuehler Wald	MH	A-F	†
-----	O liebliche Wangen	MLH	E-G	†
-----	O wuesst' ich doch den Weg zurueck	H	E-FS	†
-----	Salamander			†
-----	Salome			†
-----	Sapphische Ode	HML		†
-----	Sehnsucht	H	EF-AF	†
-----	Sommerabend			†
-----	Sonntag	H	D-G	†
-----	Spanisches Lied			†
-----	Staendchen	HL	BF-E	†
-----	Steig' auf, geliebter Schatten	HL	BF-EF	†
-----	Tambourliedchen			†
-----	Therese	HL	B-D	†
-----	Treue Liebe	LMH	DS-E	†
-----	Ueber die Haide			†
-----	Vergebliches Staendchen	LMH	E-FS	†
-----	Verzagen	MH	CS-FS	†
-----	Von ewiger Liebe	LMH	B-AF	†
-----	Wehe, so willst du mich wieder			PET
-----	Wenn du nur zuweilen laechelst			†
-----	Wie froh und frisch	HL	B-E	†
-----	Wiegenlied			
-----	Wie Melodien zieht es	HL	A-E	†
-----	Willst du, dass ich geh'?	L	C-G	†
-----	Wir wandelten	LH	EF-GF	†
Franz	Abends	HM	C-EF	†
-----	Das macht das dunkel-gruene Laub	HL		†
-----	Die blauen Fruehlingsaugen	HL		†
-----	Die helle Sonne leuchtet			
-----	Ein Stuendlein wohl vor Tag			†
-----	Er ist gekommen	HL	EF-F	†
-----	Es hat die Rose sich beklagt	LH	DF-F	†

(Franz)	Es ragt ins Meer der Runenstein	HL	G-F	†
-----	For music	ML	C-D	†
-----	Fruehling und Liebe	HL		†
-----	Im Herbst	HM	A-F	†
-----	Mutter, o sing mich zur Ruh	HL	E-G	†
-----	Sonnenuntergang	HL	CS-FS	†
-----	Staendchen	HL		GSC
-----	Sterne mit den gold'nen Fuesschen	HL	DS-E	†
Handel	Dank sei Dir, Herr	M	CS-E	†
Hassler	Gagliarda			SIM
-----	Tanzlied			SIM
Haydn	My mother bids me bind my hair	M	E-E	†
-----	She never told her love	HL	B-D	DIT
-----	The mermaid's song	M	C-F	PRE
-----	The spirit's song	M	B-GF	†
-----	The wanderer			
Himmel	Die Sendung			SIM
Hindemith	Pietà from Marienleben			AMP
Jensen	Am Ufer des Flusses des Manzanares	H	D-FS	GSC
-----	Wie so bleich			
Kahn	Es geht ein Wehen durch den Wald Violin, cello and piano			
-----	Mein Herzblut geht in Spruengen Violin, cello and piano			
-----	Waldesnacht, du wunderkuehle Violin, cello and piano			
-----	Wie bin ich nun in kuehler Nacht Violin, cello and piano			
Korngold	Love letter			AMP
Liszt	Die drei Zigeuner	LM	B-G	GSC
-----	Die Lorelei	LH	BF-BF	†
-----	Freudvoll und leidvoll			DUR
-----	Gestorben war ich			
-----	Hohe Liebe			DUR
-----	O lieb' so lang du lieben kannst	HML	B-F	†
Loewe	Canzonetta	MH	B-A	DIT
-----	Der heilige Franziskus	L	A-E	SC
-----	Die Uhr	HML	AF-EF	†
-----	Walpurgisnacht	H	G-G	SC
Mahler	Das Irdische Leben	HL	A-F	INT

38

(Mahler)	Des Antonius von Padua Fischpredigt	HL	GF-F	†
-----	Die zwei blauen Augen	M	A-G	†
-----	Ging heut Morgen uebers Feld	M	A-FS	INT
-----	Hans und Grethe	HL		INT
-----	Ich atmet' einen linden Duft	HL		INT
-----	Ich bin der Welt abhanden gekommen	HL		INT
-----	Ich hab' ein gluehend Messer	M	BF-GF	WEI
-----	Liebst du um Schoenheit	HL		INT
-----	Rheinlegendchen	M	B-FS	†
-----	Scheiden und Meiden	HL		INT
-----	Urlicht	L	DF-E	†
-----	Wenn mein Schatz Hochzeit macht			WEI
-----	Wer hat dies Liedlein erdacht?	HL	BF-E	INT
-----	Wo die schoenen Trompeten blasen	HL	GF-F	INT
Marx	An einen Herbstwald	M	CS-FS	UNI
-----	Der bescheidene Schaefer			UNI
-----	Der Rauch			UNI
-----	Der Ton	M	C-F	AMP
-----	Ein junger Dichter			AMP
-----	Hat dich die Liebe beruehrt	MH	EF-BF	AMP
Mendelssohn	An die Entfernte	M	F-F	
-----	Bei der Wiege	M	DF-EF	†
-----	Die Liebende schreibt	HL		†
-----	Nachtlied			
-----	Neue Liebe	H	CS-A	†
-----	On wings of song			†
-----	Schilflied	M	F-FS	
-----	Suleika	H	E-GS	†
-----	Volkslied	M	E-A	†
Mozart	Abendempfindung	M	E-F	
-----	Als Luise die Briefe			GSC
-----	Die Alte			
----- .	Verdankt sei es dem Glanz			DIT
-----	Warnung	HM	C-D	
-----	Wiegenlied	MH	G-G	†
Pfitzner	Gretel			BOO
-----	Venus Mater			
-----	Verrat			
Reger	Am Bruennele			
-----	Des Kindes Gebet	H	F-G	BOT

(Reger)	Mit Rosen bestreut			UNI
-----	Waldeinsamkeit	HML	A-D	BOS
Reichardt	Rhapsodie			MOS
Ries	Die blauen	HM	CS-E	GSC
	Fruehlingsaugen			
Schoenberg	Song of the wood dove			AMP
-----	Traumleben			UNI
Schubert	Am Bach im Fruehling			PET
-----	Am Feierabend	HL	BF-F	†
-----	Am Grabe Anselmos	HL	B-EF	†
-----	An den Mond	HL	F-GF	†
-----	An die Leier	LM	BF-F	†
-----	An Schwager Kronos	HL	G-E	†
-----	Auf dem Wasser zu singen	MH	EF-GF	†
-----	Aufenthalt	HLM	A-F	†
-----	Aufloesung	LH	D-A	†
-----	Aus Heliopolis			PET
-----	Ave Maria	LMH	F-F	†
-----	Bei dir allein			PET
-----	Das Wandern	HLM	E-E	†
-----	Das Wirtshaus	HL	C-D	†
-----	Dem Unendlichen	L	A-GF	†
-----	Der Atlas	HL	BF-F	†
-----	Der Doppelgaenger	HL	G-D	†
-----	Der Einsame	LH	D-G	GSC
-----	Der Erlkoenig	HML	A-E	†
-----	Der Fluss			
-----	Der Juengling an der	LH	E-A	†
	Quelle			
-----	Der Leiermann	ML	C-D	†
-----	Der Lindenbaum	HL	A-D	†
-----	Der Musensohn	LH	FS-G	†
-----	Der Neugierige	HL	CS-EF	†
-----	Der Schmetterling	LH	E-F	†
-----	Der stuermische Morgen	HL		
-----	Der Tod und das	HL	A-EF	†
	Maedchen			
-----	Der Wanderer	HML	FS-D	†
-----	Der Wanderer an den	LM	D-F	PET
	Mond			
-----	Der Wegweiser	L	D-EF	†
-----	Der Zwerg	M	A-GF	PET
-----	Des Maedchens Klage	LH	C-E	†
-----	Die Allmacht	HML	G-E	†
-----	Die boese Farbe	HL	CS-F	†
-----	Die Forelle	MLH	EF-GF	†
-----	Die junge Nonne	LH	C-GF	†
-----	Die Kraehe	HL	A-E	†
-----	Die liebe Farbe			

(Schubert)	Die Liebe hat gelogen	LM	G-F	†
-----	Die Maenner sind mechant			PET
-----	Die Mutter Erde			PET
-----	Die Nebensonnen	HL	F-D	GSC
-----	Die Post	HML	BF-EF	†
-----	Die Stadt	HL	A-E	†
-----	Die Taubenpost	HL	D-EF	†
-----	Dithyrambe	L	A-D	†
-----	Du bist die Ruh	LMH	EF-AF	†
-----	Du liebst mich nicht	LH	E-FS	†
-----	Ellens zweiter Gesang			PET
-----	Erstarrung	HL	D-F	†
-----	Fahrt zum Hades	HL	G-DF	PET
-----	Fischerweise	L	C-D	†
-----	Fragment aus dem Aeschylus			PET
-----	Fruehlingstraum	HL	C-D	†
-----	Ganymed	LH	EF-G	†
-----	Geheimes	HL	BF-EF	†
-----	Gretchen am Spinnrade	H	F-A	†
-----	Gruppe aus dem Tartarus	L	CS-EF	†
-----	Heidenroeslein			
-----	Ihr Bild	HL	C-C	†
-----	Im Abendrot	HL	C-D	†
-----	Im Fruehling	LH	D-FS	†
-----	In der Ferne	HL		†
-----	Irrlicht			
-----	Klaerchens Lied			
-----	Lachen und Weinen	HL	C-EF	†
-----	Letzte Hoffnung	HL		†
-----	Liebsebotschaft	H	E-G	†
-----	Liebhaber in allen Gestalten			PET
-----	Lied der Mignon	HL		†
-----	Lied eines Schiffers an die Dioskuren	HL	A-C	†
-----	Litanei	HLM	C-EF	†
-----	Mut	HL		†
-----	Nachtgesang			PET
-----	Nacht und Traeume	HL	C-DF	†
-----	Nur wer die Sehnsucht kennt	LH		†
-----	Rastlose Liebe	M	B-F	†
-----	Romanze aus Rosamunde			PET
-----	Schaefers Klagelied	HL	BF-D	†
-----	Sei mir gegruesst	LH	G-G	†
-----	Seligkeit			
-----	Staendchen			
-----	Suleika I	LH	DS-G	†
-----	Suleika II	LH	F-BF	†

(Schubert)	Thekla	HL	B-E	PET
-----	Ungeduld	HML		†
-----	Wehmuth	HL	B-D	†
-----	Wiegenlied (Op. 105)			PET
-----	Wohin?	HL	B-E	†
Schuetz	Aus dem 119th Psalm			
Schumann	Abends am Strande			
-----	An den Sonnenschein	HL	A-D	†
-----	Aus den Hebraeischen Gesaengen			
-----	Dein Angesicht	HL	B-EF	DIT
-----	Der Himmel hat eine Traene geweint			
-----	Der Nussbaum	LMH	D-FS	†
-----	Der Sandmann	HL	AF-DF	†
-----	Die Kartenlegerin			
-----	Die Lotusblume	HLM	BF-F	†
-----	Die Soldatenbraut	HL	AF-EF	†
-----	Die Tochter Jephthas	HL	A-E	
-----	Du bist wie eine Blume	HM	F-EF	†
-----	Du Ring an meinem Finger	HL	C-F	†
-----	Er, der Herrlichste von Allen	HL	A-EF	†
-----	Er ist's	HL	BF-EF	†
-----	Erstes Gruen	HL	D-D	†
-----	Fruehlingsfahrt	HL	B-E	†
-----	Fruehlingsnacht	L	CS-E	†
-----	Heiss' mich nicht reden			
-----	Hoch, hoch sind die Berge			
-----	Ihre Stimme	LH		†
-----	Im Walde	HL	A-D	†
-----	Im Westen	HL		†
-----	Ins freie			
-----	Liebeslied			
-----	Lied der Suleika			
-----	Lust der Sturmnacht			
-----	Marienwuermchen	HL	D-D	GSC
-----	Melancholie			
-----	Mit Myrthen und Rosen	HL	A-D	†
-----	Mondnacht	M	E-FS	†
-----	Requiem			†
-----	Schoene Wiege meiner Leiden	HL	C-EF	†
-----	Seit ich ihn gesehen	HL	DF-DF	†
-----	Stille Traenen	HL		†
-----	Waldesgespraech	HL	A-FS	†
-----	Was soll ich sagen!			†
-----	Wer machte dich so krank?			

(Schumann)	Widmung	HL	BF-F	†
Strauss	Allerseelen	HL	AS-E	†
-----	Befreit			HSC
-----	Caecilie	MH	E-B	†
-----	Dem Herzen sehnlich			
-----	Die Georgine	LH	B-A	†
-----	Die Nacht	HL		†
-----	Freundliche Vision	HL	C-F	†
-----	Fuer fuenfzehn Pfennige			†
-----	Hat gesagt bleibt's nicht dabei			†
-----	Heimkehr	HL	B-E	†
-----	Heimliche Aufforderung	HL	B-E	†
-----	Ich trage meine Minne	M		UNI
-----	Liebeshymnus			†
-----	Meinem Kinde			†
-----	Mit deinen blauen Augen	LH	C-GS	†
-----	Morgen	HML	E-F	†
-----	Nichts	LH	E-A	†
-----	Ruhe meine Seele			†
-----	Seitdem dein Aug' in meines schaute			SC
-----	Traum durch die Daemmerung	HML	BF-EF	†
-----	Wiegenliedchen			†
Trunk	In meiner Heimat			
Wagner	Der Tannenbaum			
-----	Im Treibhaus	HL		†
-----	Schmerzen	HL		†
-----	Stehe still!	HL		†
Wolf	Ach, des Knaben Augen	HL		†
-----	Ach, im Maien	HL	C-E	†
-----	Agnes	HL		†
-----	Alle gingen, Herz, zu Ruh	HL	C-EF	†
-----	An die Geliebte			†
-----	An eine Aeolsharfe			†
-----	Auch kleine Dinge	HM	D-E	†
-----	Auf dem gruenen Balkon	HL		†
-----	Auf einer Wanderung	HL		DIT
-----	Bedeckt mich mit Blumen	HL	B-D	†
-----	Bei einer Trauung			PET
-----	Cophtisches Lied 2			†
-----	Dank des Paria			PET
-----	Das Koehlerweib ist trunken			PET
-----	Das Staendchen	HL		†
-----	Das verlassene Maegdlein	HL	D-EF	†
-----	Denk' es, o Seele	LH	EF-F	†
-----	Der Freund	HM	BF-E	PET
-----	Der Gaertner	HL		†

43

(Wolf)	Der Mond hat eine schwere Klag' erhoben	HL	BF-DF	†
-----	Die ihr schwebet	HL	EF-EF	†
-----	Die Zigeunerin			†
-----	Du denkst, mit einem Faedchen			†
-----	Elfenlied	HL	D-F	†
-----	Er ist's	H	D-G	†
-----	Erstes Liebeslied eines Maedchens	H	EF-AF	†
-----	Fussreise	HL	D-E	†
-----	Ganymed	HL	CS-D	†
-----	Gebet	HL		†
-----	Geh' Geliebter, geh' jetzt			PET
-----	Gesang Weylas	HL	DF-F	†
-----	Heimweh (Moerike Lieder)			†
-----	Herbstentschluss			
-----	Ich hab' in Penna	LH		†
-----	Im Fruehling	HL	BF-F	†
-----	In dem Schatten meiner Locken	M	C-EF	†
-----	In der Fruehe	HL	C-C	†
-----	Kennst du das Land			†
-----	Klinge, klinge, mein Pandero	HL	CF-EF	†
-----	Liebe mir in Busen zuendet	M	E-F	†
-----	Lied vom Winde			†
-----	Mausfallen Spruechlein	HL	BF-E	†
-----	Mignon	LH		†
-----	Morgenstimmung	LH	C-GS	†
-----	Morgentau	HL	D-D	†
-----	Neue Liebe	LH	D-AF	†
-----	Nimmersatte Liebe	LH	CF-AF	†
-----	Nun wandre, Maria	HL	EF-D	†
-----	Rat einer Alten			†
-----	Sie blasen zum Abmarsch			
-----	Sterne mit den goldnen Fuesschen			
-----	Tretet ein, hoher Krieger	HL	B-F	†
-----	Ueber Nacht	LH	D-G	†
-----	Um Mitternacht	HL	G-EF	†
-----	Und willst du deinen Liebsten sterben	HL		†
-----	Verborgenheit	HL	B-E	†
-----	Verschling' der Abgrund			PET
-----	Verschwiegene Liebe	LH	DF-FS	†
-----	Wenn du, mein Liebster	LH	DF-GF	†

44

(Wolf)	Wenn du zu den Blumen gehst	HL	B-EF	†
-----	Wie glaenzt der helle Mond			†
-----	Zur ruh', zur Ruh'	HL	A-GF	†
Wolff	Alle Dinge haben Sprache	M	BF-GF	†
-----	Bekenntnis			
-----	Die heisse schwuele Sommernacht			HMP
-----	Die Lor' sitzt im Garten	M	C-FS	HMP
-----	Ewig			
-----	Ich bin eine Harfe			HMP
-----	Knabe und Veilchen	M	D-D	HMP
-----	Since you're near	M	BF-GF	†
-----	Voegleins Schwermut			

Italian Recital Songs

Mezzo Soprano

Alfano	Felicità			
-----	Melodia			RIC
Bimboni	Sospiri miei	M	EF-EF	GAL
Bononcini	Deh, lascia			HEU
-----	Per la gloria	HL	C-EF	†
-----	Pietà, mio caro bene	HL	C-EF	DIT
Brogi	Mattinata			
Caccini	Amarilli, mia bella	ML	C-D	†
Caldara	Alma del core			GSC
-----	Come raggio di sol	HL	D-F	†
-----	Mirti, faggi			PET
-----	Sebben crudele	HML	E-DS	†
-----	Selve amiche, ombrose piante	HM	E-E	†
Carissimi	A morire!	ML	C-D	
-----	Vittoria, mio core	HLM	B-E	†
Castelnuovo-Tedesco	Ninna Nanna			
-----	Recuerdo			
Cavalli	Donzelle fuggite	HL	C-EF	†
Cesti	Ah, quanto è vero (Il Pomo d'Oro)	HL	F-F	DIT
-----	Che angoscia, che affanno (Il Pomo d'Oro)	HL	C-DF	DIT
-----	E dove t'aggiri (Il Pomo d'Oro)	HM	D-EF	DIT
Cherubini	Ahi, che forse ai miei di (Demofonte)			RIC

45

Cimara	Fiocca la neve	H	G-G	GSC
-----	Stornellata marinara	HM		RIC
Cimarosa	Nel lasciarti			RIC
	(L'Olympiade)			
Del Leuto	Dimmi, amor	M	C-F	GSC
De Luca	Non posso disperar	HL	C-E	GSC
Donaudy	Quando ti rivedrò			RIC
-----	Spirate pur, spirate			RIC
Durante	Danza, danza fanciulla gentile	HM	BF-F	†
-----	Vergin, tutta amor	LM	C-EF	†
Falconieri	Non più d'amore	HL	C-D	DIT
-----	Nudo arciero	HL	AF-AF	DIT
Gagliano	Dormi, amore	HL	CS-E	DIT
-----	Valli profonde (Il Dannato)			HEU
Galuppi	La pastorella (Il Filosoto di Campagna)			DUR
Ghedini	La tortora			
Giordani	Caro mio ben	HML	B-D	†
Gluck	Di questa cetra (Il Parnasso Confuso)			LEM
-----	O del mio dolce ardor (Paride ed Elena)	LH	D-FS	GSC
-----	Spiagge amate (Paride ed Elena)			†
-----	Vieni che poi sereno (La Semiramide)	M	D-G	†
Guarnieri	Caro, caro il mio bambin			RIC
Handel	Affani del pensier (Ottone)			GSC
-----	Amor commanda (Floridante)	H		†
-----	Cangio d'aspetto (Admeto)			†
-----	Cara sposa (Radamisto)	M	CS-D	†
-----	Ch'io mai vi possa (Siroe)			†
-----	Crude furie de gl'orri diubissi (Serse)			
-----	Dove sei, amato bene (Rodelinda)	L	BF-EF	†
-----	Furibondo spira (Partenope)			KIS
-----	Lascia chio pianga (Rinaldo)			
-----	O rendetemi, il mio bene (Amadigi)	L	CS-EF	CFI
-----	Ombra mai fu (Serse)	HM	BF-EF	†
-----	Piangero la (Julius Caesar)			CFI
-----	Qual farfalletta (Partenope)	H	E-A	†

(Handel)	V'adoro pupille			BOO
	(Julius Caesar)			
-----	Verdi prati (Alcina)			†
Haydn	Cara speme			
	(Orfeo ed Euridice)			
Legrenzi	Che fiero costume	HML	C-D	†
Lotti	Pur dicesti, o bocca	LMH	E-FS	GSC
	bella			
Malipiero	Ballata	H		CHE
Marcello	Non m'è grave morir per	L	C-E	GSC
	amore			
Paisiello	Chi vuol la zingarella	L	C-F	GSC
-----	Nel cor più non mi sento	HL	C-EF	†
Panizza	D'une prison	H	C-G	GSC
Paradies	M'ha preso alla sua	M	EF-F	GSC
	ragna			
Pergolesi	Confusa, smarrita			GSC
-----	Ogni pena più spietata	L	B-E	GSC
-----	Se tu m'ami	LMH	C-G	GSC
Peri	Funeste piaggie (Euridice)			GSC
Piccini	O nuit, dresse du mystere			GSC
	(Le Faux Lord)			
-----	Se il ciel mi divide	M	C-F	†
	(Alessandro di Indie)			
Pignatta	Cieco si finse amor			
Pizzetti	La madre al figlio lontano			FRL
Porpora	Come la luce è tremola			
Quagliati	Apra il suo verde seno	HL	E-CS	DIT
Recli	La luna prigioniera	H		RIC
Respighi	Abbandono			BON
-----	Ballata			RIC
-----	Contrasto	M		RIC
-----	E se un giorno tornasse	M		RIC
-----	Il tramonto			RIC
-----	In alto mare			BON
-----	Invito alla danza			BON
-----	Io sono la madre	L		RIC
-----	Mattino di luce	M		RIC
-----	Nebbie			†
-----	Notte			BON
-----	Pioggia			BON
-----	Scherzo			BON
Rontani	Or ch'io non segno più	HL	CS-E	DIT
-----	Se bel rio	ML	D-C	†
Rosa	Selve, voi che le speranze	MH	D-G	DIT
-----	Vado ben spesso	ML	C-EF	†
Rossi	Ah, rendimi (Mitrane)	L	GS-FS	GSC
Rossini	La danza	MH	E-A	†
-----	La regatta Veneziana			

47

Composer	Title			
Sadero	I battitori di grano	M		CHE
Santoliquido	I canti della sera			RIC
-----	Le domandai			
Sarti	Lungi dal caro bene (Armide)	HL	G-D	GSC
Scarlatti, A.	O cessate di piagarmi	HL	DS-E	GSC
-----	Rugiadose odorose (Il Pirro e Demetrio)	HL	D-E	DIT
-----	Se Florindo è fedele	LM	EF-EF	GSC
-----	Sento nel core	M	E-F	†
Scarlatti, D.	Consolati e spara amante	L	BF-E	GSC
-----	Qual farfalletta			
Secchi	Love me or not			BOO
-----	Lungi dal caro bene	HL	A-FS	DIT
Sibella	Sotto il ciel	HM	C-F	GSC
Stradella	Col mio sangue comprenderei (Il Floridoro)	HL	E-F	DIT
-----	Per pietà (Il Floridoro)	HM	D-F	DIT
-----	Pietà, Signore	HM	C-F	GSC
Torelli	Tu lo sai	HL	BF-F	†
Tosti	Dopo!			RIC
-----	La serenata	HLM	D-EF	GSC
-----	Mattinata			RIC
Vivaldi	Da du venti (Ercole)			
-----	Onde chiare			
-----	Un certo no so che	HL	BF-EF	†

Russian Recital Songs

Mezzo Soprano

Composer	Title			
Arensky	Autumn	H	CS-FS	GSC
-----	Revery	MH	DS-FS	DIT
-----	Valse	H	DF-GF	GSC
Cui	The statue at Czarskoe-Selo	HM	DF-EF	†
Dargomijshky	I still love him			
-----	My darling girls			
Gliere	Ah, twine no blossoms	HM	CS-F	DIT
-----	Sweetly sang the nightingale			
Glinka	How sweet it is to be with you	HM		GSC
Gretchaninoff	Declaration of love			
-----	Dewdrop			
-----	Hushed the song of the nightingale	MH	E-G	DIT
-----	Il s'est tu, le charmant rossignol	H	EF-G	†

48

(Gretchaninoff)	L'amour eternel			
-----	Lullaby			
-----	My native land	L	C-EF	GSC
-----	Over the steppe	LM	C-G	GSC
-----	Wounded birch	HL	B-EF	†
Mednikoff	The hills of Gruzia	H	DS-A	LAC
Mussorgsky	After the battle			GSC
-----	Cradle song of the poor	M	B-DS	GSC
-----	Death the commander			
-----	Hopak	HM	CS-FS	GSC
-----	In the corner			INT
-----	On the Dnieper			GSC
-----	Peasant cradle song	M		GSC
-----	Serenade			BES
-----	Sphinx			BRH
-----	The classic			BRH
-----	The orphan girl			GSC
Prokofieff	Snowdrops			GSC
-----	Snowflakes			GSC
Rachmaninoff	A dream	H		BOO
-----	All things depart			BOO
-----	April			
-----	As fair is she as noonday light			GSC
-----	Floods of spring	HL		DIT
-----	In the silence of night	LH	D-A	GSC
-----	Into my open window	HL	B-FS	BOS
-----	Like blossom dew	M		BOO
-----	Lilacs	LH	EF-G	†
-----	Morning	ML	B-DS	GSC
-----	My heart trembles again			
-----	Oh cease thy singing, maiden fair	H	E-A	CFI
-----	O, do not grieve	M	BF-AF	GSC
-----	Oh, no, I pray do not depart	H		DIT
-----	O thou billowy harvest field	HL	CS-E	GSC
-----	The answer	H		BOO
-----	The island	LH	DF-F	†
-----	The raising of Lazarus			BRH
-----	The soldier's bride			†
-----	Vocalise	LH	CS-A	GSC
Rimsky-Korsakov	Clearer is the skylark's singing			
-----	On the Georgian hills	HM		GSC
Rubinstein	Der Asra	HM	B-F	GSC
Stravinsky	Pastorale			GSC
-----	The cloister (La Novice)			DIT
Tchaikovsky	At the ball	MH		GSC

49

(Tchaikovsky)	Evening	HM		GSC
-----	If you would only know			
-----	Lizochek			
-----	One word			
-----	The terrible moment			

Scandinavian Recital Songs

Mezzo Soprano

Alnaes	Der du gjekk fyre			
-----	En morgen var din grav	M	CS-D	HAN
-----	Lykken mellem to mennesker	M	B-FS	HAN
-----	Nu brister i all de kløfter	L	A-F	HAN
Backer-Gröndahl	In dreaming dance			
Grieg	A dream			†
-----	A swan			†
-----	Autumnal gale	HL	A-F	CFI
-----	By the brook			GSC
-----	Den Aergjerrige			
-----	Den blonde pige			HAN
-----	Det syng	M	C-GF	HAN
-----	Eros	LM	C-F	†
-----	From Monte Pinci			PET
-----	Goat dance			
-----	Good morning			†
-----	Hjemkomst	M	B-F	HAN
-----	I love thee	HML	E-F	†
-----	In the boat	LM	D-ES	†
-----	Jeg giver mit digt til våren.	M	CS-G	HAN
-----	Jeg lever et liv i laengsel	L	BF-E	HAN
-----	Når jeg vil dø	L	CS-EF	HAN
-----	Nu er aftenen lys og lang	L	C-E	HAN
-----	På Hamars ruiner	M	BF-G	HAN
-----	På Norges nøgne fjelde	M	D-F	HAN
-----	På skogstien	H	E-G	HAN
-----	Radiant night			
-----	Saint John's eve	L	DF-E	CFI
-----	Snegl, Snegl	M	B-F	HAN
-----	Solvejgs' cradle song	M	CS-FS	GSC
-----	Spring rain			PET
-----	Thanks for thy counsel			DIT
-----	The mother sings			DIT
-----	The tryst			DIT
-----	The wounded heart			PET

(Grieg)	Til en I	L	B-CS	HAN
-----	Til en II	M	E-F	HAN
-----	Til min dreng		C-E	
-----	Turisten	M	CS-F	HAN
-----	Udvandreren	M	EF-F	HAN
-----	Vaer hilset, I Damer	M	D-F	HAN
-----	Ved Moders grav	M	C-F	HAN
-----	Verse for an album			
-----	With a water lily	HM	CS-EF	†
Heise	Arnes sang			
-----	Sol deroppe ganger under lide			
Henriques	Vaaren er kommen			
Kjerulf	Synnove's song	M	C-F	GSC
-----	The cuckoo calls	M		AMP
Lange-Mueller	Gjenboens først vise			
-----	Himlen ulmer svagt i flammerødt			
Lie	Soft-footed snow	HM		DIT
Nielson	Pigen højt i taarnet sad			
Rangstroem	Melodie			
Sibelius	Black roses	M	A-ES	AMP
-----	Diamonds on the March snow			
-----	Hymn to Thais the unforgettable			
-----	In the field a maiden sings			
-----	On a balcony by the sea			
-----	Reeds, reeds rustle			
-----	Song of the Jewish girl			
-----	Spring is fleeting			DIT
-----	The first kiss	M		AMP
-----	The silent town			AMP
-----	The tryst	M		AMP
-----	The young huntsman			
-----	Was it a dream?			BRH
Sinding	I hear the gull			JCH
-----	The daisies secret			
Sjoeberg	Visions	MH	F-AF	GAL
Soderberg	Fågelns visa			
Vehanen	Cantilena			
Weyse	I skovens dybe, stille ro			
-----	Natten er saa stille			
-----	Pigen paa gjaerdet			

Spanish Recital Songs

Mezzo Soprano

Alvarez	La partida	HL	DS-E	GSC
Falla	Psyché String quartet, harp and flute	M		CHE
Ferrazzano	El lago			
Ginastera	Chacarera			RIC
-----	Triste			RIC
Granados	El majo discreto	H		INT
Guastavino	Encantamiento			
-----	La rose y la sauce			RIC
Nin	Cloris hermosa			
-----	El amor es como un niño			ESC
-----	El vito			ESC
-----	Paño murciano			ESC
-----	Villancico vasco			ESC
Obradors	Coplas de curro dulce			
-----	El vito			
-----	Malagueña de la magruga			
-----	Romance de los pelegrinitos			
Ravel	Chanson espagnole			DUR
Turina	Farruca	M	A-F	UME

Miscellaneous Recital Songs

Mezzo Soprano

Bach-Gounod	Ave Maria			
Bartok	Tears of autumn	M	C-F	GSC
Bizet	Agnus Dei	HLM	C-AF	
Chajes	Adarim			TRA
Chopin	Lithuanian song	ML	C-C	GSC
-----	Melancholy	HL		GSC
-----	My beloved	HL		GSC
-----	The maiden's wish	LM	CS-E	GSC
Dvořák	Clouds and darkness			
-----	God is my shepherd			AMP
-----	Hear my prayer, O Lord			AMP
-----	I will sing new songs of gladness	HL		
-----	Lord, Thou art my refuge and shield			AMP
-----	Sing ye a joyful song			AMP
-----	Songs my mother taught me	HM	E-E	
-----	Tune thy fiddle gypsy			SIM
-----	Turn Thee to me			AMP

Enesco	Aux demoiselles paresseuses			
-----	Etienne à Anne			
Fisher	Eili, Eili	LMH	E-G	DIT
Franck	Panis angelicus	LM		
Luzzi	Ave Maria	HL	BF-EF	GSC
Mignone	Cantiga de ninar			SUM
-----	Dona janaina			
Ravel	Mayerke mein suhn			RAV
Saint-Saëns	Ave Maria	HM		DIT
-----	Ave Verum			DUR
Villa-Lobos	Abril			
-----	Adeus Ema			AMP
-----	Bachianas Brazileiras,			AMP
	no. 5 8 Celli and bass			
-----	Canção do carreiro			
-----	Canção do marinheiro			
-----	Desejo			
-----	Evocacao			
-----	Miau (A gatinha parda)			
-----	Modinha (Love song)			
-----	No paz do outono			
-----	Nozani-na			AMP
-----	Papae curumiassu			AMP
-----	Saudades da minha vida			
-----	Sino da aldeia			
-----	Xango			AMP

British Songs and Arias for Opening Recitals

Mezzo Soprano

Green	My lips shall speak the praise M	E-F	OXF
-----	Salvation belongeth unto M	F-EF	OXF
	the Lord		
Handel	Art thou troubled M	F-F	GSC
	(Rodelinda)		
-----	Have mercy, Lord HM		†
	(Te Deum)		
-----	Let me wander not unseen M	D-G	†
	(L'Allegro)		
-----	Lord to Thee each night L	C-E	†
	and day (Theodora)		
-----	O sleep why dost thou H	DS-GS	†
	leave me (Semele)		
Purcell	Ah, how pleasant 'tis to love		AUG
-----	Hark, the echoing air		BAF
	(The Fairy Queen)		
-----	If music be the food of love M	D-G	BOO

(Purcell)	Music for a while (Oedipus)	LH		SC
-----	Not all my torments			NOV
-----	There's not a swain on on the plain	M	B-G	BAF
-----	When I am laid in earth (Dido and Aeneas)	LH	C-G	†

German Songs For Opening Recitals

Mezzo Soprano

Bach, J.S.	Bist du bei mir	HML	A-EF	†
-----	O Jesulein suess			
Beethoven	Andenken			†
-----	Bonnie laddie, highland laddie			†
-----	Ich liebe dich	HL	BF-DF	†
Brahms	Nachtigall	MHL	BF-FS	†
-----	Verzagen	MH	CS-FS	†
Buxtehude	Singet dem Herrn Violin and piano			
Handel	Dank sei dir, Herr	M	CS-E	†
Haydn	She never told her love	HL	B-D	DIT
-----	The mermaid's song	M	C-F	PRE
Schubert	Das Wandern	HLM	E-E	†
-----	Ganymed	LH	EF-G	†
-----	Liebesbotschaft	H	E-G	†
Schumann	Mit Myrthen und Rosen	HL	A-D	†
Wolf	Ueber Nacht	LH	D-G	†

Italian Songs and Arias For Opening Recitals

Mezzo Soprano

Caccini	Amarilli, mia bella	ML	C-D	†
Caldara	Sebben crudele	HML	E-DS	†
Carissimi	Vittoria, mio core	HLM	B-E	†
Cavalli	Donzelle fuggite	HL	C-EF	†
Cesti	Ah, quanto è vero (Il Pomo d'Oro)	HL	F-F	DIT
-----	Che angoscia, che affanno (Il Pomo d'Oro)	HL	C-DF	DIT
Cherubini	Ahi, che forse ai miei di (Demofonte)			RIC
Cimara	Stornellata marinara	HM		RIC

54

Cimarosa	Nel lasciarti			RIC
	(L'Olympiade)			
Donaudy	Quando ti rivedrò			RIC
Durante	Vergin, tutta amor	LM	C-EF	†
Gluck	O del mio dolce ardor	LH	D-FS	GSC
	(Paride ed Elena)			
-----	Spiagge amate			†
	(Paride ed Elena)			
Handel	Affani del pensier (Ottone)			†
-----	Cangio d'aspetto (Admeto)			†
-----	Cara sposa (Radamisto)	M	CS-D	†
-----	Ch'io mai vi possa (Siroe)			†
-----	Dove sei, amato bene	L	BF-EF	CFI
	(Rodelinda)			
-----	Furibondo spira			KIS
	(Partenope)			
-----	Lascia ch'io pianga	HM	EF-F	†
	(Rinaldo)			
-----	O rendetemi il mio bene	L	CS-EF	CFI
	(Amadigi)			
-----	Ombra mai fu (Serse)	HM	BF-EF	†
-----	Piangero la sorte mia			CFI
	(Julius Caesar)			
-----	V'adoro pupille			BOO
	(Julius Caesar)			
Haydn	Cara speme (Orfeo ed Euridice)			
Lotti	Pur dicesti, o bocca bella	LMH	E-FS	GSC
Mozart	Ch'io mi scordi di te			BOO
-----	Non più di fiori			†
	(La Clemenza di Tito)			
-----	Parto, parto (La Clemenza	H		AMP
	di Tito) B flat clarinet and			
	piano			
Paisiello	Chi vuol la zingarella	L	C-F	GSC
-----	Nel cor più non mi sento	HL	C-EF	†
Pergolesi	Se tu m'ami	LMH	C-G	GSC
Piccini	O nuit, dresse du mystere			GSC
	(Le Faux Lord)			
Pignatta	Cieco si finse amor			
Rosa	Vado ben spesso	ML	C-EF	BOO
Sarti	Lungi dal caro bene	HL	G-D	GSC
	(Armide)			
Scarlatti, A.	Sento nel core	M	E-F	†
Stradella	Per pietà (Il Floridoro)	HM	D-F	DIT
-----	Pietà, Signore	HM	C-F	GSC
Vivaldi	Un certo no so che	HL	BF-EF	†

Mezzo Soprano

Barber	I hear an army	LH	D-AF	GSC
-----	Sure on this shining night	MH	D-G	GSC
Bassett	Take joy home	LH	EF-BF	GSC
Bernstein	La bonne cuisine	H	B-B	GSC
Bibb	A rondel of spring	HL	BF-D	GSC
Bowles	Sugar in the cane	M	D-FS	GSC
Branscombe	At the postern gate	MH	DF-AF	ASC
Browning	Phoenix			
Carpenter	Light, my light	M	C-G	GSC
-----	Serenade	LH	CS-A	GSC
Castelnuovo- Tedesco	Springtime	M		CHE
Clough- Leighter	My lover he comes on the skee	HM	D-F	BOS
Diack	Little Jack Horner			CFI
Dougherty	Everyone sang			
-----	Song for autumn			
Duke	Evening			
-----	On a March day	M	B-GF	BOH
-----	XXth century	M		VLP
Dukelsky	The ladies of St. James			
Enders	Russian picnic	HM	C-G	GSC
Giannini	Sing to my heart a song	H	D-B	ELV
Golde	Who knows?	HM	BF-F	GSC
Hageman	At the well	LH	EF-AF	GSC
-----	Miranda	HL		GAL
Kingsford	Command	HLM	EF-G	GSC
-----	Courage	M	C-F	GSC
Kramer	Allah			
La Forge	Song of the open	MH	EF-AF	DIT
-----	To a messenger	HLM	CF-G	GSC
Levitzki	Ah, thou beloved one	H	EF-AF	GSC
Mana-Zucca	Rachem	HML		CHA
Rogers	The last song	MLH	E-AF	GSC
-----	Time for making songs	HM	CS-F	DIT
Rummel	Ecstasy	LMH	GF-AF	GSC
Sacco	Rapunzel	MH	FS-BF	GSC
Salter	The cry of Rachel	LH	C-AF	GSC
Sargent	Twentieth century	H	EF-GS	LEE
Schuman	Holiday song	M	C-F	GSC
Silberta	You shall have your red rose			
Speaks	Morning	HML	BF-D	GSC
Swanson	Joy	M	BF-EF	Lee

Tyson	Sea moods	LH	E-AF	GSC
Ware	This day is mine	MH	EF-AF	BOS
Warren	Fulfilment	H	D-BF	GAL
-----	We two	LH	E-A	GSC
Watts	Green branches	HM		DIT
-----	Joy	HL	D-F	GSC
Worth	Midsummer	LM	E-A	GSC

(See also Negro Spirituals and Folk Songs.)

Miscellaneous Songs For
Closing Recitals

Mezzo Soprano

Bizet	Adieu de l'hôtesse arabe	H	BF-G	†
Bliss	The buckle			CUR
Brahms	Meine Liebe ist gruen	MLH	ES-A	†
-----	Wenn du nur zuweilen laechelst			†
-----	Wie froh und Frisch	HL	B-E	†
-----	Willst du, dass ich geh'?	L	C-G	†
Bridge	Love went a-riding	HL		BOS
Britten	A charm	L	AS-E	BOO
-----	Oliver Cromwell			BOH
Cimara	Canto di primavera		D-G	FRL
Debussy	Chevaux de bois	H	C-G	†
Delius	Love's philosophy			†
Elgar	The swimmer			BOO
Falla	Jota	LH		AMP
-----	Polo	HL		AMP
Gretchaninoff	My native land	L	C-EF	GSC
Grieg	By the brook			GSC
-----	Good morning			†
-----	Jeg lever et liv i laengsel	L	BF-E	HAN
-----	Vaer hilset, I Damer	M	D-F	HAN
Head	A piper	HL		BOO
Hely Hutchinson	Old mother Hubbard	HL	B-E	CFI
Henschel	Morning-hymn	MH	DS-GS	†
Kennedy-Fraser	Song of the sea-reivers			
Marx	Der Ton	M	C-F	AMP
Nin	El vito			ESC
Obradors	Coplas de curro dulce			
-----	El vito			
Poulenc	Air vif	H	C-AF	ROU

Quilter	Blow, blow, thou winter wind	HL	C-E	BOO
Rachmaninoff	Floods of spring	HL		DIT
-----	Oh, no, I pray do not depart	H		DIT
Respighi	Pioggia			BON
Ronald	Southern song			ENO
Schubert	Aufloesung	LH	D-A	†
-----	Die Forelle	MLH	EF-GF	†
Schumann	Er ist's	HL	BF-EF	†
Shaw	Romance			
Sibelius	The tryst	M		AMP
-----	Was it a dream			BRH
Turina	Farruca	M	A-F	UME
Villa-Lobos	Canção do carreiro			
Wolf	Er ist's	H	D-G	†
-----	Morgenstimmung	LH	C-GS	†

American Atmospheric Songs

Mezzo Soprano

Barber	Rain has fallen	HM	D-E	GSC
-----	Sleep now	MH	EF-AF	GSC
Burleigh	Sometimes I feel like a motherless child	HML		RIC
Carpenter	Go, lovely rose	M	DF-EF	GSC
-----	On the seashore of endless worlds	M	C-FS	GSC
-----	Slumber song	ML	BF-F	GSC
-----	The day is no more	M	GS-DS	GSC
-----	The green river	M	B-E	GSC
-----	The pools of peace	M	D-F	GSC
-----	When I bring to you colour'd toys	LM	CS-FS	GSC
Carter	Dust of snow	M	D-E	AMP
Charles	Clouds	HML	C-EF	GSC
-----	When I have sung my songs	HM	BF-EF	GSC
Crist	Into a ship dreaming	LMH	EF-GS	CFI
Davis	Nancy Hanks	H	D-G	GAL
Dello Joio	New born	M	C-D	CFI
Dougherty	Loveliest of trees	HM	C-E	BOH
Duke	I can't be talkin' of love	H	CS-G	GSC
-----	Loveliest of trees	L	C-D	GSC
Ganz	A memory	HM	B-D	GSC
Griffes	Night on ways unknown has fallen	L	GS-F	GSC

(Griffes)	The dreamy lake	H	BS-GS	GSC
Hageman	Do not go, my love	HL	B-EF	GSC
Harris	Fog	M	D-F	CFI
-----	Vanished summer	M	C-E	GAL
Hovaness	How I adore thee	M		WHB
Kramer	Our lives together	HL	D-E	GAL
-----	Swans	HL		RIC
MacGimsey	Sweet little Jesus boy	ML	D-D	CFI
Naginski	Look down, fair moon			
-----	Night song at Amalfi	M	D-EF	GSC
Niles	I wonder as I wander	HL	BF-D	GSC
-----	Jesus, Jesus rest your head	HL	A-D	GSC
Sacco	The ragpicker	MH	C-AF	GSC
Silbert a	Aylia, dancer of Kashmir	M	B-F	GSC
Tureman	A winter sunset	L	BF-E	GSC
Tyson	Noon and night	LH	F-AF	GSC

British Atmospheric Songs

Mezzo Soprano

Benjamin	Calm sea and mist			CUR
Dunhill	The cloths of heaven	LM	EF-G	STB
Elgar	Sea pictures	L	A-A	BOO
Handel	O sleep why dost thou leave me (Semele)	H	DS-GS	†
Harty	My lagan love	ML	BF-EF	BOO
Holst	The heart worships	ML	BF-D	STB
Hughes	A Ballynure ballad	L	BF-D	BOH
-----	O men from the fields	M	F-F	BOO
Quilter	Dream valley	H	EF-GF	ROG
Sanderson	Quiet	ML	AF-EF	BOH
Vaughan Williams	Bright is the ring of words	L		BOH
Warlock	Sleep			OXF

French Atmospheric Songs

Mezzo Soprano

Chaminade	The silver ring	HM	BF-F	GSC
Chausson	Les papillons	M	C-F	GSC
Debussy	C'est l'extase	LH	CS-A	†
Duparc	La vie antérieure	HL		†
Ferrari	Le miroir	M	E-F	GSC
Février	L'intruse	M	B-DF	HEU
Gounod	Sérénade	LMH	D-A	GSC

59

Hahn	A Chloris	H	DS-FS	HEU
-----	D'une prison	L	BF-EF	HEU
-----	L'heure exquise	M	DF-F	†
-----	Paysage	MH	EF-G	HEU
Leguerney	L'adieu	M	B-FS	DUR
Paladilhe	Psyché	HM	BF-F	GSC
Poulenc	Fleurs	M	DF-F	ROU
Ravel	Sainte	M	C-G	ELV
-----	Sur l'herbe	MH	C-G	DUR
Roussel	Le jardin mouillé	M	C-FS	ROU

German Atmospheric Songs

Mezzo Soprano

Brahms	Steig' auf, geliebter Schatten	HL	BF-EF	†
Franz	Sterne mit den gold'nen Fuesschen	HL	DS-E	†
Haydn	She never told her love	HL	B-D	DIT
Schubert	Der Tod und das Maedchen	HL	A-EF	†
-----	Nacht und Traeume	HL	C-DF	†
Schumann	Dein Angesicht	HL	B-EF	†
-----	Der Nussbaum	LMH	D-FS	†
-----	Im Walde	HL	A-D	†
Strauss	Die Nacht	HL		†
-----	Traum durch die Daemmerung	HML	BF-EF	†
Wolf	In dem Schatten meiner Locken	M	C-EF	†
-----	Verborgenheit	HL	B-E	†

Miscellaneous Atmospheric Songs

Mezzo Soprano

Alnaes	Lykken mellem to mennesker	M	B-FS	HAN
Cimara	Fiocca la neve	H	G-G	GSC
Cui	The statue at Czarskoe-Selo	HM	DF-EF	†
Grieg	A dream			†
-----	A swan			†
-----	Det syng	M	C-GF	HAN
-----	Digte af Vilhelm Krag			HAN
-----	In the boat	LM	D-ES	†
-----	Julens vuggesang			

60

(Grieg)	Når jeg vil dø	L	CS-EF	HAN
-----	På Norges nøgne fjelde	M	D-F	HAN
-----	På skogstien	H	E-G	HAN
-----	Radiant night			
-----	Snegl, Snegl	M	B-F	HAN
-----	Spring rain			PET
-----	Til En I	L	B-CS	HAN
-----	Til En II	M	E-F	HAN
-----	Udvandreren	M	EF-F	HAN
Kjerulf	Synnove's song	M	C-F	GSC
Lie	Soft-footed snow	HM		DIT
Rachmaninoff	Lilacs	LH	EF-G	BOS
-----	Morning	ML	B-DS	GSC
Sibelius	Reeds, reeds rustle			

American Dramatic Songs

Mezzo Soprano

Barber	I hear an army	LH	D-AF	GSC
Beach	Ah, love but a day			ASC
Campbell-Tipton	A spirit flower	LHM	B-G	GSC
-----	The crying of water	LH	FS-GS	GSC
Carpenter	Berceuse de guerre	M	C-G	GSC
-----	I am like a remnant of a cloud of autumn	L	BF-F	GSC
-----	Light, my light	M	C-G	GSC
-----	Slumber song	ML	BF-F	GSC
-----	The green river	M	B-E	GSC
-----	To one unknown	M	A-DS	GSC
Duke	Evening			
-----	On a March day	M	B-GF	BOH
Elwell	Renouncement	M	G-G	GSC
Enders	Russian picnic	HM	C-G	GSC
Giannini	Sing to my heart a song	H	D-B	ELV
Griffes	Sorrow of Mydath	M		GSC
-----	The lament of Ian the proud	MH	DS-AS	GSC
-----	We'll to the woods and gather May	M	D-F	GSC
Hageman	Do not go, my love	HL	B-EF	GSC
-----	Music I heard with you	MH	E-A	GAL
Hindemith	Envoy	M	EF-F	AMP
Johnson	Roll Jerd'n roll	M	EF-F	GSC
La Forge	Song of the open	MH	EF-AF	DIT
Parker	Gens duce splendida (Hora Novissima)			NOV

Protheroe	Ah, love but a day	LMH	F-AF	GAM
Rogers	The last song	MLH	E-AF	GSC
-----	Time for making songs	HM	CS-F	DIT
Salter	The cry of Rachel	LH	C-AF	GSC
Schuman	Holiday song	M	C-F	GSC
Silberta	Aylia, dancer of Kashmir	M	B-F	GSC
Speaks	Morning	HML	BF-D	GSC
Tyson	Sea moods	LH	E-AF	GSC
Ware	This day is mine	MH	EF-AF	BOS
Warren	Fulfilment	H	D-BF	GAL
-----	We two	LH	E-A	GSC
Worth	Midsummer	LM	E-A	GSC

British Dramatic Songs

Mezzo Soprano

Bainton	Ring out, wild bells	M	C-EF	OXF
Bridge	O that it were so	LMH	D-G	CHA
Clarke	Eight o'clock			ROG
-----	The seal man	M		BOH
Coleridge-Taylor	Life and death	HML		ASC
Delius	Twilight fancies	M	D-FS	CFI
Del Riego	Homing	HML	BF-E	CHA
Elgar	Sea pictures	L	A-A	BOO
-----	The swimmer			BOO
Henschel	Morning-hymn	MH	DS-GS	†
Purcell	When I am laid in earth (Dido and Aeneas)	LH	C-G	†
Quilter	Blow, blow, thou winter wind	HL	C-E	BOO

French Dramatic Songs and Arias

Mezzo Soprano

Berlioz	Le spectre de la rose			CST
-----	Les nuits d'été			AUG
Bizet	Habanera (Carmen)	HM	D-F	†
Chausson	Chanson perpétuelle String quartet	H	CS-GS	ROU
-----	Poème de l'amour et de la mer	H		INT
Debussy	Air de Lia (L'Enfant Prodigue)	H	E-A	DUR
-----	Chevaux de bois	H	C-G	†

62

(Debussy)	Colloque sentimental			DUR
-----	Noël des enfants qui n'ont plus de maisons			DUR
Duparc	Au pays où se fait la guerre			SAL
-----	La vague et la cloche			ROU
-----	La vie antérieure	HL		†
-----	Le manoir de Rosamunde	HL	B-F	BOS
-----	Phidylé	MH	EF-AF	BOS
-----	Testament	HL		INT
Fauré	Automne	MH	D-FS	GSC
-----	Poème d'un jour			HAM
-----	Prison	LH		†
-----	Toujours	LH	F-AF	†
Février	L'intruse	M	B-DF	HEU
Gounod	O ma lyre immortelle (Sappho)	M	C-G	†
Hahn	D'une prison	L	BF-EF	HEU
-----	Offrande	M	D-D	†
Halévy	Humble fille des champs (Charles VI)			GSC
Honegger	Les cloches			SEN
Hue	J'ai pleuré en Rêve	HL	D-E	BOS
Indy	Lied maritime	LH	B-G	†
Lenormand	Quelle souffrance	HM	AF-F	HAM
Massenet	Il est doux, il est bon (Hérodiade)	MH	EF-BF	GSC
-----	Werther! qui m'aurait dit (Air de lettres) (Werther)			HEU
Meyerbeer	Ah! mon fils (Le Prophète)	M	B-AS	†
Paladilhe	Lamento provinçal	M	CS-FS	HOM
Poldowski	Dansons la gigue	M	EF-G	MAR
Saint-Saëns	Amour, viens aider (Samson et Dalila)	HM	AF-G	†
-----	L'attente			DUR
Severac	Chanson pour le petit cheval			ROU

German Dramatic Songs

Mezzo Soprano

Brahms	Ach, wende diesen Blick			†
-----	Am Sonntag Morgen	L	CS-FS	†
-----	Nicht mehr zu dir zu gehen			†
-----	Treue Liebe	LMH	DS-E	†
-----	Von ewiger Liebe	LMH	B-AF	†
Franz	Im Herbst	HM	A-F	†
Liszt	Die drei Zigeuner	LM	B-G	GSC
-----	Die Lorelei	LH	BF-BF	†

63

Loewe	Walpurgisnacht	H	G-G	SC
Mahler	Das Irdische Leben	HL	A-F	INT
-----	Ich hab' ein gluehend Messer	M	BF-GF	WEI
-----	Lieder eines fahrenden Gesellen	M		INT
Marx	An einen Herbstwald	M	CS-FS	UNI
-----	Hat dich die Liebe beruehrt	MH	EF-BF	AMP
Mendelssohn	Schilflied	M	F-FS	
Schubert	Am Feierabend	HL	BF-F	†
-----	An Schwager Kronos	HL	G-E	†
-----	Aufenthalt	HLM	A-F	†
-----	Dem Unendlichen	L	A-GF	†
-----	Der Atlas	HL	BF-F	†
-----	Der Doppelgaenger	HL	G-D	GSC
-----	Der Erlkoenig	HML	A-E	†
-----	Der Lindenbaum	HL	A-D	†
-----	Der Tod und das Maedchen	HL	A-EF	†
-----	Der Zwerg	M	A-GF	PET
-----	Die Allmacht	HML	G-E	†
-----	Die junge Nonne	LH	C-GF	†
-----	Die Kraehe	HL	A-E	†
-----	Die Liebe hat gelogen	LM	G-F	†
-----	Die Stadt	HL	A-E	†
-----	Du liebst mich nicht	LH	E-FS	†
-----	Erstarrung	HL	D-F	†
-----	Fahrt zum Hades	HL	G-DF	PET
-----	Fragment aus dem Aeschylus			PET
-----	Fruehlingstraum	HL	C-D	†
-----	Ganymed	LH	EF-G	†
-----	Gruppe aus dem Tartarus	L	CS-EF	†
-----	In der Ferne	HL		†
-----	Mut	HL		†
-----	Schaefers Klagelied	HL	BF-D	†
Schumann	Der arme Peter	HL	B-G	†
-----	Fruehlingsfahrt	HL	B-E	†
-----	Heiss' mich nicht reden			
-----	Mit Myrthen und Rosen	HL	A-D	†
-----	Schoene Wiege meiner Leiden	HL	C-EF	GSC
-----	Waldesgespraech	HL	A-FS	†
Strauss	Caecilie	MH	E-B	†
-----	Ruhe meine Seele			†
Wagner	Schmerzen	HL		†
Wolf	Alle gingen, Herz zu Ruh	HL	C-EF	†
-----	Das Koehlerweib ist trunken			PET
-----	Denk' es, o Seele	LH	EF-F	†

(Wolf)	Der Freund	HM	BF-E	PET
-----	Die ihr schwebet	HL	EF-EF	†
-----	Geh' Geliebter, geh' jetzt			PET
-----	Liebe mir in Busen zuendet	M	E-F	†
-----	Ueber Nacht	LH	D-G	†
-----	Zur Ruh', zur Ruh'	HL	A-GF	†

Italian Dramatic Songs and Arias

Mezzo Soprano

Cimara	Canto di primavera		D-G	FRL
Donizetti	O mio Fernando	M	B-A	†
	(La Favorita)			
Durante	Vergin, tutta amor	LM	C-EF	†
Mascagni	Voi lo sapete	H	B-A	†
	(Cavalleria Rusticana)			
Pergolesi	Confusa, smarrita			GSC
Piccini	O nuit, dresse du mystere			GSC
	(Le Faux Lord)			
Pizzetti	La madre al figlio lontano			FRL
Ponchielli	Stella del marinar	M	B-A	RIC
	(La Gioconda)			
-----	Voce di donna (La Gioconda)			
Respighi	In alto mare			BON
-----	Io sono la madre	L		RIC
-----	Nebbie			†
Verdi	Condotta ell' era in ceppi			GSC
	(Il Trovatore)			
-----	O don fatale (Don Carlos)	MH	CF-CF	†
-----	Stride la vampa	M	B-G	†
	(Il Trovatore)			

Miscellaneous Dramatic Songs and Arias

Mezzo Soprano

Alvarez	La partida	HL	DS-E	GSC
Dvořák	Hear my prayer, O Lord			AMP
Gliere	Ah, twine no blossoms	HM	CS-F	DIT
Granados	La maja dolorosa	M		INT
Gretchaninoff	Over the steppe	LM	C-G	GSC
-----	Wounded birch	HL	B-EF	†
Grieg	A dream			†
-----	A swan			†
-----	Autumnal gale	HL	A-F	CFI
-----	Den Aergjerrige			

(Grieg)	Digte af Vilhelm Krag			HAN
-----	Eros	LM	C-F	†
-----	Hjemkomst	M	B-F	HAN
-----	In the boat	LM	D-ES	†
-----	Jeg lever et liv i laengsel	L	BF-E	HAN
-----	Vaer hilset, I damer	M	D-F	HAN
-----	Verse for an album			
Mussorgsky	After the battle			GSC
-----	Divination by water (Khovantchina)	L	GS-FS	GSC
-----	Hopak	HM	CS-FS	GSC
-----	Matha's song (Khovantchina)	ML		GSC
-----	On the Dnieper			GSC
-----	The orphan girl			GSC
Rachmaninoff	As fair is she as noonday light			GSC
-----	Christ is risen	LM	D-F	GAL
-----	Floods of spring	HL		DIT
-----	O, do not grieve	M	BF-AF	GSC
-----	Oh, no, I pray do not depart	H		DIT
-----	O thou billowy harvest field	HL	CS-E	GSC
-----	The soldier's bride			†
-----	To the children	MH	F-G	DIT
Rimsky-Korsakov	On the Georgian hills	HM		GSC
Sibelius	Black Roses	M	A-ES	AMP
-----	The tryst	M		AMP
-----	Was it a dream			BRH
Stravinsky	The cloister (La novice)			DIT
Tchaikovsky	Adieu forêts (Jeanne D'Arc)	HM	BF-FS	GSC
-----	None but the lonely heart	HLM	C-F	DIT
-----	Pauline's romance (Pique Dame)	M	BF-AF	GSC

American Humorous Songs

Mezzo Soprano

Bernstein	I hate music	H	C-A	WIT
-----	La bonne cuisine	H	B-B	GSC
Carpenter	Don't ceare	M	C-D	GSC
-----	If	M	D-E	GSC
-----	To a young gentleman	M	C-F	GSC
Crist	Chinese mother goose rhymes	H	C-G	CFI

Davis	Deaf old woman			GAL
Diack	Little Jack Horner			CFI
-----	Little Polly Flinders			CFI
Dougherty	Declaration of independence	L	C-C	GSC
-----	Love in the dictionary	M	C-G	GSC
Duke	I can't be talkin' of love	H	CS-G	GSC
Enders	Russian picnic	HM	C-G	GSC
Griselle and Young	The cuckoo clock	LH	EF-G	GSC
Hadley	My shadow			ASC
Hageman	Animal crackers	HL	C-D	GSC
Kountz	The little French clock	LH	D-G	GAL
Nordoff	Serenade	H	CS-FS	AMP
-----	There shall be more joy	M	CS-FS	AMP
Rawls	The balloon man	L	A-FS	AMP
Rich	American lullaby	LH	C-F	GSC
Sacco	Mexican serenade	HL	D-EF	BOS
Schuman	Holiday song	M	C-F	GSC
Slonimsky	Gravestones at Hancock, New Hampshire	H	D-G	AXE
Spross	Will o' the wisp			JCH
Stein	The puffin	M		CFI
Wolf	Jack in the box			

British Humorous Songs

Mezzo Soprano

Arne, T.	Why so pale and wan			GSC
Bax	Oh dear, what can the matter be?	M	D-EF	CHE
Bliss	The buckle			CUR
Britten	Oliver Cromwell			BOH
Clarke	Shy one	HL	BF-G	BOH
Gibbs	Five eyes	HL	D-D	BOS
Hely-Hutchinson	Old mother Hubbard	HL	B-E	CFI
Hughes	A Ballynure ballad	L	BF-D	BOH
Johnston	Because I were shy	L	B-E	CRA
Lehmann	The cuckoo	HH	D-B	BOH
Novello	The little damozel	LHM	C-G	BOO

French Humorous Songs

Mezzo Soprano

Chabrier	Villanelle des petits canards	HML	B-E	†
Debussy	Ballade des femmes de Paris			DUR
Pierné	Ils etaient trois petits chats blancs			MAR
Poulenc	Le bestiaire String quartet, flute, clarinet and bassoon	M		AMP
Ravel	Sur l'herbe	MH	C-G	DUR
Satie	La statue de bronze			ROU
-----	Le chapelier			ROU

German Humorous Songs and Arias

Mezzo Soprano

Bach, J.S.	Patron, das macht der Wind (Phoebus and Pan)	M	C-G	GSC
Brahms	Der Kranz			†
-----	Vergebliches Staendchen	LHM	E-FS	†
Mahler	Des Antonius von Padua Fischpredigt	HL	GF-F	†
-----	Rheinlegendchen	M	B-FS	†
-----	Wer hat dies Liedlein erdacht?	HL	BF-E	INT
Marx	Der bescheidene Schaefer			UNI
Mozart	Die Alte			
-----	Warnung	HM	C-D	
Reger	Waldeinsamkeit	HML	A-D	BOS
Reichardt	Rhapsodie			MOS
Schubert	Die Maenner sind mechant			PET
-----	Heidenroeslein			
Strauss	Fuer fuenfzehn Pfennige			†
Wolf	Elfenlied	HL	D-F	†
-----	Ich hab' in Penna	LH		†
-----	Nimmersatte Liebe	LH	CF-AF	†
-----	Tretet ein, hoher Krieger	HL	B-F	†

Miscellaneous Humorous Songs

Mezzo Soprano

Grieg	My Johann	HL	BF-EF	GSC
-----	Til min dreng		C-E	
Paisiello	Chi vuol la zingarella	L	C-F	GSC
Rontani	Or ch'io non segno più	HL	CS-E	DIT

American Folk Songs (Arr.)

Mezzo Soprano

Bacon	Adam and Eve	M	B-D	CFI
-----	Common Bill			
Bartholomew	Dearest Billie	M	E-E	GSC
Brockway	Barbara Allen			
-----	Frog went-a-courting			
-----	Sourwood Mountain			
-----	The nightingale			GRA
-----	The old maid's song			GRA
Davis	Deaf old woman			GAL
-----	He's gone away	M	C-E	GAL
Hughes	Birds' courting song			GSC
Matteson	The blue eyed boy			GSC
Niles	Down in the valley			GSC
-----	Go 'way from my window	MH	C-G	GSC
-----	Hi, ho the preacher man			GSC
-----	I wonder as I wander	HL	BF-D	GSC
-----	If I had a ribbon bow			GSC
-----	Jesus, Jesus rest your head	M		JFI
Powell	The rich old woman	M		JFI
Scott	Wailie, wailie	M	D-E	JCH
Shaw	Black is the color of my true love's hair	M	C-F	DIT
-----	He's gone away	M	C-E	DIT
Taylor	Twenty, eighteen	HM	D-E	JFI
Young	Red rosey bush	M		CFI

British Folk Songs (Arr.)

Mezzo Soprano

Bax	Oh dear, what can the matter be?	M	D-EF	CHE
Benjamin	Linstead market	M		BOO

Britten	A charm	L	AS-E	BOO
-----	O waly, waly			
-----	Oliver Cromwell			BOH
-----	The ash grove			BOH
-----	The miller of Dee			
-----	The Sally gardens			BOH
-----	The trees they grow so high			
Butterworth	Roving in the dew			AUG
Clayton	O men from the fields	M	C-F	BOS
Harty	My lagan love	ML	BF-EF	BOO
-----	The lowlands of Holland			OXF
Hopekirk	Coming through the rye			DIT
-----	Loch Lomond			DIT
Hughes	A Ballynure ballad	L	BF-D	BOH
-----	Down by the Sally gardens			BOO
-----	Hey diddle diddle			CRA
-----	I know my love			BOO
Johnson	Because I were shy	L	B-E	CRA
Kennedy- Fraser	An Eriskay love lilt			BOO
-----	Kishmul's galley			BOO
-----	Song of the sea reivers			
-----	The bens of Jura			BOO
Kreisler	Loch Lomond			
Lawson	Turn ye to me	M	B-E	GSC
McGill	Lord Randall			BOO
-----	Lord Thomas			BOO
Page	The harp that once through Tara's halls			DIT
Peterkin	I wish and I wish	M	B-E	OXF
Quilter	Ye banks and braes	M	DF-EF	BOH
Reid	Turn ye to me			BOO
Shaw	The land of heart's desire	M	C-E	CUR
Stevens	Early one morning			
Vaughan Williams	And all in the morning	L	D-E	GAL
-----	King William	L	D-D	OXF
-----	Lullaby of the Madonna	L	BF-D	GRA
-----	Robin Hood and the pedlar	M	D-E	OXF
-----	Rolling in the dew			OXF
Welsh	All through the night			
Wilson	Come let's be merry			BOO

Miscellaneous Folk Songs (Arr.)

Mezzo Soprano

Beethoven	Bonnie laddie, Highland laddie			†
-----	Enchantress farewell			
-----	Sally in our alley			
-----	Sunset			
-----	The lovely lass of Inverness			
Brahms	Mein Maedel hat einen Rosenmund	M	F-F	†
Canteloube	Bailèro			HEU
-----	Brezaviola			HEU
-----	L'aïo de rotso			HEU
-----	L'antouèno			HEU
-----	Malurous qu'o uno fenno			HEU
-----	Passo pel prat			HEU
Dvořák	Gypsy songs	LH	D-A	AMP
Falla	Asturiana	HL		AMP
-----	El paño moruno	HL		AMP
-----	Jota	LH		AMP
-----	Nana	HL		AMP
-----	Polo	HL		AMP
-----	Seguidilla murciana	HL		AMP
Greek Folk	Neranzula			
Obradors	Con amores a mi madre			RIC
Ravel	Chanson espagnole	LH	D-BF	DUR
-----	Cinq mélodies populaires grecques			CUR
-----	Quel galant!	M	D-F	DUR
-----	Tout gai	MH	EF-F	DUR
Schumann	Drei Gesaenge (Hebrew melodies) Harp or piano			
Weckerlin	Maman, dites-moi	M	E-FS	BOS
-----	Menuet d'Exaudet	H	D-G	GSC
-----	O, ma tendre musette	LM	A-E	GSC
-----	Venez, agréable printemps	M	C-F	

Negro Spirituals

Mezzo Soprano

Boatner	Oh, what a beautiful city!	HL	D-E	GSC
-----	On mah journey	LH	EF-EF	RIC
-----	Trampin', tryin' to make Heaven my home	L	D-F	ELK

71

Brown	Dere's no hidin' place down dere			CFI
-----	Every time I feel de spirit	L		AMP
-----	Sometimes I feel like a motherless child	L		AMP
Burleigh	Balm in Gilead	HL		RIC
-----	De gospel train	HL		RIC
-----	Deep river	HML		RIC
-----	Go down, Moses	HL		RIC
-----	Hard trials	M		RIC
-----	Joshua fit de battle ob Jericho	LH	DS-E	RIC
-----	My Lord what a mornin'?			
-----	Nobody knows de trouble I've seen	HL		RIC
-----	Oh Peter, go ring-a-dem bells			RIC
-----	Ride on, King Jesus	H		RIC
-----	Sometimes I feel like a motherless child	HML		RIC
-----	Were you there?	HML		RIC
Dett	Sit down servant			GSC
Fisher	He's de lily of de valley			
Johnson	At the feet of Jesus	L		
-----	City called Heaven			ROB
-----	Dere's no hidin' place down dere			
-----	Hold on			ROB
-----	Honor, honor	HM	C-E	CFI
-----	My good Lord done been here	HM	BF-F	CFI
-----	Ride on, King Jesus			CFI
-----	Roll Jerd'n roll	M	EF-F	GSC
-----	Witness	HM	D-F	CFI
Kerby- Forrest	He's got the whole world in His hands	M	G-E	MLS
Lawrence	Let us break bread together	HML	BF-EF	MCR
MacGimsey	Sweet little Jesus boy	ML	D-D	CFI
Niles	Does you call dat religion?			GSC
-----	Hold on			GSC
-----	My little black star			GSC
Payne	Crucifixion	L	C-C	GSC
Price	My soul's been anchored in the Lord			GAM
Ryder	Let us break bread together	LH	D-G	JFI

Saunders	The Lord's prayer	L	BF-C	BOH
White	Wake up, Jacob			PRE

American Songs Employing Agility

Mezzo Soprano

Bernstein	La bonne cuisine	H	B-B	GSC
Cough- Leighter	My lover he comes on the skee	HM	D-F	BOS
Crist	O come hither	HM	B-GS	CFI
Curran	Ho! Mr. Piper	LH	D-G	GSC
Diack	Little Jack Horner			CFI
Griffes	We'll to the woods and gather May	M	D-F	GSC
Hageman	Miranda	HL		GAL
Nevin	One spring morning	MH	DS-F	BOS
Nordoff	There shall be more joy	M	CS-FS	AMP
Parker	The lark now leaves her watery nest	LH	D-BF	JCH
Speaks	In May time	HL	D-E	JCH

British Songs and Arias Employing Agility

Mezzo Soprano

Arne, T.	Where the bee sucks	HM		†
German	Charming Chloe	HML		NOV
Green	My lips shall speak the praise	M	E-F	OXF
-----	Salvation belongeth unto the Lord	M	F-EF	OXF
Handel	In the battle, fame pursuing (Deborah)	L	A-D	†
-----	Lord, to thee each night and day (Theodora)	L	C-E	†
-----	O thou that tellest good tidings to Zion (The Messiah)	L	A-C	†
Hely- Hutchinson	Old mother Hubbard	HL	B-E	CFI
Morley	It was a lover and his lass	HM		DIT
Purcell	From rosy bow'rs (Don Quixote)			AUG
-----	Hark! how all things with one sound rejoice			NOV

(Purcell)	Hark! the echoing air			BAF
	(The Fairy Queen)			
-----	Nymphs and shepherds	HM	C-F	†
	(The Libertine)			
Wilson	Come let's be merry			BOO
-----	Phillis has such charming	ML	CS-EF	BOO
	graces			

French Songs and Arias Employing Agility

Mezzo Soprano

Bizet	Adieu de l'hotesse arabe			
-----	Ouvre ton coeur	MH	DS-GS	†
-----	Seguidilla (Carmen)	HM	B-FS	†
Campra	Charmant papillon	MH	D-G	GSC
	(Les Fêtes Venitiennes)			
Chausson	Les papillons	M	C-F	GSC
Debussy	Fêtes galantes	LH	CS-A	†
Delibes	Le rossignol	M		GSC
-----	Passepied	LH	DS-CS	GSC
Dupont	Cendrillon	M		
Falla	Polo	HL		AMP
Fauré	Mandoline	HL	F-E	†
Georges	La pluie	HL		INT
Gounod	Que fais-tu blanche			JCH
	tourterelle? (Roméo et Juliette)			
Meyerbeer	O prêtres de Baal			BRO
	(Le Prophète)			
Poulenc	Air vif	H	C-AF	ROU
Thomas	Je connais un pauvre	H	C-B	†
	enfant (Mignon)			

German Songs and Arias Employing Agility

Mezzo Soprano

Bach, J.S.	Gelobet sei der Herr			AUG
	(Cantata 129) Oboe d'Amore			
-----	Hochgelobter Gottessohn			NOV
	(Cantata 6) English horn or			
	viola or violin			
-----	It is finished	L	B-D	†
	(St. John Passion)			
-----	Mein glaeubiges Herze	HML		†
	(Cantata 68)			
Brahms	Botschaft	HL	D-F	†

(Brahms)	Das Maedchen spricht	H	E-FS	†
-----	O liebliche Wangen	MLH	E-G	†
Haydn	My mother bids me bind my hair	M	E-E	†
-----	The mermaid's song	M	C-F	PRE
Jensen	Am Ufer des Flusses des Manzanares	H	D-FS	GSC
Mahler	Des Antonius von Padua Fischpredigt	HL	GF-F	†
-----	Rheinlegendchen	M	B-FS	†
-----	Wer hat dies Liedlein erdacht?	HL	BF-E	INT
Schubert	Das Wandern	HLM	E-E	†
-----	Irrlicht			
-----	Ungeduld	HML		†
Schumann	Fruehlingsnacht	L	CS-E	†
-----	Waldesgespraech	HL	A-FS	†
Strauss	Fuer fuenfzehn Pfennige			†
Wolf	Die Zigeunerin			PET

Italian Songs and Arias Employing Agility

Mezzo Soprano

Carissimi	Vittoria, mio core	HLM	B-E	†
Cimara	Canto di primavera		D-G	FRL
Cimarosa	Nel lasciarti (L'Olympiade)			RIC
Donaudy	Spirate pur, spirate			RIC
Donizetti	Il segreto per esser felici (Lucrezia Borgia)	M	C-G	†
Durante	Danza, danza fanciulla gentile	HM	BF-F	†
Handel	Amor commanda (Floridante)	H		†
-----	Ch'io mai vi possa (Siroe)			†
-----	Furibondo spira (Partenope)			KIS
-----	Qual farfalletta (Partenope)	H	E-A	†
Lotti	Pur dicesti, o bocca bella	LMH	E-FS	GSC
Pergolesi	Ogni pena più spietata	L	B-E	GSC
Rossini	Bel raggio lusinghier (Semiramide)	H	CS-A	GSC
-----	La danza	MH	E-A	†
-----	Non più mesta (La Cenerentola)	M	A-B	GSC
-----	Una voce poco fa (Il Barbiere di Siviglia)	HM	GS-E	GSC

Scarlatti, A.	Rugiadose odorose	HL	D-E	DIT
	(Il Pirro e Demetrio)			
-----	Se Florindo è fedele	LM	EF-EF	GSC
Scarlatti, D.	Consolati e spara amante	L	BF-E	GSC
-----	Qual farfalletta			
Vivaldi	Un certo no so che	HL	BF-EF	†

Miscellaneous Songs and Arias
Employing Agility

Mezzo Soprano

Alvarez	La partida	HL	DS-E	GSC
Bach, J.S.	Qui sedes ad dexteram			†
	Patris (Mass in B Minor)			
	Oboe d'amore			
Chopin	The maiden's wish	LM	CS-E	GSC
Falla	Nana	HL		AMP
-----	Seguidilla murciana	HL		AMP
Granados	El majo discreto	H		INT
Grieg	Good morning			†
Mozart	Laudamus Te			PET
	(C Minor Mass)			
Stravinsky	The cloister (La novice)			DIT
Turina	Farruca	M	A-F	UME

American Songs Employing
Crescendo and Diminuendo

Mezzo Soprano

Bacon	Is there such a thing as	M	DS-FS	AMP
	day?			
Barber	Rain has fallen	HM	D-E	GSC
-----	Sleep now	MH	EF-AF	GSC
-----	The daisies	M	C-F	GSC
Beach	Ah, love but a day			ASC
Branscombe	Across the blue Aegean	M	G-G	GAL
Cadman	From the land of the			WHI
	sky-blue water			
Campbell-				
Tipton	A spirit flower	LHM	B-G	GSC
-----	The crying of water	LH	FS-GS	GSC
Carpenter	Go, lovely rose	M	DF-EF	GSC
-----	The day is no more	M	GS-DS	GSC
-----	The pools of peace	M	D-F	GSC

(Carpenter)	The sleep that flits on baby's eyes	M	B-FS	GSC
-----	Watercolors	M	C-F	GSC
-----	When I bring to you colour'd toys	LM	CS-FS	GSC
Charles Clough- Leighter	Clouds	HML	C-EF	GSC
	Who knows?	M		GSC
Duke	Loveliest of trees	L	C-D	GSC
Engel	Sea shell	M	EF-EF	GSC
Fairchild	A memory			BOS
Hopkinson	Beneath a weeping willow's shade	H	D-G	†
-----	My days have been so wondrous free	LH	EF-G	
Howe	Berceuse	HM	EF-F	GSC
Naginski	The pasture	M	BF-EF	GSC
Niles	I wonder as I wander	HL	BF-D	GSC
-----	Jesus, Jesus rest your head	HL	A-D	GSC
Nordoff	Serenade	H	CS-FS	AMP
Rogers	At parting	LH	CS-FS	GSC
Silberta	Aylia, dancer of Kashmir	M	B-F	GSC
Thompson	Velvet shoes	M	C-E	ECS

British Songs and Arias Employing
Crescendo and Diminuendo

Mezzo Soprano

Bantock	Yung Yang	MH	E-G	GAL
Bax	A lullaby			
-----	Cradle song			CHA
Benjamin	Calm sea and mist			CUR
Clarke	Shy one	HL	BF-G	BOH
Goossens	Melancholy	M		CHE
Gurney	Under the greenwood tree			ROG
Handel	Art thou troubled (Rodelinda)	M	F-F	GSC
-----	He shall feed His (The Messiah)	L	C-D	†
-----	He was despised (The Messiah)	L	B-D	†
-----	Let me wander not unseen (L'Allegro)	M	D-G	†
-----	O sleep why dost thou leave me (Semele)	H	DS-GS	†
Head	The ships of Arcady	ML	BF-EF	BOH

77

Horn	Cherry ripe	M	D-G	†
-----	I've been roaming	L	B-E	†
Ireland	Bed in summer			CUR
Peterkin	The garden of bamboos	M	EF-F	OXF
Purcell	I attempt from love's sickness to fly (The Indian Queen)	MH	CS-E	†
Quilter	Dream valley	H	EF-GF	ROG
-----	The fuchsia tree			BOO
Shaw	Song of the Palanquin bearers	LH	E-F	CUR

French Songs and Arias Employing Crescendo and Diminuendo

Mezzo Soprano

Berlioz	Villanelle	H	E-FS	†
Chabrier	Romance de l'étoile			ENO
Chaminade	The silver ring	HM	BF-F	GSC
David	Charmant oiseau (La Perle du Brésil)	M	D-E	†
Debussy	Air de Lia (L'Enfant Prodigue)	H	E-A	DUR
-----	C'est l'extase	LH	CS-A	†
-----	En sourdine	M	C-FS	†
-----	La flûte de Pan		B-B	†
-----	Le tombeau des Naïades			JOB
-----	Les ingénus			DUR
Duparc	Chanson triste	MH	FS-AF	†
-----	L'invitation au voyage	HM	E-F	†
-----	Phidylé	MH	EF-AF	BOS
Fauré	Adieu	MH	F-F	†
-----	Arpège	MH	E-FS	HAM
-----	Clair de lune	MH	C-G	†
-----	En prière	H	F-F	†
-----	Le secret	LH	F-G	†
-----	Spleen	H	E-FS	MAR
Koechlin	L'hiver	H	E-G	†
Martini	Plaisir d'amour	M	BF-EF	GSC
Meyerbeer	Nobles Seigneurs, salut! (Les Huguenots)	LH	C-C	†
Mouret	Doux plaisirs (Pirithous)			CHE
Paladilhe	Psyché	HM	BF-F	GSC
Rameau	A l'amour rendez les armes (Hippolyte et Aricie)			CHO
-----	Dans ces doux asiles (Castor et Pollux)			LEM

Rhené-Baton	Berceuse			DUR
Satie	Daphénéo			ROU

German Songs Employing
Crescendo and Diminuendo

Mezzo Soprano

Beethoven	Andenken			†
Brahms	Auf dem See	HL	D-F	†
-----	Sonntag	H	D-G	†
-----	Spanisches Lied			†
-----	Therese	HL	B-D	†
-----	Wie Melodien zieht es	HL	A-E	†
Franz	Die blauen Fruehlingsaugen	HL		†
-----	Es hat die Rose sich beklagt	LH	DF-F	†
-----	Fruehling und Liebe	HL		†
-----	Sterne mit den gold'nen Fuesschen	HL	DS-E	†
Mahler	Ich atmet' einen linden Duft	HL		INT
Reger	Des Kindes Gebet	H	F-G	BOT
-----	Mit Rosen bestreut			UNI
-----	Waldeinsamkeit	HML	A-D	BOS
Schubert	An den Mond	HL	F-GF	†
-----	Auf dem Wasser zu singen	MH	EF-GF	†
-----	Der Einsame	LH	D-G	†
-----	Der Musensohn	LH	FS-G	†
-----	Der Schmetterling	LH	E-F	†
-----	Der Wanderer	HML	FS-D	GSC
-----	Der Wanderer an den Mond	LM	D-F	PET
-----	Die Taubenpost	HL	D-EF	†
-----	Fruehlingstraum	HL	C-D	†
-----	Geheimes	HL	BF-EF	†
-----	Gretchen am Spinnrade	H	F-A	†
-----	Im Fruehling	LH	D-FS	†
-----	Lachen und Weinen	HL	C-EF	†
-----	Liebesbotschaft	H	E-G	†
-----	Nacht und Traeume	HL	C-DF	†
Schumann	Der Nussbaum	LMH	D-FS	†
-----	Der Sandmann	HL	AF-DF	†
-----	Die Soldatenbraut	HL	AF-EF	†
-----	Erstes Gruen	HL	D-D	†
-----	Lieder der Braut	H	D-A	†

79

(Schumann)	Marienwuermchen	HL	D-D		†
Strauss	Die Nacht	HL			†
Wolf	Auch kleine Dinge	HM	D-E		†
-----	Der Gaertner	HL			†
-----	In dem Schatten meiner Locken	M	C-EF		†
-----	Mausfallen Spruechlein	HL	BF-E		†
-----	Morgentau	HL	D-D		†
-----	Nun wandre, Maria	HL	EF-D		†
-----	Und willst du deinen Liebsten sterben	HL			†
-----	Verschwiegene Liebe	LH	DF-FS		†
-----	Wenn du zu den Blumen gehst	HL	B-EF	DIT
Wolff	Knabe und Veilchen	M	D-D	HMP

Italian Songs and Arias Employing
Crescendo and Diminuendo

Mezzo Soprano

Bononcini	Per la gloria	HL	C-EF		†
Caldara	Alma del core			GSC
-----,-	Sebben crudele	HML	E-DS		†
-----	Selve amiche, ombrose piante	HM	E-E		†
De Luca	Non posso disperar	HL	C-E	GSC
Gluck	Vieni che poi sereno (La Semiramide)	M	D-G		†
Handel	Affani del pensier (Ottone)				†
-----	Cangio d'aspetto (Admeto)				†
-----	Ombra mai fu (Serse)	HM	BF-EF		†
Marcello	Non m'è grave morir per amore	L	C-E	GSC
Monteverdi	Lasciatemi morire (Arianna)	ML	D-D		†
Pergolesi	Se tu m'ami	LMH	C-G	GSC
Respighi	Contrasto	M		RIC
Rontani	Se bel rio	ML	D-C		†
Rosa	Selve, voi che le speranze	MH	D-G	DIT
-----	Vado ben spesso	ML	C-EF		†
Scarlatti, A.	Sento nel core	M	E-F		†
Secchi	Love me or not			BOO

Miscellaneous Songs and Arias Employing
Crescendo and Diminuendo

Mezzo Soprano

Bach, J.S.	Esurientes implevit bonis (Magnificat in D Major)			†
Backer-Grondahl	In dreaming dance			
Gretchaninoff	My native land	L	C-EF	GSC
Grieg	In the boat	LM	D-ES	†
-----	Nu er aftenen lys og lang	L	C-E	HAN
-----	With a water lily	HM	CS-EF	†
Mussorgsky	Oriental chant (Josua Navine Cantata)	ML	BF-E	GSC
Rachmaninoff	Lilacs	LH	EF-G	†
-----	The island	LH	DF-F	†
Stravinsky	Pastorale			GSC

American Songs Employing
Piano Singing

Mezzo Soprano

Barber	Rain has fallen	HM	D-E	GSC
-----	Sleep now	MH	EF-AF	GSC
Campbell-Tipton	A spirit flower	LHM	B-G	GSC
-----	The crying of water	LH	FS-GS	GSC
Carpenter	Go, lovely rose	M	DF-EF	GSC
-----	May the maiden			DIT
-----	On the seashore of endless worlds	M	C-FS	GSC
-----	The day is no more	M	GS-DS	GSC
-----	The green river	M	B-E	GSC
-----	The pools of peace	M	D-F	GSC
-----	The sleep that flits on baby's eyes	M	B-FS	GSC
-----	Watercolors	M	C-F	GSC
-----	When I bring to you colour'd toys	LM	CS-FS	GSC
Charles	Clouds	HML	C-EF	GSC
-----	When I have sung my songs	HM	BF-EF	GSC
Clough-Leighter	Who knows?	M		GSC
Davis	Nancy Hanks	H	D-G	GAL
Duke	To Karen, singing	M	CS-G	ELV

Engel	A sprig of rosemary	M	EF-F	GSC
-----	Sea shell	M	EF-EF	GSC
Fairchild	A memory			BOS
Gaines	My heart hath a mind			
Ganz	A memory	HM	B-D	GSC
Giannini	Tell me, o blue, blue sky	H		RIC
Griffes	O'er the Tarn's unruffled mirror	HL	G-E	GSC
-----	The dreamy lake	H	BS-GS	GSC
Guion	Mam'selle Marie	M	D-E	GSC
Hageman	Do not go, my love	HL	B-EF	GSC
Howe	Berceuse	HM	EF-F	GSC
Kingsford	Wallpaper for a little girl's room	M	BF-F	GSC
Kramer	Swans	HL		RIC
MacGimsey	Sweet little Jesus boy	ML	D-D	CFI
Manning	In the Luxembourg gardens	HML	BF-D	GSC
-----	Shoes	M	EF-F	GSC
Menotti	Lullaby (The Consul)			GSC
Naginski	Night song at Amalfi	M	D-EF	GSC
-----	The pasture	M	BF-EF	GSC
Niles	I wonder as I wander	HL	BF-D	GSC
-----	Jesus, Jesus rest your head	HL	A-D	GSC
Nordoff	Serenade	H	CS-FS	AMP
Schuman	Orpheus with his lute	M	C-FS	GSC
Thompson	Velvet shoes	M	C-E	ECS

British Songs Employing
Piano Singing

Mezzo Soprano

Bax	Cradle song			CHA
Benjamin	Calm sea and mist			CUR
Clarke	Shy one	HL	BF-G	BOH
Coleridge-Taylor	She rested by the broken brook	HL		DIT
Delius	Twilight fancies	M	D-FS	CFI
Dunhill	The cloths of heaven	LM	EF-G	STB
Elgar	Sea pictures	L	A-A	BOO
Handel	Let me wander not unseen (L'Allegro)	M	D-G	†
Harty	My lagan love	ML	BF-EF	BOO
Head	The ships of Arcady	ML	BF-EF	BOH
Peterkin	The garden of bamboos	M	EF-F	OXF

Pilkington	Rest, sweet nymphs			STB
Quilter	Dream valley	H	EF-GF	ROG
Sanderson	Quiet	ML	AF-EF	BOH
Scott	Lullaby	MML	BF-DF	GAL
Shaw	The land of heart's desire	M	C-E	CUR
Vaughn				
Williams	Silent noon			GSC
-----	The twilight people	L	BF-EF	OXF

French Songs and Arias Employing
Piano Singing

Mezzo Soprano

Berlioz	Villanelle	H	E-FS	†
Bizet	Pastorale	H	C-FS	GSC
Chabrier	Romance de l'étoile			ENO
Chaminade	The silver ring	HM	BF-F	GSC
Chausson	Dans la forêt	HL		INT
Debussy	En sourdine	M	C-FS	†
-----	Il pleure dans mon coeur	LH	CS-GS	†
-----	L'ombre des arbres			†
-----	La flûte de Pan		B-B	†
-----	La grotte			DUR
-----	La mort des amants			†
-----	Le tombeau des naïades			JOB
-----	Recueillement			DUR
Fauré	Adieu	MH	F-F	†
-----	Après un rêve	HM	C-F	†
-----	C'est l'extase	HL	C-FF	GSC
-----	Clair de lune	MH	C-G	†
-----	Dans les ruines d'une abbaye	M	E-FS	†
-----	En prière	H	F-F	†
-----	Le secret	LH	F-G	†
Ferrari	Le miroir	M	E-F	GSC
Fevrier	L'intruse	M	B-DF	HEU
Franck	Le mariage des roses	M	E-FS	BOS
Godard	Cachés dans cet asile (Jocelyn) Violin or cello	MH	DF-F	GSC
Gossec	Dors, mon enfant (Rosine)	L		CHE
Gounod	Au rossignol	LMH	D-G	CHO
-----	Sérénade	LMH	D-A	GSC
Hahn	A Chloris	H	DS-FS	HEU
-----	D'une prison	L	BF-EF	HEU
-----	L'heure exquise	M	DF-F	†
-----	Offrande	M	D-D	†
-----	Paysage	MH	EF-G	HEU

83

Lully	Au clair de la lune	H	E-D	CFI
-----	Bois épais (Amadis)	ML	C-EF	†
Massanet	Crépuscule	M	D-E	GSC
Mouret	Doux plaisirs (Pirithous)			CHE
Paladilhe	Psyché	HM	BF-F	GSC
Pessard	L'adieu du matin	ML	BF-D	GSC
Rameau	Dans ces doux asiles (Castor et Pollux)			LEM
Ravel	D'Anne qui me jecta	HM	CS-FS	GSC
-----	La flûte enchantée	M	DS-FS	DUR
-----	Noël des jouets	M	BS-FS	MAT
-----	Sainte	M	C-G	ELV
-----	Sur l'herbe	MH	C-G	DUR
-----	Trois beaux oiseaux du paradis			DUR
-----	Trois poemes de Mallarme 2 Flutes, 2 clarients, 4 strings and piano	M	BF-G	DUR
Roussel	Le jardin mouillé	M	C-FS	ROU
Saint-Saëns	Mai	H	G-FS	DUR
Severac	Ma poupée chérie			ROU
Weckerlin	Menuet d'Exaudet	H	D-G	GSC
-----	O ma tendre musette	LM	A-E	GSC
Widor	Je ne veux pas autre chose	HL	C-EF	HAM

German Songs and Arias Employing
Piano Singing

Mezzo Soprano

Bach, J.S.	Jesus schlaeft (Cantata 81)	L	A-D	GSC
Beethoven	Ich liebe dich	HL	BF-DF	†
Brahms	Es traeumte mir			†
-----	Five songs of Ophelia	HL	B-EF	†
-----	In Waldeseinsamkeit	H	ES-G	†
-----	Lerchengesang	LH	FS-GS	†
-----	Sapphische Ode	HML		†
-----	Spanisches Lied			†
-----	Staendchen	HL	BF-E	†
-----	Steig, auf geliebter Schatten	HL	BF-EF	†
Franz	Abends	HM	C-EF	†
-----	Die blauen Fruelingsaugen	HL		†
-----	Ein Stuendlein wohl vor Tag			†
-----	Es hat die Rose sich beklagt	LH	DF-F	†

(Franz)	Sterne mit den gold'nen Fuesschen	HL	DS-E	†
Hassler	Tanzlied			SIM
Mahler	Die zwei blauen Augen	M	A-G	†
-----	Ich atmet' einen linden Duft	HL		INT
-----	Ich bin der Welt abbanden gekommen	HL		INT
-----	Liebst du um Schoenheit	HL		INT
-----	Wo die schoenen Trompeten blasen	HL	GF-F	INT
Marx	Der Rauch			UNI
Mendelssohn	Bei der Wiege	M	DF-EF	†
-----	O rest in the Lord (Elijah)	L	B-D	†
Reger	Des Kindes Gebet	H	F-G	BOT
Schubert	Auf dem Wasser zu singen	MH	EF-GF	†
-----	Ave Maria	LMH	F-F	†
-----	Der Einsame	LH	D-G	†
-----	Der Schmetterling	LH	E-F	†
-----	Der Tod und das Maedchen	HL	A-EF	†
-----	Der Wanderer an den Mond	LM	D-F	PET
-----	Die Taubenpost	HL	D-EF	†
-----	Du bist die Ruh	LMH	EF-AF	†
-----	Fruehlingstraum	HL	C-D	†
-----	Geheimes	HL	BF-EF	†
-----	Im Abendrot	HL	C-D	†
-----	Im Fruehling	LH	D-FS	†
-----	Lachen und Weinen	HL	C-EF	†
-----	Liebesbotschaft	H	E-G	†
-----	Nacht und Traeume	HL	C-DF	†
Schumann	Der Nussbaum	LMH	D-FS	†
-----	Der Sandmann	HL	AF-DF	†
-----	Marienwuermchen	HL	D-D	†
-----	Mondnacht	M	E-FS	†
-----	Requiem			†
Strauss	Allerseelen	HL	AS-E	†
-----	Die Nacht	HL		DIT
-----	Freundliche Vision	HL	C-F	†
-----	Heimkehr	HL	B-E	†
-----	Ich trage meine Minne	M		†
-----	Meinem Kinde			†
-----	Traum durch die Daemmerung	HML	BF-EF	†
-----	Wiegenliedchen			†
Trunk	In meiner Heimat			
Wagner	Im Treibhaus	HL		†

Wolf	Ach, des Knaben Augen	HL		†
-----	An die Geliebte			†
-----	Der Gaertner	HL		†
-----	Du denkst, mit einem Faedchen			†
-----	In dem Schatten meiner Locken	M	C-EF	†
-----	Mausfallen Spruechlein	HL	BF-E	†
-----	Morgentau	HL	D-D	†
-----	Schlafendes Jesuskind	HL	AS-F	†
-----	Verborgenheit	HL	B-E	†
-----	Verschwiegene Liebe	LH	DF-FS	†
-----	Wie glaenzt der helle Mond			†
Wolff	Ich bin eine Harfe			HMP
-----	Knabe und Veilchen	M	D-D	HMP

Italian Songs and Arias Employing
Piano Singing

Mezzo Soprano

Castelnuovo-Tedesco	Ninna Nanna			
Cimara	Fiocca la neve	H	G-G	GSC
Gagliano	Dormi, amore (La Flora)	HL	CS-E	DIT
Gluck	O del mio dolce ardor (Paride ed Elena)	LH	D-FS	GSC
Monteverdi	Lasciatemi morire (Arianna)	ML	D-D	†
Respighi	Mattino di luce	M		RIC
-----	Notte			BON
Rontani	Se bel rio	ML	D-C	†
Secchi	Lungi dal caro bene	HL	A-FS	DIT

Miscellaneous Songs Employing
Piano Singing

Mezzo Soprano

Alnaes	En morgen var din grav	M	CS-D	HAN
-----	Lykken mellem to mennesker	M	B-FS	HAN
Arensky	Revery	MH	DS-FS	DIT
-----	Valse	H	DF-GF	GSC
Cui	The statue at Czarskoe-Selo	HM	DF-EF	†
Dvořák	God is my shepherd			AMP

(Dvořák)	Songs my mother taught me	HM	E-E	†
Gretchaninoff	Hushed the song of the nightingale	MH	E-G	DIT
Grieg	A dream			†
-----	A swan			†
-----	In the boat	LM	D-ES	†
-----	Radiant night			
-----	Snegl, Snegl	M	B-F	HAN
-----	Til En II	M	E-F	HAN
Lie	Soft-footed snow	HM		DIT
Mednikoff	The hills of Gruzia	H	DS-A	LAC
Rachmaninoff	In the silence of night	LH	D-A	GSC
-----	Into my open window	HL	B-FS	BOS
Sibelius	The tryst	M		AMP
Tchaikovsky	Evening	HM		GSC

American Songs Employing Rapid Enunciation

Mezzo Soprano

Bernstein	La bonne cuisine	H	B-B	GSC
Boatner	Oh, what a beautiful city!	HL	D-E	GSC
Burleigh	Joshua fit de battle ob Jericho	LH	DS-E	RIC
Carpenter	Don't ceare	M	C-D	GSC
-----	The cock shall crow	M	B-E	GSC
Clough-Leighter	My lover he comes on the skee	HM	D-F	BOS
Curran	Ho! Mr. Piper	LH	D-G	GSC
Deis	Come down to Kew			
Hadley	My shadow			ASC
Hageman	At the well	LH	EF-AF	GSC
-----	Miranda	HL		GAL
Kountz	The sleigh	HL	D-FS	GSC
Nevin	One spring morning	MH	DS-F	BOS
Sacco	Mexican serenade	HL	D-EF	BOS
Spross	Will o' the wisp			JCH
Warner	Hurdy gurdy	M	D-F	CFI

British Songs Employing
Rapid Enunciation

Mezzo Soprano

Bantock	A feast of lanterns	HM	D-F	GAL
Bax	Oh dear, what can the matter be?	M	D-EF	CHE
Brewer	The fairy pipers	HML		BOH
Britten	Oliver Cromwell			BOH
German	Charming Chloe	HML		NOV
Gibbs	Five eyes	HL	D-D	BOS
Head	A piper	HL		BOO
Hughes	Hey diddle diddle			CRA
Morley	It was a lover and his lass	HM		DIT
Purcell	There's not a swain on the plain	M	B-G	BAF
Vaughn Williams	A piper			OXF
-----	The water mill	L	C-D	OXF

French Songs and Arias Employing
Rapid Enunciation

Mezzo Soprano

Bizet	Habanera (Carmen)	HM	D-F	†
Chabrier	Les cigales	HML		†
-----	Villanelle des petits canards	HML	B-E	†
Debussy	Ballade des femmes de Paris			DUR
-----	Chevaux de bois	H	C-G	†
-----	Fantoches	H	D-A	JOB
-----	Fêtes galantes	LH	CS-A	†
-----	Le temps a laissié son manteau			DUR
-----	Mandoline	HM	BF-F	†
-----	Placet futile			DUR
Fauré	Mandoline	HL	F-E	†
-----	Notre amour	H	DS-B	†
-----	Poème d'un jour			HAM
-----	Toujours	LH	F-AF	†
Fourdrain	Carnaval	M	C-F	RIC
Gounod	Flower song (Faust)			†
Koechlin	La lune	M	C-F	ROU
Milhaud	La tourterelle	M	B-G	DUR

Pierné	Ils étaient trois petits chats blancs			MAR
Poldowski	Dansons la gigue	M	EF-G	MAR
Ravel	Manteau de fleurs	H		INT
-----	Nicolette	L	B-FS	ELK
-----	Tout gai	MH	EF-F	DUR
Saint-Saëns	L'attente			DUR
-----	Tournoiement			DUR
Severac	Chanson pour le petit cheval			ROU
Weckerlin	Maman, dites-moi	M	E-FS	BOS

German Songs Employing
Rapid Enunciation

Mezzo Soprano

Bach, J.S.	Patron, das macht der Wind (Phoebus and Pan)	M	C-G	GSC
Brahms	Blinde Kuh			†
-----	Das Maedchen spricht	H	E-FS	†
-----	Der Jaeger	HL		†
-----	Dort in den Weiden	LH	A-A	†
-----	Meine Liebe ist gruen	MLH	ES-A	†
-----	O liebliche Wangen	MLH	E-G	†
-----	Tambourliedchen			†
-----	Vergebliches Staendchen	LHM	E-FS	†
Loewe	Walpurgisnacht	H	G-G	SC
Mendelssohn	An die Entfernte	M	F-F	
-----	Neue Liebe	H	CS-A	†
Mozart	Warnung	HM	C-D	
Schubert	Am Feierabend	HL	BF-F	†
-----	Das Wandern	HLM	E-E	†
-----	Die Forelle	MLH	EF-GF	†
-----	Die Post	HML	BF-EF	†
-----	Erstarrung	HL	D-F	†
-----	Fischerweise	L	C-D	†
-----	Ungeduld	HML		†
-----	Wohin?	HL	B-E	†
Schumann	Die Kartenlegerin			
Strauss	Fuer fuenfzehn Pfennige			†
Wolf	Elfenlied	HL	D-F	INT
-----	Ich hab' in Penna	LH		†

Italian Songs and Arias Employing
Rapid Enunciation

Mezzo Soprano

Carissimi	Vittoria, mio core	HLM	B-E	†
Cavalli	Donzelle figgite	HL	C-EF	†
Donizetti	Il segreto per esser felici (Lucrezia Borgia)	M	C-G	†
Durante	Danza, danza fanciulla gentile	HM	BF-F	†
Falconieri	Non più d'amore	HL	C-D	DIT
-----	Nudo arciero	HL	AF-AF	DIT
Handel	Ch'io mai vi possa (Siroe)			†
Legrenzi	Che fiero costume	HML	C-D	†
Leoncavallo	Da quel suon soavemento (La Boheme)			SON
Malipiero	Ballata	H		CHE
Mozart	Non so più cosa son (Le Nozze di Figaro)	H	EF-G	†
-----	Voi che sapete (Le Nozze di Figaro)	M	C-F	†
Paisiello	Chi vuol la zingarella	L	C-F	GSC
Paradies	M'ha preso alla sua ragna	M	EF-F	GSC
Rontani	Or ch'io non segno più	HL	CS-E	DIT
Rossini	La danza	MH	E-A	†

Miscellaneous Songs Employing
Rapid Enunciation

Mezzo Soprano

Falla	Cancion del amor dolido			CHE
-----	Seguidilla murciana	HL		AMP
Grieg	My Johann	HL	BF-EF	GSC
-----	Simpel sang			
-----	With a water lily			GSC
-----	Til min dreng		C-E	
Mussorgsky	The evening prayer		MC-E	GSC
-----	The magpie and the gypsy dancer			GSC

American Songs Employing
Sustained Singing

Mezzo Soprano

Barber	A nun takes the veil	MH	G-G	GSC
-----	Sure on this shining night	MH	D-G	GSC
Burleigh	Deep river	HML		RIC
-----	Sometimes I feel like a motherless child	HML		RIC
-----	Were you there?	HML		RIC
Carpenter	Slumber song	ML	BF-F	GSC
-----	The player queen	M	BF-EF	GSC
-----	To one unknown	M	A-DS	GSC
Chadwick	Allah	LH	CS-GS	ASC
Dello Joio	New born	M	C-D	CFI
Edwards	By the bend of the river	HML	C-E	GSC
-----	Into the night	HML	C-DF	GSC
Foote	On the way to Kew			ASC
Giannini	Be still my heart			ELV
Golde	O beauty, passing beauty	MH	CS-GS	GSC
Griffes	By a lonely forest pathway	HML	A-EF	GSC
-----	The lament of Ian the proud	MH	DS-AS	GSC
Hageman	Music I heard with you	MH	E-A	GAL
Harris	Fog	M	D-F	CFI
Hindemith	Envoy	M	EF-F	AMP
-----	The wildflower's song	MH	E-G	AMP
Horsman	In the yellow dusk	MH	FS-A	GSC
Kramer	For a dream's sake	HL		JFI
MacDowell	The swan bent low	LH		ELK
Metcalf	At nightfall	HML	C-DF	ASC
Porter, Q.	Music, when soft voices die	HM	D-C	MUP
Rasbach	Trees	LMH	CS-GS	GSC
Rogers	Wind song	LM	C-G	GSC
Scott	Think on me	HML	D-EF	GAL
Tyson	Noon and night	LH	F-AF	GSC
Watts	Transformation	ML	AS-DS	GSC

British Songs and Arias Employing
Sustained Singing

Mezzo Soprano

Arne, T.	In infancy			NOV
Bantock	Silent strings	MH	F-G	BOO

Bridge	All things that we clasp	HL		BOS
-----	O that it were so	LMH	D-G	CHA
Britten	The Sally gardens			BOH
Butterworth	Loveliest of trees			AUG
Clarke	Eight o'clock			ROG
Coleridge- Taylor	Life and death	HML		ASC
Del Riego	Homing	HML	BF-E	CHA
Dowland	Flow, my tears	M	D-E	STB
-----	Sorrow, sorrow stay	M	D-D	BOS
Dunhill	To the Queen of Heaven	M	C-G	GSC
Elgar	Pleading	HML		NOV
Handel	In gentle murmurs will I mourn (Jephtha)	L	B-E	†
-----	Thou shalt bring them in (Israel in Egypt)	L	B-D	†
Henschel	Morning-hymn	MH	DS-GS	†
Holst	The heart worships	ML	BF-D	STB
Johnson	Dear, do not your fair beauty wrong			DIT
Milford	So sweet love seemed	HL	D-D	GRA
	Cello			
Murray	I'll walk beside you			CHA
Purcell	If music be the food of love	M	D-G	BOO
-----	Music for a while (Oedipus)	LH		SC
-----	When I am laid in earth (Dido and Aeneas)	LH	C-G	†
Quilter	Drink to me only	LMH	GF-GF	BOH
Ronald	The dove			ENO
Scott	The unforeseen	HML		GAL
Stephenson	Love is a sickness	HML	C-D	BOO
Vaughn Williams	Bright is the ring of words	L		BOH
-----	Linden Lea	HML	C-D	BOS
Warlock	Sleep			OXF
Welsh	All through the night			

French Songs and Arias Employing
Sustained Singing

Mezzo Soprano

Bemberg	Chant hindou	HML	A-EF	†
Berlioz	La captive	HL		GSC
-----	Le spectre de la rose			CST
-----	Les nuits d'été			AUG

Bizet	Adieu de l'hôtesse arabe	H	BF-G	†
Caplet	Les prières			DUR
Chaminade	Chant slave			GSC
Chausson	Chanson perpétuelle	H	CS-GS	ROU
-----	Le charme	HM	BF-EF	HAM
-----	Le colibri	M	F-GF	BOS
-----	Le temps des lilas	MH	D-GS	†
Debussy	Ballade que fait Villon à la requeste de sa mère			DUR
-----	Beau soir	LH	C-FS	†
-----	Chansons de Bilitis	M	C-FS	†
-----	Colloque sentimental			DUR
-----	Je tremble en voyant ton visage			DUR
-----	La chevelure	M	CF-FS	†
-----	Le son du cor	HL		†
Duparc	Au pays où se fait la guerre			SAL
-----	La vie antérieure	HL		†
-----	Lamento	ML	EF-EF	†
Fauré	Au cimetière	LH	D-F	
-----	Automne	MH	D-FS	GSC
-----	Le jardin clos	M	C-E	DUR
-----	Le parfum impérissable	LH	GF-GF	
-----	Les berceaux	LMH	BF-G	†
-----	Nocturne	H	F-A	MAR
-----	Prison	LH		†
-----	Rencontre	H	EF-AF	†
-----	Soir	LH	D-GS	†
Franck	Nocturne	HL		†
Georges	Hymne au soleil	LH	E-A	HOM
Gluck	Divinités du Styx (Alceste)	MH	DF-AF	†
Godard	Florian's song	LMH	D-FS	GSC
Gounod	O ma lyre immortelle (Sappho)	M	C-G	†
Honegger	Chanson (Ronsard) Flute and string quartet			SEN
Hue	J'ai pleuré en rêve	HL	D-E	BOS
Indy	Lied maritime	LH	B-G	†
Lalo	Chant breton	M	E-E	HAM
Leguerney	L'adieu	M	B-FS	DUR
Lenormand	Quelle souffrance	HM	AF-F	HAM
Leroux	Le nil Cello or violin	LH	E-A	†
Lully	Fermez-vous pour jamais (Amadis)			LEM
Massenet	Elégie	LM	C-GF	GSC
-----	Il est doux, il est bon (Hérodiade)	MH	EF-BF	GSC

Meyerbeer	Ah! mon fils	M	B-AS	GSC
	(Le Prophète)			
Paladilhe	Lamento provinçal	M	CS-FS	HOM
Poulenc	A sa guitare	M	D-FS	DUR
-----	Air grave			ROU
-----	Fleurs	M	DF-F	ROU
-----	Violon			ROU
Ravel	Kaddisch	H	C-G	DUR
-----	Le martin-pêcheur			DUR
-----	Le paon	M	C-F	DUR
-----	Vocalise en forme de	MH	BF-G	MAR
	habanera			
Saint-Saëns	Aimons-nous			DUR
-----	Amour, viens aider	HM	AF-G	†
	(Samson et Dalila)			
-----	La cloche	LH	DF-AF	†
-----	Le lever de la lune			DUR
-----	Mon coeur s'ouvre à ta	HLM	BF-GF	†
	voix (Samson et Dalila)			
-----	Printemps qui commence	M	B-E	†
	(Samson et Dalila)			
Thomas	Connais-tu le pays?	HML	C-F	†
	(Mignon)			
Tremisot	Nuit d'été			
Weckerlin	Venez, agréable printemps	M	C-F	

German Songs and Arias Employing
Sustained Singing

Mezzo Soprano

Ahle	Bruenstiges Verlangen	M	E-E	GSC
Bach, J.S.	Bist du bei mir	HML	A-EF	†
Beethoven	Das Geheimnis			
-----	Die Ehre Gottes	HL	AF-EF	†
-----	Faithfu' Johnie			
-----	Vom Tode	L	A-EF	GSC
-----	Wonne der Wehmut			†
Bohm	Calm as the night	HML	A-EF	†
Brahms	An eine Aeolsharfe	H	EF-AF	†
-----	Auf dem Kirchhofe	HL	BF-EF	†
-----	Dein blaues Auge	MH	BF-G	†
-----	Der Tod, das ist die	L	AF-F	†
	kuehle Nacht			
-----	Die Mainacht	HL	BF-FF	†
-----	Feldeinsamkeit	HL	C-EF	†
-----	Immer leiser wird mein	LH	DF-A	†
	Schlummer			

(Brahms)	Liebestreu	ML	C-F	†
-----	Mit vierzig Jahren	HL	FS-D	†
-----	Mondenschein	LH	D-GF	†
-----	Muss es eine Trennung geben?	LH	FS-FS	†
-----	Nachtigall	MHL	BF-FS	†
-----	O kuehler Wald	MH	A-F	†
-----	O wuesst' ich doch den Weg zurueck	H	E-FS	†
-----	Sommerabend			†
-----	Treue Liebe	LMH	DS-E	GSC
-----	Ueber die Haide			†
-----	Verzagen	MH	CS-FS	†
-----	Wenn du nur zuweilen laechelst			†
-----	Wir wandelten	LH	EF-GF	†
Bruch	Penelope's sorrow (Odysseus)			SIM
Franz	Dedication	HML	BF-C	†
-----	Es ragt ins Meer der runenstein	HL	G-F	†
-----	For music	ML	C-D	†
-----	Im Herbst	HM	A-F	†
-----	Mutter, o sing mich zur Ruh	HL	E-G	†
Haydn	She never told her love	HL	B-D	DIT
Himmel	Die Sendung			SIM
Hindemith	Pietà from Marienleben			AMP
Jensen	Wie so bleich			
Korngold	Love letter			AMP
Lehar	Vilia (The Merry Widow)			CHA
Liszt	Freudvoll und leidvoll			DUR
Loewe	Canzonetta	MH	B-A	DIT
-----	Der heilige Franziskus	L	A-E	SC
Mahler	Wenn mein Schatz Hochzeit macht			WEI
Marx	Der Ton	M	C-F	AMP
-----	Hat dich die Liebe beruehrt	MH	EF-BF	AMP
Mendelssohn	But the Lord is mindful of His own (Saint Paul)	L	A-D	GSC
-----	Nachtlied			
-----	On wings of song			†
-----	Woe unto them who forsake him (Elijah)	L	B-E	†
Mozart	Abendempfindung	M	E-F	
-----	Verdankt sei es dem Glanz			DIT
-----	Wiegenlied	MH	G-G	†
Reichardt	In the time of roses			†

Schoenberg	Song of the wood dove			AMP
Schubert	Am Bach im Fruehling			PET
-----	Am Grabe Anselmos	HL	B-EF	†
-----	An die Leier	LM	BF-F	†
-----	An die Musik	HL	A-DS	†
-----	Das Wirtshaus	HL	C-D	†
-----	Der Doppelgaenger	HL	G-D	†
-----	Der Leiermann	ML	C-D	†
-----	Der Lindenbaum	HL	A-D	†
-----	Der Neugierige	HL	CS-EF	†
-----	Der Wegweiser	L	D-EF	†
-----	Des Maedchens Klage	LH	C-E	†
-----	Die Allmacht	HML	G-E	†
-----	Die Kraehe	HL	A-E	†
-----	Die Liebe hat gelogen	LM	G-F	†
-----	Die Maenner sind mechant			PET
-----	Die Nebensonnen	HL	F-D	†
-----	Die Stadt	HL	A-E	†
-----	Du liebst mich nicht	LH	E-FS	†
-----	Ganymed	LH	EF-G	†
-----	Ihr Bild	HL	C-C	†
-----	In der Ferne	HL		†
-----	Lied eines Schiffers an die Dioskuren	HL	A-C	†
-----	Litanei	HLM	C-EF	†
-----	Nachtgesang			PET
-----	Nur wer die Sehnsucht kennt	LH		†
-----	Schaefers Klagelied	HL	BF-D	†
-----	Sei mir gegruesst	LH	G-G	†
-----	Thekla	HL	B-E	PET
-----	Wehmuth	HL	B-D	†
Schuetz	Aus dem 119th Psalm			
Schumann	An den Sonnenschein	HL	A-D	†
-----	Aus den Hebraeischen Gesaengen			
-----	Dein Angesicht	HL	B-EF	†
-----	Der Himmel hat eine Traene geweint			
-----	Die Lotusblume	HLM	BF-F	†
-----	Du bist wie eine Blume	HM	F-EF	†
-----	Du ring an meinem Finger	HL	C-F	†
-----	Hoch, hoch sind die Berge			
-----	Ihre Stimme	LH		†
-----	Im Westen	HL		†
-----	Lied der Suleika			
-----	Mit Myrthen und Rosen	HL	A-D	†
-----	Seit ich ihn gesehen	HL	DF-DF	†
-----	Stille Traenen	HL		†

96

(Schumann)	Wer machte dich so krank?			
Strauss	Befreit			HSC
-----	Liebeshymnus			†
-----	Mit deinen blauen Augen	LH	C-GS	†
-----	Morgen	HML	E-F	†
-----	Ruhe meine Seele			†
-----	Seitdem dein Aug' in meines schaute			SC
Wagner	Five Wesendonck songs			GSC
-----	Schmerzen	HL		†
Wolf	Agnes	HL		†
-----	Alle gingen, Herz, zu Ruh	HL	C-EF	†
-----	An eine Aeolsharfe			†
-----	Bedeckt mich mit Blumen	HL	B-D	†
-----	Das Staendchen	HL		†
-----	Das verlassene Maegdlein	HL	D-EF	†
-----	Denk' es, o Seele	LH	EF-F	INT
-----	Der Mond hat eine schwere Klag' erhoben	HL	BF-DF	†
-----	Gebet	HL		†
-----	Gesang Weylas	HL	DF-F	†
-----	Herr, was traegt der Boden	HL	B-DS	†
-----	Im Fruehling	HL	BF-F	†
-----	In der Fruehe	HL	C-C	†
-----	Morgenstimmung	LH	C-GS	†
-----	Neue Liebe	LH	D-AF	†
-----	Um Mitternacht	HL	G-EF	†
-----	Zur ruh', zur Ruh'	HL	A-GF	†
Wolff	Alle Dinge haben Sprache	M	BF-GF	†
-----	Ewig			

Italian Songs and Arias Employing Sustained Singing

Mezzo Soprano

Bellini	Scombra è la sacra selva (Norma)			RIC
Bimboni	Sospiri miei	M	EF-EF	GAL
Bononcini	Deh, lascia			HEU
-----	Pietà, mio caro bene	HL	C-EF	DIT
Caccini	Amarilli, mia bella	ML	C-D	†
Caldara	Come raggio di sol	HL	D-F	†
Cesti	Che angoscia, che affanno (Il Pomo d'Oro)	HL	C-DF	DIT

97

Cherubini	Ahi, che forse ai miei di (Demofonte)			RIC
Cimara	Stornellata marinara	HM		RIC
Del Leuto	Dimmi, amor	M	C-F	GSC
Donaudy	Quando ti rivedrò			RIC
Donizetti	O mio Fernando (La Favorita)	M	B-A	†
Durante	Vergin, tutta amor	LM	C-EF	†
Giordano	O grandi occhi lucenti (Fedora)			BRO
Gluck	Che farò senza Euridice (Orphée)	ML	BF-F	†
-----	Spiagge amate (Paride ed Elena)			†
Handel	Dove sei, amato bene (Rodelinda)	L	BF-EF	†
-----	Lascia ch'io pianga (Rinaldo)	HM	EF-F	DIT
-----	O rendetemi il mio bene (Amadigi)	L	CS-EF	CFI
-----	V'adoro pupille (Julius Caesar)			BOO
-----	Verdi prati (Alcina)			†
Mascagni	Voi lo sapete (Cavalleria Rusticana)	H	B-A	†
Monteverdi	Tu se' morta (Orfeo)	M	C-E	GSC
Mozart	Ch'io mi scordi di te			BOO
-----	Deh, se piacer mi vuoi (La Clemenza di Tito)			RIC
-----	Non più di fiori (La Clemenza di Tito)			†
-----	Parto, parto (La Clemenza di Tito) B flat clarinet and piano	H		AMP
Paisiello	Nel cor più non mi sento	HL	C-EF	†
Peri	Funeste piaggie (Euridice)			GSC
Piccini	O nuit, dresse du mystere (Le Faux Lord)			GSC
Pizzetti	La madre al figlio lontano			FRL
Ponchielli	Voce di donna (La Gioconda)	HM	A-G	GSC
Respighi	Abbandono			BON
-----	Ballata			RIC
-----	Io sono la madre	L		RIC
-----	Nebbie			GSC
Scarlatti, A.	O cessate di piagarmi	HL	DS-E	†
Stradella	Col mio sangue comprenderei (Il Floridoro)	HL	E-F	DIT

(Stradella)	Per pietà (Il Floridoro)	HM	D-F	DIT
-----	Pietà Signore	HM	C-F	GSC
Torelli	Tu lo sai	HL	BF-F	†

Miscellaneous Songs Employing Sustained Singing

Mezzo Soprano

Arensky	Autumn	H	CS-FS	GSC
Bach-Gounod	Ave Maria			†
Dvořák	Hear my prayer, O Lord			AMP
-----	Lord thou art my refuge and shield			AMP
-----	Turn Thee to me			AMP
Gliere	Ah, twine no blossoms	HM	CS-F	DIT
Granados	La maja dolorosa	M		INT
Gretchaninoff	Over the steppe	LM	C-G	GSC
-----	Wounded birch	HL	B-EF	†
Grieg	I love thee	HML	E-F	†
-----	The mother sings			DIT
Kjerulf	Synnove's song	M	C-F	GSC
Mussorgsky	Cradle-song of the poor	M	B-DS	GSC
-----	Martha's song (Khovantchina)	ML		GSC
-----	On the Dnieper			GSC
-----	Sphinx			BRH
Rachmaninoff	As fair is she as noonday light			GSC
-----	Christ is risen	LM	D-F	GAL
-----	Oh cease thy singing, maiden fair	H	E-A	CFI
-----	O, do not grieve	M	BF-AF	GSC
-----	O thou billowy harvest field	HL	CS-E	GSC
-----	The soldier's bride			†
-----	To the children	MH	F-G	DIT
-----	Vocalise	LH	CS-A	GSC
Rimsky-Korsakov	On the Georgian hills	HM		GSC
Sibelius	Black roses	M	A-ES	AMP
-----	The first kiss	M		AMP
-----	Was it a dream			BRH
Sinding	I hear the gull			JCH
-----	The daisies secret			
Tchaikovsky	A legend	M	D-E	GSC
-----	Adieu forêts (Jeanne d'Arc)	HM	BF-FS	GSC

(Tchaikovsky)	None but the lonely heart	HLM	C-F	DIT
-----	Pauline's romance (Pique Dame)	M	BF-AF	GSC

American Songs Employing Spirited Singing

Mezzo Soprano

Barber	I hear an army	LH	D-AF	GSC
Bassett	Take joy home	LH	EF-BF	GSC
Boatner	Oh, what a beautiful city!	HL	D-E	GSC
Burleigh	Joshua fit de battle ob Jericho	LH	DS-E	RIC
Carpenter	Dansons la gigue	M	B-E	GSC
-----	Don't ceare	M	C-D	GSC
-----	If	M	D-E	GSC
-----	Light, my light	M	C-G	GSC
-----	Serenade	LH	CS-A	GSC
-----	The cock shall crow	M	B-E	GSC
-----	To a young gentleman	M	C-F	GSC
Clough-Leighter	My lover he comes on the skee	HM	D-F	BOS
Crist	O come hither	HM	B-GS	CFI
Curran	Ho! Mr. Piper	LH	D-G	GSC
Deis	Come down to Kew			
Duke	I can't be talkin' of love	H	CS-G	GSC
-----	On a March day	M	B-GF	BOH
Elwell	The road not taken	M	B-FS	GSC
Enders	Russian picnic	HM	C-G	GSC
Giannini	Sing to my heart a song	H	D-B	ELV
Griffes	We'll to the woods, and gather May	M	D-F	GSC
Hadley	My shadow			ASC
Hageman	At the well	LH	EF-AF	GSC
-----	Miranda	HL		GAL
-----	Voices			
Johnson	Roll Jerd'n roll	M	EF-F	GSC
Kountz	The sleigh	HL	D-FS	GSC
La Forge	Song of the open	MH	EF-AF	DIT
Levitzki	Ah, thou beloved one	H	EF-AF	GSC
Nevin	One spring morning	MH	DS-F	BOS
Nordoff	There shall be more joy	M	CS-FS	AMP
Rawls	The balloon man	L	A-FS	AMP
Rogers	The last song	MLH	E-AF	GSC
Rummel	Ecstasy	LMH	GF-AF	GSC

Sacco	Mexican serenade	HL	D-EF	BOS
-----	Rapunzel	MH	FS-BF	GSC
Salter	The cry of Rachel	LH	C-AF	GSC
Schuman	Holiday song	M	C-F	GSC
Speaks	Morning	HML	BF-D	GSC
Spross	Will o' the wisp			JCH
Warner	Hurdy gurdy	M	D-F	CFI

British Songs and Arias Employing Spirited Singing

Mezzo Soprano

Arne, T.	Why so pale and wan			GSC
Bantock	A feast of lanterns	HM	D-F	GAL
Bax	Oh dear what can the matter be?	M	D-EF	CHE
Benjamin	Hedgerow			CUR
Bliss	The buckle			CUR
Brewer	The fairy pipers	HML		BOH
Bridge	Love went a-riding	HL		BOS
Butterworth	When I was one and twenty			AUG
Dowland	Come again! sweet love	M	D-E	STB
Elgar	The swimmer			BOO
German	Charming Chloe	HML		NOV
Gibbs	Five eyes	HL	D-D	BOS
Harty	Across the door			NOV
Head	A piper	HL		BOO
Johnston	Because I were shy	L	B-E	CRA
Lehmann	The cuckoo	HH	D-B	BOH
Morley	It was a lover and his lass	HM		DIT
Novello	The little damozel	LHM	C-G	BOO
Purcell	Hark! how all things with one sound rejoice			NOV
-----	Hark! the echoing air (The Fairy Queen)			BAF
-----	Nymphs and shepherds (The Libertine)	HM	C-F	†
-----	There's not a swain on the plain	M	B-G	BAF
Quilter	Blow, blow, thou winter wind	HL	C-E	BOO
-----	O mistress mine	HML		BOO
Ronald	Love, I have won you	HML	EF-EF	ENO
Vaughn Williams	A piper			OXF

101

Mezzo Soprano

Bizet	Habanera (Carmen)	HM	D-F	†
-----	Ouvre ton coeur	MH	DS-GS	†
-----	Seguidilla (Carmen)	HM	B-FS	†
Chabrier	Les cigales	HML		†
-----	Villanelle des petits canards	HML	B-E	†
Chausson	Les papillons	M	C-F	GSC
Debussy	Ballade des femmes de Paris			DUR
-----	Chevaux de bois	H	C-G	†
-----	De grève	HL		†
-----	De soir	HL		†
-----	Fantoches	H	D-A	JOB
-----	Fêtes galantes	LH	CS-A	†
-----	La mer est plus belle	HL		†
-----	Le faune			DUR
-----	Le temps a laissié son manteau			DUR
-----	Mandoline	HM	BF-F	†
-----	Noël des enfants qui n'ont plus de maisons			DUR
Duparc	Le manoir de Rosamunde	HL	B-F	BOS
-----	Testament	HL		INT
Fauré	Mandoline	HL	F-E	†
-----	Noël	LH	EF-AF	GSC
-----	Notre amour	H	DS-B	†
-----	Poème d'un jour			HAM
-----	Toujours	LH	F-AF	MAR
Georges	La pluie	HL		INT
Gluck	Amours, sors pour jamais (Armide)			PET
Gounod	Au printemps	LMH	DF-AF	GSC
-----	Flower song (Faust)			†
-----	Que fais-tu blanche tourterelle? (Romeo et Juliette)			JCH
-----	Vénise	HL		INT
Hahn	Si mes vers avaient des ailes	HLM	B-FS	†
Honegger	Les cloches			SEN
Koechlin	La lune	M	C-F	ROU
Milhaud	La tourterelle	M	B-G	DUR
Pierné	Ils étaient trois petits chats blancs			MAR
-----	Le moulin	ML	C-E	BOS

Poldowski	Colombine	H	D-GF	CHE
-----	Dansons la gigue	M	EF-G	MAR
Poulenc	Air vif	H	C-AF	ROU
Ravel	Chanson espagnole	LH	D-BF	DUR
-----	Manteau de fleurs	H		INT
-----	Nicolette	L	B-FS	ELK
-----	Quel galant!	M	D-F	DUR
-----	Tout gai	MH	EF-F	DUR
Saint-Saëns	L'attente			DUR
-----	Tournoiement			DUR
Severac	Chanson pour le petit cheval			ROU
Thomas	Je connais un pauvre enfant (Mignon)	H	C-B	GSC

German Songs and Arias Employing Spirited Singing

Mezzo Soprano

Bach, J.S.	Mein glaebiges Herze (Cantata 68)	HML		†
-----	Patron, das macht der Wind (Phoebus and Pan)	M	C-G	GSC
Beethoven	An die Geliebte	M	E-E	†
-----	Busslied			†
-----	Die Trommel geruehret			†
-----	Mignon (Kennst du das Land)	M	E-FS	AUG
Brahms	Alte Liebe	HL	C-F	†
-----	Bei dir sind meine Gedanken	MH	E-FS	†
-----	Blinde Kuh			†
-----	Botschaft	HL	D-F	†
-----	Das Maedchen spricht	H	E-FS	†
-----	Der Gang zur Liebsten	HL		†
-----	Der Jaeger	HL		†
-----	Der Schmied	HL	EF-EF	†
-----	Dort in den Weiden	LH	A-A	†
-----	Klage	LH	FS-FS	†
-----	Meine Liebe ist gruen	MLH	ES-A	†
-----	O komm holde Sommernacht			†
-----	O liebliche Wangen	MLH	E-G	†
-----	Salome			†
-----	Sehnsucht	H	EF-AF	GSC
-----	Tambourliedchen			†
-----	Vergebliches Staendchen	LHM	E-FS	†
-----	Wie froh und frisch	HL	B-E	†

Franz	Er ist gekommen	HL	EF-F		†
-----	Sonnenuntergang	HL	CS-FS		†
Hassler	Gagliarda			SIM	
Haydn	The mermaid's song	M	C-F	PRE	
Jensen	Am Ufer des Flusses des Manzanares	H	D-FS	GSC	
Loewe	Walpurgisnacht	H	G-G	SC	
Mahler	Das Irdische Leben	HL	A-F	INT	
-----	Ging heut Morgen uebers Feld	M	A-FS	INT	
-----	Hans und Grethe	HL		INT	
-----	Ich hab' ein gluehend Messer	M	BF-GF	WEI	
-----	Lieder eines fahrenden Gesellen	M		INT	
-----	Rheinlegendchen	M	B-FS		†
-----	Wer hat dies Liedlein erdacht?	HL	BF-E	INT	
Marx	Der bescheidene Schaefer			UNI	
Mendelssohn	An die Entfernte	M	F-F		
-----	Neue Liebe	H	CS-A		†
-----	Suleika	H	E-GS		†
Schubert	Am Feierabend	HL	BF-F		†
-----	Aufenthalt	HLM	A-F		†
-----	Die Forelle	MLH	EF-GF		†
-----	Die Post	HML	BF-EF	GSC	
-----	Ellens zweiter Gesang			PET	
-----	Erstarrung	HL	D-F		†
-----	Fischerweise	L	C-D		†
-----	Heidenroeslein				
-----	Mut	HL			†
-----	Rastlose Liebe	M	B-F		†
-----	Suleika I	LH	DS-G		†
-----	Suleika II	LH	F-BF		†
-----	Wohin?	HL	B-E		†
Schumann	Er, der Herrlichste von Allen	HL	A-EF		†
-----	Er ist's	HL	BF-EF		†
-----	Fruehlingsnacht	L	CS-E		†
-----	Im Walde	HL	A-D		†
-----	Schoene Wiege meiner Leiden	HL	C-EF		†
-----	Waldesgespraech	HL	A-FS		†
-----	Widmung	HL	BF-F		†
Strauss	Caecilie	MH	E-B		†
-----	Fuer fuenfzehn Pfennige				†
-----	Heimliche Aufforderung	HL	B-E		†
Wagner	Stehe still!	HL			†

Weber	Bethoerte, die an meine Liebe glaubt (Euryanthe)			PET
Wolf	Ach, im Maien	HL	C-E	†
-----	Auf dem gruenen Balkon	HL		†
-----	Auf einer Wanderung	HL		DIT
-----	Das Koehlerweib ist trunken			PET
-----	Die ihr schwebet	HL	EF-EF	†
-----	Die Zigeunerin			†
-----	Er ist's	H	D-G	†
-----	Erstes Liebeslied eines Maedchens	H	EF-AF	†
-----	Fussreise	HL	D-E	†
-----	Geh' Geliebter, geh' jetzt			PET
-----	Ich hab' in Penna	LH		†
-----	Klinge, klinge, mein Pandero	HL	CF-EF	†
-----	Liebe mir in Busen zuendet	M	E-F	†
-----	Lied vom Winde			†
-----	Nimmersatte Liebe	LH	CF-AF	†

Italian Songs and Arias Employing
Spirited Singing

Mezzo Soprano

Carissimi	Vittoria, mio core	HLM	B-E	†
Castelnuovo-Tedesco	Recuerdo			
Cavalli	Donzelle fuggite	HL	C-EF	†
Cimara	Canto di primavera		D-G	FRL
Donaudy	Spirate pur, spirate			RIC
Donizetti	Il segreto per esser felici (Lucrezia Borgia)	M	C-G	†
Durante	Danza, danza fanciulla gentile	HM	BF-F	†
Falconieri	Non più d'amore	HL	C-D	DIT
-----	Nudo arciero	HL	AF-AF	DIT
Handel	Amor commanda (Floridante)	H		†
-----	Ch'io mai vi possa (Siroe)			†
-----	Furibondo spira (Partenope)			KIS
-----	Piangero la sorte mia (Julius Caesar)			CFI
-----	Qual farfalletta (Partenope)	H	E-A	†
Legrenzi	Che fiero costume	HML	C-D	†
Leoncavallo	Da quell suon soavemento (La Boheme)			SON
Mozart	Non so più cosa son	H	EF-G	†

(Mozart)	(Le Nozze di Figaro) Voi che sapete	M	C-F	†
Paisiello	(Le Nozze di Figaro) Chi vuol la zingarella	L	C-F	GSC
Paradies	M'ha preso alla sua ragna	M	EF-F	GSC
Pergolesi	Confusa, smarrita			GSC
Piccini	Se il ciel mi divide	M	C-F	†
Ponchielli	(Alessandro di Indie) Stella del marinar	M	B-A	RIC
Respighi	(La Gioconda) In alto mare			BON
-----	Invito alla danza			BON
-----	Pioggia			BON
-----	Scherzo			BON
Rontani	Or ch'io non segno più	HL	CS-E	DIT
Rossi	Ah, rendimi (Mitrane)	L	GS-FS	GSC
Rossini	Bel raggio lusinghier	H	CS-A	GSC
-----	(Semiramide) Una voce poco fa (Il	HM	GS-E	GSC
Scarlatti, A.	Barbiere di Siviglia) Se Florindo è fedele	LM	EF-EF	GSC
Scarlatti, D.	Consolati e spara amante	L	BF-E	GSC
-----	Qual farfalletta			

Miscellaneous Songs Employing Spirited Singing

Mezzo Soprano

Alnaes	Nu brister i alle de kløfter	L	A-F	HAN
Dvořák	I will sing new songs of gladness	HL		†
-----	Sing ye a joyful song			AMP
-----	Tune thy fiddle gypsy			SIM
Falla	El paño moruno	HL		AMP
-----	Seguidilla murciana	HL		AMP
-----	Siete canciones	HL		AMP
Granados	El majo discreto	H		INT
Grieg	Good morning			†
-----	Jeg lever et liv i laengsel	L	BF-E	HAN
-----	My Johann	HL	BF-EF	GSC
-----	På Hamars ruiner	M	BF-G	HAN
-----	7 children's songs			HAN
-----	Til min dreng		C-E	
-----	Turisten	M	CS-F	HAN
-----	Vaer hilset, I damer	M	D-F	HAN
Mussorgsky	Hopak	HM	CS-FS	GSC

(Mussorgsky)	In the corner			INT
Rachmaninoff	Floods of spring	HL		DIT
-----	Oh, no, I pray do not depart	H		DIT
Stravinsky	The cloister (La novice)			DIT
Tchaikovsky	At the ball	MH		GSC
Turina	Farruca	M	A-F	UME

Songs and Arias Employing Staccato

Mezzo Soprano

Arne, T.	Where the bee sucks	HM		†
Delibes	Passepied	LH	DS-CS	GSC
Fourdrain	Carnaval	M	C-F	RIC
Haydn	My mother bids me bind my hair	M	E-E	†
Rossini	Non più mesta (La Cenerentola)	M	A-B	GSC
Scarlatti, A.	Rugiadose odorose (Il Pirro e Demetrio)	HL	D-E	DIT
Schubert	Der Juengling an der Quelle	LH	E-A	
Weckerlin	Maman, dites-moi	M	E-FS	BOO

American and British Songs of Popular Appeal

Mezzo Soprano

Bassett	Take joy home	LH	EF-BF	GSC
Beach	Ah, love but a day			ASC
Besley	The second minuet	HL		BOO
Bliss	The buckle			CUR
Brahe	Bless this house	HML	A-EF	BOO
Cadman	From the land of the sky-blue water			WHI
Campbell-Tipton	A spirit flower	LHM	B-G	GSC
Charles	When I have sung my songs	HM	BF-EF	GSC
Clarke	Shy one	HL	BF-G	BOH
Curran	Ho! Mr. Piper	LH	D-G	GSC
Del Riego	Homing	HML	BF-E	CHA
D'Hardelot	My message			
Diack	Little Jack Horner			CFI
-----	Little Polly Flinders			CFI

Dougherty	Everyone sang			
-----	Love in the dictionary	M	C-G	GSC
Duke	I can't be talkin' of love	H	CS-G	GSC
Edwards	By the bend of the river	HML	C-E	GSC
-----	Into the night	HML	C-DF	GSC
Enders	Russian picnic	HM	C-G	GSC
Fox	The hills of home	HML	BF-DF	CFI
Friml	L'amour, toujours l'amour			HAR
Gade	Jalousie			HAR
German	Who'll buy my lavender	HML		BOO
Giannini	Sing to my heart a song	H	D-B	ELV
Goulding	The lovely song my heart is singing	ML	A-D	GSC
Griffes	We'll to the woods and gather May	M	D-F	GSC
Grisell and Young	The cuckoo clock	LH	EF-G	GSC
Guion	Mam'selle Marie	M	D-E	GSC
Hely-Hutchinson	Old mother Hubbard	HL	B-E	CFI
Henschel	Morning-hymn	MH	DS-GS	†
Kountz	Prayer of the Norwegian child	ML	C-C	GSC
-----	The little French clock	LH	D-G	GAL
LaForge	Song of the open	MH	EF-AF	DIT
-----	To a messenger	HLM	CF-G	GSC
Lehmann	The cuckoo	HH	D-B	BOH
Levitzki	Ah, thou beloved one	H	EF-AF	GSC
Manning	In the Luxembourg gardens	HML	BF-D	GSC
-----	Shoes	M	EF-F	GSC
Murray	I'll walk beside you			CHA
Novello	The little damozel	LHM	C-G	BOO
Quilter	Drink to me only	LMH	GF-GF	BOH
Rasbach	Trees	LMH	CS-GS	GSC
Rich	American lullaby	LH	C-F	GSC
Rodgers	Lover			FAM
Rogers	At parting	LH	CS-FS	GSC
Ronald	Love, I have won you	HML	EF-EF	ENO
Schuman	Holiday song	M	C-F	GSC
Scott	Think on me	HML	D-EF	GAL
Silberta	Aylia, dancer of Kashmir	M	B-F	GSC
Speaks	In May time	HL	D-E	JCH
-----	Morning	HML	BF-D	GSC
Spross	Will o' the wisp			JCH
Strelezki	Dreams	LMH	B-A	GSC
Tyson	Noon and night	LH	F-AF	GSC
Ware	This day is mine	MH	EF-AF	BOS
Warren	Fulfilment	H	D-BF	GAL

Weatherly	Danny boy	LMH		BOO
Wolf	Jack in the box			
Wood	A brown bird singing	HLM	FS-G	CHA
Woodford- Finden	Kashmiri song			BOO
Worth	Midsummer	LM	E-A	GSC

(See also Humorous Songs, Negro Spirituals,
Folk Songs, Operetta Songs and Opera Arias.)

Miscellaneous Songs of Popular Appeal

Mezzo Soprano

Alvarez	La partida	HL	DS-E	GSC
Bach- Gounod	Ave Maria			†
Bizet	Agnus Dei	HLM	C-AF	†
-----	Ouvre ton coeur	MH	DS-GS	†
Böhm	Calm as the night	HML	A-EF	†
Cavalli	Donzelle fuggite	HL	C-EF	†
Cimara	Canto di primavera		D-G	FRL
Delibes	Passepied	LH	DS-CS	GSC
Denza	Funiculi, funicula			†
Dvořák	Songs my mother taught me	HM	E-E	†
Franz	Dedication	HML	BF-C	†
Gounod	Au printemps	LMH	DF-AF	GSC
-----	Sérénade	LMH	D-A	GSC
Grieg	A dream			†
-----	I love thee	HML	E-F	†
-----	My Johann	HL	BF-EF	GSC
Hahn	Si mes vers avaient des ailes	HLM	B-FS	†
Lara	Novillero			
Lecuona	Siboney			FEI
Leroux	Le nil Cello or violin	LH	E-A	†
Louiquy	La vie en rose			
Massenet	Elégie	LM	C-GF	GSC
Mendelssohn	On wings of song			†
Pestalozza	Ciribiribin			Dit
Ponce	Estrellita	LH		†
Poulenc	Les chemins de l'amour	M		AMP
Rachmaninoff	To the children	MH	F-G	DIT
Reichardt	In the time of roses			†
Rossini	La danza	MH	E-A	†
Roy	How do I love thee	HM	C-G	GSC
Schubert	An die Musik	HL	A-DS	†

(Schubert)	Ave Maria	LMH	F-F	†
-----	Staendchen			
Schumann	Widmung	HL	BF-F	†
Sieczynski	Vienna, city of my dreams			HAR
Sjoberg	Visions	MH	F-AF	GAL
Tchaikovsky	None but the lonely heart	HLM	C-F	DIT
Tosti	Marechiare	M	D-FS	GSC
Velázquez	Bésame mucho	M	CS-D	SOU

(See also Humorous Songs, Negro Spirituals,
Folk Songs, Operetta Songs and Opera Arias.)

Arias From British Operas

Mezzo Soprano

Handel	Art thou troubled (Rodelinda)	M	F-F	GSC
Purcell	Celia has a thousand charms (The Rival Sisters)			
-----	From rosy bow'rs (Don Quixote)			AUG
-----	Hark! the echoing air (The Fairy Queen)			BAF
-----	I attempt from love's sickness to fly (The Indian Queen)	MH	CS-E	†
-----	Music for a while (Oedipus)	LH		SC
-----	Nymphs and shepherds (The Libertine)	HM	C-F	†
-----	When I am laid in earth (Dido and Aeneas)	LH	C-G	†
Vaughn Williams	Greensleeves (Sir John in Love)			OXF

Arias From French Operas

Mezzo Soprano

Bizet	Card scene (Carmen)			
-----	Habanera (Carmen)	HM	D-F	†
-----	Seguidilla (Carmen)	HM	B-FS	†
Campra	Charmant papillon (Les Fêtes Venitiennes)	MH	D-G	GSC

110

David	Charmant oiseau (La	M	D-E	†
	Perle du Brésil)			
Debussy	Voici ce qu'il ecrit			BRO
	(Pelléas et Mélisande)			
Gluck	Amours, sors pour jamais			PET
	(Armide)			
-----	Divinités du Styx	MH	DF-AF	†
	(Alceste)			
Godard	Cachés dans cet asile	MH	DF-F	GSC
	(Jocelyn) Violin or cello			
Gossec	Dors, mon enfant (Rosine)	L		CHE
Gounod	Flower song (Faust)			†
-----	O ma lyre immortelle	M	C-G	†
	(Sappho)			
-----	Que fais-tu blanche tourterelle?			JCH
	(Romeo and Juliette)			
-----	Si le bonheur (Faust)			†
Grétry	La danse n'est pas ce que			JOB
	j'aime (Richard Coeur-de-Lion)			
Halévy	Humble fille des champs			GSC
	(Charles VI)			
Lully	Air de Persée (Persée)			
-----	Ariette de Cloris			
	(Divertissement de Chambord)			
-----	Bois épais (Amadis)	ML	C-EF	†
-----	Fermez-vous pour jamais			LEM
	(Amadis)			
Massenet	Il est doux, il est bon	MH	EF-BF	GSC
	(Hérodiade)			
-----	Ne me refuse pas (Hérodiade)			HEU
-----	Va laisse, les couler (Werther)			
-----	Werther! qui m'aurait dit (Air			
	de lettres) (Werther)			
Meyerbeer	Ah! mon fils (Le Prophète)	M	B-AS	B †
-----	Nobles Seigneurs, salut!	LH	C-C	†
	(Les Huguenots)			
-----	O prêtres de Baal			BRO
	(Le Prophète)			
Mouret	Doux plaisirs (Pirithous)			CHE
Offenbach	Ah, quel dîner (La Périchole)			
-----	Couplets de l'aveu			
	(La Périchole)			
-----	Mon Dieu, que les hommes sont			
	bêtes (La Périchole)			
-----	O mon cher amant, je te jure			
	(La Périchole)			
Rameau	A l'amour rendez les armes			CHO
	(Hippolyte et Aricie)			

(Rameau)	Air de Vénus (Dardanus)			LEM
-----	Dans ces doux asiles (Castor et Pollux)			LEM
Saint-Saëns	Amour, viens aider (Samson et Dalila)	HM	AF-G	†
-----	Mon coeur s'ouvre à ta voix (Samson et Dalila)	HLM	BF-GF	†
-----	Printemps qui commence (Samson et Dalila)	M	B-E	†
Thomas	Connais-tu le pays? (Mignon)	HML	C-F	†
-----	Je connais un pauvre enfant (Mignon)	H	C-B	†

Arias From German Operas

Mezzo Soprano

Bruch	Penelope's sorrow (Odysseus)		SIM
Wagner	Einsam wachend in der Nacht (Tristan und Isolde)	FS-FS	PET
-----	Entweihte Goetter! Helft jetzt meiner Rache! (Lohengrin)	FS-AS	GSC
-----	Geliebter, komm', sieh' dort die Grotte (Tannhaeuser)	F-A	PET
-----	Hoere mit Sinn, was ich dir sage (Die Goetterdaemmerung)	G-G	PET
-----	In seiner Bluete bleicht mein Leben (Rienzi)		PET
-----	So ist es denn aus mit den ewigen Goettern (Die Walkuere)	CS-GS	GSC
Weber	Bethoerte! Die an meine Liebe glaubt (Euryanthe)		

Arias From Italian Operas

Mezzo Soprano

Bellini	Scombra è la sacra selva (Norma)			RIC
Cilea	O vagabonda stella d'oriente (Adriana Lecouvreur)			AMP
Donizetti	Il segreto per esser felici (Lucrezia Borgia)	M	C-G	†
-----	O mio Fernando (La Favorita)	M	B-A	†

Giordano	O grandi occhi lucenti (Fedora)			BRO
Gluck	Che farò senza Euridice (Orphée)	ML	BF-F	†
Leoncavallo	Da quel suon soavemento (La Boheme)			
Mascagni	Lacere miseri (L'Amico Fritz)			GSC
-----	O pallida che un giorno (L'Amico Fritz)			
-----	Voi lo sapete (Cavalleria Rusticana)	H	B-A	†
Monteverdi	Lasciatemi morire (Arianna)	ML	D-D	†
-----	Tu se' morta (Orfeo)	M	C-E	GSC
Mozart	Al desio di chi t'adora (Appendix, Nozze di Figaro)			
-----	Deh, se piacer mi vuoi (La Clemenza di Tito)			RIC
-----	Non più di fiori (La Clemenza di Tito)			†
-----	Non so più cosa son (Le Nozze di Figaro)	H	EF-G	GSC
-----	Parto, parto (La Clemenza di Tito) B flat clarinet and piano	H		AMP
-----	Voi che sapete (Le Nozze di Figaro)	M	C-F	†
Pittaluga	Romanza de solita (La Romeria de los Cornudos)			
Ponchielli	Stella del marinar (La Gioconda)	M	B-A	RIC
-----	Voce di donna (La Gioconda)	HM	A-G	GSC
Respighi	Maria Egiziaca-Prelude and aria (Maria Egiziaca)			RIC
Rossini	Bel raggio lusinghier (Semiramide)	H	CS-A	GSC
-----	Cruda sorte, amor tiranno! (L'Italiana in Algeri)			
-----	Non più mesta (La Cenerentola)	M	A-B	GSC
-----	Pensa alla patria (L'Italiana in Algeri)			RIC
-----	Una voce poco fa (Il Barbiere di Siviglia)	HM	GS-E	GSC
Verdi	Aria of Abigail (Nabucco)			RIC
-----	Condotta ell'era in ceppi (Il Trovatore)			GSC

113

(Verdi)	Giunta all' albergo della Giarettiera (Falstaff)	L	G-G	RIC
-----	O don fatale (Don Carlos)	MH	CF-CF	†
-----	Stride la vampa (Il Trovatore)	M	B-G	GSC

Miscellaneous Opera Arias

Mezzo Soprano

Cadman	Song of the Robin Woman (Shanewis)	MH	CS-GS	MOR
Gershwin	A woman is a sometime thing (Porgy and Bess)			GER
Menotti	Lullaby (The Consul)			GSC
-----	The black swan (The Medium)	M	D-G	GSC
Mussorgsky	Divination by water (Khovantchina)	L	GS-FS	GSC
-----	Martha's song (Khovantchina)	ML		GSC
-----	Song of Khivria (The Fair at Sorotchinsk)			GSC
Rimsky-Korsakov	Song of the shepherd lehl (Snegourotchka)	LM		DIT
Stravinsky	Jacasta's aria (Oedipus Rex)			BOO
Tchaikovsky	Adieu forêts (Jeanne d'Arc)	HM	BF-FS	GSC
-----	It is near to midnight (Pique Dame)			GSC
-----	Pauline's romance (Pique Dame)	M	BF-AF	GSC

Arias From Oratorios and Latin Works

Mezzo Soprano

Bach, J.S.	Agnus Dei (Mass in B Minor) Violin			†
-----	Esurientes implevit bonis (Magnificat in D Major)			†
-----	Et exultavit spiritus meus (Magnificat in D)			
-----	It is finished (St. John Passion)	L	B-D	†

114

(Bach, J.S.)	Prepare thyself, Zion (Christmas Oratorio)			
-----	Qui sedes ad dexteram Patris (Mass in B Minor) Oboe d'amore			†
Bennett	O Lord, thou hast searched (Woman of Samaria)			
Gaul	Thou art the guide (Ten Virgins)			
Handel	Chi sprezzando il somo bene (La Passione)			
-----	Come and trip it (L'Allegro)	M	C-F	†
-----	Father, whose blessing (Ode from St. Cecelia's Day)			
-----	He shall feed His flock (The Messiah)	L	C-D	†
-----	He was despised (The Messiah)	L	B-D	†
-----	In gentle murmurs will I mourn (Jephtha)	L	B-E	†
-----	In the battle, fame pursuing (Deborah)	L	A-D	GSC
-----	Let me wander not unseen (L'Allegro)	M	D-G	†
-----	Lord, to thee each night and day (Theodora)	L	C-E	†
-----	O sleep why dost thou leave me (Semele)	H	DS-GS	†
-----	O thou that tellest good tidings to Zion (The Messiah)	L	A-C	†
-----	Return, O God of hosts (Samson)	L	B-E	GSC
-----	The parent bird in search of food (Susanna)			
-----	The smiling hours a joyful train (Hercules)			
-----	Thou shalt bring them in (Israel in Egypt)	L	B-D	†
-----	Weep no more (Hercules)			†
Hindemith	Sing on there in the swamp (When Lilacs in the Dooryard Bloomed)			
Mendelssohn	But the Lord is mindful of His own (Saint Paul)	L	A-D	†
-----	I will sing of Thy great mercies (Saint Paul)	H	E-F	†

(Mendelssohn)	O rest in the Lord (Elijah)	L	B-D	†
-----	Woe unto them who forsake him (Elijah)	L	B-E	†
Mozart	Laudamus Te (C Minor Mass)			PET
Parker	Gens duce splendida (Hora Novissima)			NOV
Rossini	Fac ut portem (Stabat Mater)	L	B-G	DIT
Saint-Saëns	Expectans Dominum (Christmas Oratorio)			GSC
-----	Patiently (Christmas Oratorio)			
Sullivan	Love not the world (The Prodigal Son)	L		GSC
Verdi	Liber scriptus (The Requiem)			GSC

Cantata Arias

Mezzo Soprano

Bach, J.S.	Christi Glieder, ach bedenket (Cantata 132) Violin			
-----	Gelobet sei der Herr (Cantata 129) Oboe d'amore			AUG
-----	Jesu lass Dich finden (Cantata 154)			
-----	Jesus macht mich geistlich reich (Cantata 75) Violin			
-----	Jesus schlaeft (Cantata 81)	L	A-D	GSC
-----	Mein glaeubiges Herze (Cantata 68)	HML		†
-----	Oh, yes, just so (Phoebus and Pan)			NOV
-----	Patron, das macht der Wind (Phoebus and Pan)	M	C-G	GSC
-----	Sheep may safely graze (Cantata 208) 2 Flutes and continuo	LM	EF-GF	GAL
Debussy	Air de Lia (L' Enfant Prodigue)	H	E-A	DUR
Gaul	Eye hath not seen (The Holy City)	ML	B-D	GSC
Gretchaninov	Credo from Liturgica Domestica			BOO

116

Handel	Have mercy, Lord	HM		†
	(Te Deum)			
Mussorgsky	Oriental chant	ML	BF-E	GSC
	(Josua Navine Cantata)			
Prokofieff	Song after the battle	M		AMP
	(Alexander Nevsky)			
Tchaikovsky	Prayer (Moscow Cantata)	M	A-GF	GAL

Operetta, Musical Comedy
or Show Songs

Mezzo Soprano

Arlen	Right as the rain			CHA
	(Bloomer Girl)			
Berlin	It's a lovely day tomorrow			BER
	(Louisiana Purchase)			
Bowers	Chinese lullaby			FFI
	(East is West)			
Brown	Temptation (Going Hollywood)			ROB
Coward	I'll see you again	M	C-F	HAR
	(Bitter Sweet)			
-----	Zigeuner (Bitter Sweet)	H	CF-G	HAR
De Koven	Oh promise me	HML	C-D	†
	(Robin Hood)			
Forrest-Grieg	Strange music			CHA
	(Song of Norway)			
Friml	Give me one hour			MRT
	(The White Eagle)			
Gershwin	The man I love			BRO
	(Strick Up the Band)			
Herbert	A kiss in the dark			WIT
	(Orange Blossoms)			
-----	Ah! sweet mystery of life	LMH	A-A	WIT
	(Naughty Marietta)			
-----	I can't do that sum			WIT
	(Babes in Toyland)			
-----	I'm falling in love with someone (Naughty Marietta)			WIT
-----	If only you were mine			WIT
	(The Singing Girl)			
-----	Kiss me again	LHM	CS-A	WIT
	(Mlle. Modiste)			
-----	Moonbeams (The Red Mill)			WIT
-----	'Neath the southern moon (Naughty Marietta)			

(Herbert)	Rose of the world (The Rose of Algeria)			WIT
-----	Sweetheart waltz (Sweethearts)			GSC
-----	Tell it all over again (The Only Girl)			WIT
-----	Thine alone (Eileen)			WIT
Kern	Can't help lovin' dat man (Show Boat)	L	BF-EF	HAR
-----	Look for the silver lining (Sally)			CHA
-----	Smoke gets in your eyes (Roberta)			HAR
-----	The night was made for love (The Cat and the Fiddle)	M	C-F	HAR
-----	The song is you (Music in the Air)	M	C-F	HAR
-----	The touch of your hand (Roberta)			CHA
-----	They didn't believe me (Girl from Utah)			HAR
-----	Yesterdays (Roberta)			CHA
Lehar	Meine Lippen, sie kuessen so heiss (Giuditta)			GLO
-----	My little nest of heavenly blue (Frasquita)	HML		MAR
-----	Vilia (The Merry Widow)			CHA
Milloecker	I give my heart (Mme. Dubarry)			CHA
Porter	Ev'rything I love (Let's Face It)			CHA
-----	Begin the Beguine (Jubilee)	L	BF-F	HAR
-----	I love you (Mexican Hayride)			CHA
-----	In the still of the night (Rosalie)			CHA
-----	I've got you under my skin (Born to Dance)			CHA
-----	Night and Day (Gay Divorcee)	M	BF-EF	HAR
-----	What is this thing called love? (Wake Up and Dream)			HAR
Rodgers	Bali ha'i (South Pacific)			CHA
-----	Fallin in love with love (The Boys from Syracuse)			WIL
-----	It might as well be spring (State Fair)			CHA
-----	My heart stood still (Connecticut Yankee)			HAR

118

(Rodgers)	People will say we're in love (Oklahoma)			CHA
-----	What's the use of wond'rin'? (Carousel)			WIL
-----	Where or when? (Babes in Arms)			CHA
Romberg	Lover come back to me (New Moon)	H	D-G	HAR
-----	Mother (My Maryland)			HAR
-----	When I grow too old to dream (The Night is Young)	HLM	C-G	ROB
Schwarz	Dancing in the dark (The Band Wagon)			HAR
-----	You and the night and the music (Revenge with Music)			HAR
Tierney	Alice Blue Gown (Irene)			FEI
Weill	September song (Knickerbocker Holiday)			CHA
Youmans	Through the years (Through the Years)	HML	A-F	MLR
-----	Time on my hands you in my arms (Smiles)	M	C-E	MLR
-----	You're everywhere (Through the Years)			MLR

Song Cycles (Or Groups of Songs)

Mezzo Soprano

Bantock	Muse of the golden throne			
-----	Sappho			
Bax	Celtic song cycle	MH	BF-A	CHE
Beethoven	Sechs geistliche Lieder			
Berger	Four sonnets Piano or string quartet	M	A-G	GSC
Berlioz	Les nuits d'été			AUG
Bernstein	I hate music	H	C-A	WIT
-----	La bonne cuisine	H	B-B	GSC
Bloch	Poèmes d'automne	M	B-G	GSC
Brahms	Five songs of Ophelia	HL	B-EF	†
-----	Two songs for alto, viola and piano	L		AMP
Caplet	Les prieres			DUR
Carpenter	Gitanjali	M	B-G	GSC
-----	Watercolors	M	C-F	GSC
Chanler	The children (9 songs)	M	C-G	GSC
Chausson	Poème de l'amour et de la mer	H		INT

Cornelius	Bridal songs			INT
-----	Six Christmas songs	HL		BOS
Crist	Chinese mother goose rhymes	H	C-G	CFI
-----	Coloured stars	HM		CFI
Debussy	Chansons de Bilitis	M	C-FS	†
-----	Fêtes galantes	LH	CS-A	†
-----	Proses lyriques	HL		JOB
Dvořák	Biblical songs	HL		AMP
-----	Gypsy songs	LH	D-A	AMP
Elgar	Sea pictures	L	A-A	BOO
Falla	El amor brujo	M		BRO
-----	Siete canciones	HL		AMP
Fauré	Le jardin clos	M	C-E	DUR
-----	Poème d'un jour			HAM
Granados	La maja dolorosa	M		INT
Grieg	Digte af Vilhelm Krag			HAN
-----	Elegiske digte af John Paulsen			HAN
-----	Haugtussa	M	B-GF	PET
-----	7 children's songs			HAN
Hindemith	Das Marienleben	H		AMP
Holst	Four songs for voice and violin	M	C-G	CHE
Honegger	Quatre chansons pour voix grave			SAL
-----	Trois chansons String quartet and flute			SEN
Kabelevsky	Seven merry songs			
Kilpinen	Lieder um den Tod	M		AMP
Mahler	Kindertotenlieder	L	G-GF	INT
-----	Lieder eines fahrenden Gesellen	M		INT
Milhaud	Trois poèmes de Jean Cocteau			SIR
Mussorgsky	Songs and dances of death			INT
-----	Sunless			CHE
-----	The nursery	M	C-G	INT
Poulenc	Chansons villageoises	M	C-G	ESC
-----	Cinq poèmes de Ronsard			HEU
-----	Le bestiaire	M		AMP
-----	Tel jour, telle nuit	M	B-A	DUR
Ravel	Chansons madécasses Flute, cello and piano			DUR
-----	Cinq mélodies populaires grecques			CUR
-----	Quatre chants populaires	M		DUR
-----	Shéhérazade	M	CS-G	DUR

(Ravel)	Trois poèmes de Mallarmé	M	BF-G	DUR
	2 flutes, 2 clarinets, 4 strings & piano			
Schumann	Der arme Peter	HL	B-G	†
-----	Frauenliebe und Leben	HL		†
-----	Lieder der Braut	H	D-A	†
Slonimsky	Gravestones at Hancock, New Hampshire	H	D-G	AXE
Still	Songs of separation			LEE
Strauss	Drei Liebeslieder			PET
Stravinsky	Trois histoires pour enfants			CHE
Villa-Lobos	Serestas			
Wagner	Five Wesendonck songs			GSC
Woodford-Finden	Indian love lyrics			BOO

Solo Cantatas

Mezzo Soprano

Pergolesi	Salve Regina			
Stradella	Se amor m'annoda	L	BF-F	

(See Solo Cantatas of Pergolesi, Handel and
Scarlatti, Kirchenkantaten of Buxtehude and
Symphoniae Sacrae of Schuetz.)

Concert Aria

Mezzo Soprano

Mozart	Ch'io mi scordi di te			BOO

Christmas Songs

Mezzo Soprano

Adam	O Holy night			†
Andrews	I heard the bells on Christmas day	L	A-E	GAL
Bach, J. S.	Prepare thyself, Zion (Christmas Oratorio)			
-----	Schlafe mein Liebster (Christmas Oratorio)			
Bacon	Ancient Christmas carol			NEM
Baldwin	Little Lordeen	L	BF-EF	WIT
Bax	A Christmas carol	H	DF-A	CHE
Berlin	White Christmas (Holiday Inn)			BER

Brahms	Geistliches Wiegenlied			†
	Piano and viola			
Branscombe	Hail ye time of holidays			
Bush	I saw a maiden fair	L	C-DF	GRA
Candlyn	The song of Mary	M	B-D	GRA
Carr	As on the night	M	E-FS	GSC
Chaminade	Christmas carol of the	MH	D-A	GSC
	birds			
De Koven	The white Christ	L	C-D	GSC
Dickinson	Joseph, tender Joseph	M		GRA
Dunhill	To the Queen of Heaven	M	C-G	GSC
Elmore and				
Reed	Come all ye who weary	L	C-C	JFI
Evans	The Virgin had a baby	L	C-EF	BOH
Fauré	Noël	LH	EF-AF	GSC
France	A Christmas lullaby	M	DS-F	GAL
Grieg	Christmas song			AUG
-----	Jule Sne	M	C-G	HAN
-----	Julens Vuggesang			
Handel	O thou that tellest good	L	A-C	†
	tidings to Zion			
	(The Messiah)			
Harker	A child is born in	LH	D-G	GSC
	Bethlehem			
-----	There's a song in the	HL	BF-D	GSC
	air			
Harris	The feast of Christmas	M	C-F	OXF
Head	Slumber song of the	HL		BOO
	Madonna			
-----	The little road to	MH	EF-AF	BOO
	Bethlehem			
-----	The robin's carol	H	C-AF	BOH
-----	The three mummers			BOO
Herbert	Toyland (Babes in Toyland)			WIT
Holmes	Noël d'Irlande	HL		DIT
Ireland	The Holy boy	MH	D-G	BOO
Ives	A Christmas carol			NEM
Jewell	The vision of the	HL	A-D	ASC
	shepherds			
Lehmann	No candle was there and	MH	EF-G	CHA
	no fire			
Lynn	Gently little Jesus	L	BF-BF	DIT
-----	The magic night of	M	D-D	DIT
	Christmas			
MacGimsey	A new Christmas morning	M	DF-F	CFI
	hallelujah			
Martin	The Holy Child	HML	G-G	ENO
Matthews	Voices of the sky	HL	BF-D	GSC
McKinney	The Holy Mother sings	MH	AF-AF	JFI

Murphy	O little town of Bethlehem	M	D-F	SUM
Neidlinger	The birthday of a king	LMH	C-F	GSC
-----	The manger cradle	L	EF-F	GSC
Niles	Our lovely Lady singing	M	EF-F	GSC
-----	The cherry tree			GSC
Nin	Jesus de Nazareth			ESC
Prokoff	Christmas cradle song	LM	D-E	CHA
Ravel	Noël des jouets	M	BS-FS	MAT
Reger	The Virgin's slumber song	MMH	G-G	†
Reimann	Joseph tender Joseph mine	M	F-F	GRA
Rodney	A dream of Bethlehem	MML	G-DF	ENO
Russell	Child Redeemer	HL		GAL
Sadero	Fa la nana, bambin			RIC
Saint-Saëns	Expectans Dominum (Christmas Oratorio)			GSC
Schubert	Ave Maria	LMH	F-F	†
-----	They sang that night in Bethlehem	LMH	EF-EF	GSC
Taylor	Christmas folk song	L	BF-EF	GRA
Thiman	I saw three ships	L		NOV
-----	In the bleak midwinter	L	A-E	NOV
Thorp	Come, Mary take courage	M	DS-FS	GAL
Trunk	The Christ child in the manger	HM		AMP
Warlock	The first mercy	M	F-F	BOO
Warren	Christmas candle	HML	D-E	GSC
Wentzel	Lamkins Cello and piano			GRA
West	It came upon a midnight	MM	E-FS	SUM
Wild	The Christ child	M	EF-EF	CFI
Wolf	Schlafendes Jesuskind	HL	AS-F	†
Wright	A Babe lies in His cradle warm	MD	D-D	GSC
Yon	Gesu Bambino	HL	B-E	JFI

Easter Songs

Mezzo Soprano

Bach, J.S.	Hochgelobter Gottessohn (Cantata 6) English horn or viola or violin			NOV
-----	Jesus from the grave is risen	M	F-EF	CFI
Bantock	Easter hymn	M	FS-F	CHE
Barnes	Easter	HM	D-EF	GSC
Chaffin	Easter message	MH	D-G	FLA
Curran	Crucifixion			
Davis	Christ is risen today	M		GAL

123

Dennee	Easter song	HM	B-F	ASC
Diack	All in the April evening	LMH	D-G	BOO
Granier	Hosanna	HH	F-BF	DIT
Gretchaninoff	The Christ is risen			
Guion	At the cry of the first bird	H	D-G	GSC
Hageman	Christ went up into the hills	LH	EF-AF	CFI
Huhn	Christ is risen	HM	C-E	ASC
Kountz	Palm Sunday	HL		GAL
La Forge	Before the Crucifix	HML	BF-EF	GSC
MacFarlane	On wings of living light	MH	D-G	GSC
O'Hara	There is no death	LMH	EF-AF	CHA
Rachmaninoff	Christ is risen	LM	D-F	GAL
Rorem	The resurrection			
Scott	Angels roll the rock away	MH	E-G	HUN
-----	The first Easter morn	LH	F-G	GSC
Tchaikovsky	A legend	M	D-E	GSC
Turner	Hail your risen Lord	HL	C-D	GSC
Wolf	Herr, was traegt der Boden	HL	B-DS	†
Yon	Christ triumphant	MH	E-A	JFI
-----	O faithful Cross	HM	C-EF	JFI
-----	Our Paschal joy	LH	AF-AF	JFI

Patriotic Songs

Mezzo Soprano

Bone and Fenton	Prayer for a waiting world	L		CFI
Bowles	An American hero	M	E-E	AXE
Cadman	Glory	H	EF-G	GAL
Chadwick	He maketh wars to cease	ML		ASC
Dungan	Eternal life	HL		PRE
Foster, F.	The Americans come	MH	F-BF	JFI
Lester	Greater love hath no man	LH	B-E	CFI
O'Hara	There is no death	LMH	EF-AF	CHA
Steffe	Battle hymn of the Republic			
Ward- Stephens	Phantom legions	MHH	EF-BF	CHA

Sacred Songs

Mezzo Soprano

Bach, J.S.	Come, Christians, greet this day	L	BF-F	CFI

124

(Bach, J. S.)	Draw near to me	HML		GSC
Beethoven	The worship of God in nature			
Bitgood	Be still and know that I am God	ML		GRA
-----	The greatest of these is love	M		GRA
Bizet	O Lord be merciful	HL		GSC
Bone and Fenton	First Psalm	LM	DF-F	CFI
-----	Thy word is a lamp	LH	C-F	ROW
Brown	The twenty third Psalm	LH	E-G	GRA
Browning	For I am persuaded	LM	DF-G	CFI
-----	The beatitudes	HM	C-F	CFI
Buck	Fear not ye, O Israel	HLM		GSC
Campbell-Tipton	I will give thanks unto the Lord	LMH	DF-AF	GSC
Candlyn	God that madest earth and heaven	M	C-F	GRA
Chadwick	A ballad of trees and the Master	HML	A-F	DIT
Charles	Incline Thine ear	HL	BF-D	GSC
Clokey	God is in everything	LH	D-G	JFI
Davis	Be ye kind, one to another	L		GAL
-----	Let not your heart be troubled	HML		WOO
-----	Trust in the Lord	MH	CS-G	GAL
Dickinson	Roads	L		GRA
Dvořák	God is my shepherd			AMP
-----	Hear my prayer, O Lord			AMP
-----	Sing ye a joyful song			AMP
-----	Turn Thee to me			AMP
Edmunds	Praise we the Lord	HL	D-D	ROW
Goodhall	The mountain	M	D-E	GAL
Gounod	O Divine Redeemer	LMH	B-DS	GSC
Guion	Prayer	HL		GSC
-----	The cross bearer	HM	B-DS	GSC
Hamblen	Trust in Him	LH	D-G	GSC
Handel	Thanks be to Thee	M	CS-E	†
Harker	How beautiful upon the mountains	MLH	EF-G	GSC
Hartley	Charity	HM	DF-EF	HUN
Henschel	Morning-hymn	MH	DS-GS	†
Hinchliffe	Tranquillity	M	E-F	CFI
Holst	The heart worships	ML	BF-D	STB
Kountz	What shall I ask?	L		GAL
La Forge	They that trust in the Lord	HL	BF-EF	GAL

125

Lederer	Psalm 104	L	A-E	CFI
Liddle	How lovely are Thy dwellings	HML		BOS
MacDermid	In my Father's house are many mansions	HML		FRS
MacGimsey	Think on these things	LM	BF-EF	CFI
Malotte	The beatitudes	LH	E-G	GSC
-----	The Lord's prayer			
-----	The twenty-third Psalm	HLM	C-F	GSC
McFeeters	A Psalm of praise	M		CFI
Mendelssohn	But the Lord is mindful of His own (Saint Paul)	L	A-D	†
-----	I will sing of Thy great mercies (Saint Paul)	H	E-F	†
-----	O rest in the Lord (Elijah)	L	B-D	†
-----	Woe unto them who forsake him (Elijah)	L	B-E	†
Noble	Souls of the righteous	M		GRA
O'Connor-Morris	Fill thou my life, O Lord	L	BF-EF	CFI
Rorem	Song of David	M		AMP
Sanderson	Green pastures	HL	BF-EF	BOO
Schubert	The Omnipotent			
-----	To the Infinite			
Scott	Come ye blessed	LMH	EF-AF	GSC
-----	Ride on, ride on	HML		FLA
Speaks	The Lord is my light	HML		GSC
-----	Thou wilt keep him in perfect peace	HML		GSC
Stevenson	I sought the Lord	HL	D-F	DIT
-----	Praise	M	F-F	CFI
Stickles	Saith the Lord	LH	D-F	CHA
Sullivan	Love not the world (The Prodigal Son)	L		GSC
Tchaikovsky	Lord, Almighty God (Moscow Cantata)	M		GRA
Thiman	My Master hath a garden	HL		NOV
Thompson	My Master hath a garden	M		ECS
Voris	Song of mothers	LH	D-FS	GRA
Watts	Intreat me not to leave thee	L	A-F	GSC
Weaver	Build thee more stately mansions	M	C-E	GAL
Wilder	Psalm 137			
Wolf	Morning prayer (Morgenstimme)			
-----	Prayer (Gebet)			

Wedding Songs

Mezzo Soprano

Barnby	O perfect love	M	C-G	DIT
Beethoven	Ich liebe dich	HL	BF-DF	†
Bond	I love you truly			BOS
Clough-				
Leighter	Possession	MH	DF-AF	GSC
Cornelius	Bridal songs			INT
De Koven	Oh promise me	HML	C-D	†
	(Robin Hood)			
Grieg	I love Thee	HML	E-F	†
La Forge	How much I love you	HM	DF-F	GSC
Lippe	How do I love Thee?			BOS
Manney	Consecration	MHH	E-A	DIT
Marx	Hat dich die Liebe	MH	EF-BF	AMP
	beruehrt			
Ronald	Love, I have won you	HML	EF-EF	ENO
Rowley	Here at thine altar, Lord			NOV
Roy	How do I love thee	HM	C-G	GSC
Sacco	With this ring	M	F-F	BVC
Schubert	Du bist die Ruh	LMH	EF-AF	†
-----	Ungeduld	HML		†
Schumann	Du Ring an meinem Finger	MHL		†
-----	Widmung	HL	BF-F	†
Sowerby	O perfect love	MH	BF-F	†
Strauss	Seitdem dein Aug' in			SC
	meines Schaute			
Thiman	The God of love my	ML	A-D	NOV
	Shepherd is			
Willan	O perfect love	HM	E-FS	GRA
Youmans	Through the Years	HML	A-F	MLR
	(Through the Years)			

Songs and Arias With Added Accompanying Instrument

Mezzo Soprano

Bach, J. S.	Christi Glieder ach bedenket	
	(Cantata 132) Violin	
-----	Gelobet sei der Herr	AUG
	(Cantata 129) Oboe d'amore	
-----	Hochgelobter Gottessohn	NOV
	(Cantata 6) English horn or	
	viola or violin	

127

(Bach, J.S.)	Jesus macht mich geistlich reich (Cantata 75) Violin			
Barber	Dover Beach String quartet	M	BF-F	GSC
Brahms	Geistliches Wiegenlied Piano and viola			†
-----	Gestillte Sehnsucht Viola and piano			†
Buxtehude	Singet dem Herrn (Violin)			
Chausson	Chanson perpétuelle String quartet	H	CS-GS	ROU
-----	Le colibri Violin or cello	M	F-GF	BOS
Falla	Psyché String quartet, harp and flute	M		CHE
Godard	Cachés dans cet asile (Jocelyn) Violin or cello	MH	DF-F	GSC
Honegger	Chanson (Ronsard) Flute and string quartet			SEN
Kahn	Es geht ein Wehen durch den Wald Violin, cello and piano			
-----	Mein Herzblut geht in Spruengen Violin, cello and piano			
-----	Waldesnacht, du wunderkuehle Violin, cello and piano			
-----	Wie bin ich nun in kuehler Nacht Violin, cello and piano			
Leroux	Le nil Cello or violin	LH	E-A	†
Mana-Zucca	Rachem Trumpet	HML		CHA
Milford	So sweet love seemed Cello	HL	D-D	GRA
Mozart	Parto, parto (La Clemenza di Tito) B flat clarinet and piano	H		AMP
Rorem	Music for voice and strings			
Peterkin	A curse on a closed gate Voice and viola	M	D-E	OXF
Rorem	Music for voice and strings			
Villa-Lobos	Bachianas Brazileiras, no. 5 8 Celli and bass			AMP
Wentzel	Lamkins Cello and piano			GRA

Contralto

Alberti	The gypsy			
Bacon	A clear midnight			NEM
Barber	A nun takes the veil	MH	G-G	GSC
-----	Dover Beach	M	BF-F	GSC
	String quartet			
-----	I hear an army	LH	D-AF	GSC
-----	Nocturne	HM	DS-FS	GSC
-----	Sleep now	MH	EF-AF	GSC
-----	Sure on this shining night	MH	D-G	GSC
Bauer	Swan	M		AMP
-----	The harp			AMP
Beach	Ah, love but a day			ASC
Bellini	My Persian garden	HL	EF-EF	GSC
Bone and				
Fenton	Everything that I can spy	M	E-GF	CFI
Bowles	Once a lady was here	ML	C-EF	GSC
Braine	Dawn awakes	HML	A-D	ASC
Buchhauser	Beyond the stars			
Bucky	Hear the wind whispering			BOO
Campbell				
Tipton	The crying of water	LH	FS-GS	GSC
Carpenter	Don't ceare	M	C-D	GSC
-----	Go, lovely rose	M	DF-EF	GSC
-----	Highway men	M	C-F	GSC
-----	If	M	D-E	GSC
-----	Light, my light	M	C-G	GSC
-----	May the maiden			DIT
-----	Odalisque	M	EF-EF	GSC
-----	On a screen	L	BF-DF	GSC
-----	Serenade	LH	CS-A	GSC
-----	Slumber song	ML	BF-F	GSC
-----	The cock shall crow	M	B-E	GSC
-----	The day is no more	M	GS-DS	GSC
-----	The green river	M	B-E	GSC
-----	The Lawd is smilin'	L	B-E	GSC
	through the do'			
-----	The player queen	M	BF-EF	GSC
-----	The sleep that flits on	M	B-FS	GSC
	baby's eyes			
-----	To a young gentleman	M	C-F	GSC
-----	To one unknown	M	A-DS	GSC
-----	When I bring to you	LM	CS-FS	GSC
	colour'd toys			
Castelnuovo-				
Tedesco	Am Teetisch			

129

(Castelnuovo-Tedesco)	Apemantus grace			CHE
-----	New York			
Chadwick	The danza	HM		ASC
Chanler	Once upon a time	M	C-G	GSC
Charles	Clouds	HML	C-EF	GSC
-----	The white swan	HL	C-F	GSC
-----	When I have sung my songs	HM	BF-EF	GSC
Clokey	The storke	M	C-D	JFI
Crist	Nina Bobo	HL		CFI
Dello Joio	Mill doors	M	D-E	CFI
-----	New born	M	C-D	CFI
Dougherty	Love in the dictionary	M	C-G	GSC
-----	Loveliest of trees	HM	C-E	BOH
-----	Pianissimo	M	C-G	GSC
-----	Portrait	HM	BF-G	GSC
-----	Sonatina	M	E-FS	GSC
-----	The bird and the beast			
Duke	Calvary	L	G-F	CFI
-----	Loveliest of trees	L	C-D	GSC
-----	Luke Havergal	M	BF-F	CFI
-----	On a March day	M	B-GF	BOH
-----	Wild swans	H	D-A	MER
Edmunds	Billy boy	ML	BF-EF	ROW
Elwell	Music I heard	M		AMP
-----	Renouncement	M	G-G	GSC
Engel	Sea shell	M	EF-EF	GSC
Fairchild	A memory			BOS
Farwell	These saw visions			GAL
Ferrata	Night and the curtains drawn			JFI
Foote	Tranquillity	HL	BF-E	ASC
Foster, S.C.	Ah, may the red rose live always			GSC
Ganz	A memory	HM	B-D	GSC
Giannini	I did not know	H		ELV
Golde	Calls	HL	BF-EF	GSC
-----	The deeper love			
Griffes	By a lonely forest pathway	HML	A-EF	GSC
-----	Evening song	H	DS-GS	GSC
-----	Night on ways unknown has fallen	L	GS-F	GSC
-----	We'll to the woods and gather May	M	D-F	GSC
Guion	When you go			
-----	Wild geese	M	D-F	CFI
Hadley	My shadow			ASC
Hageman	Do not go, my love	HL	B-EF	GSC
-----	Miranda	HL		GAL

130

(Hageman)	Music I heard with you	MH	E-A	GAL
Harris	Agatha Morley	M	C-D	CFI
-----	Fog	M	D-F	CFI
Hawley	Ah, 'tis a dream	L	G-C	JCH
Helm	Prairie waters by night			
Hindemith	The wildflower's song	MH	E-G	AMP
Horsman	The bird of the wilderness	LMH	DF-BF	GSC
Hovaness	How I adore thee	M		WBM
Huhn	O that it were so	HLM	D-E	GSC
Ilgenfritz	As we part			SCH
Ives	Evening			CSC
Kettering	The turtle			
Kingsford	Command	HLM	EF-G	GSC
Kramer	Faltering dusk			DIT
Kurstiner	Invocation to Eros			
La Forge	Hills	HL		RIC
-----	Into the light	HL		RIC
-----	The sand			
Lockwood	O, lady, let the sad tears fall	M		MER
Malotte	One, two, three	M	C-F	GSC
-----	Upstream	M	C-F	GSC
Mana-Zucca	Mirror of my soul			
-----	Rachem Trumpet	HML		CHA
-----	Speak to me			
-----	Today is mine			CNG
Metcalf	At nightfall	HML	C-DF	ASC
Moore	Sigh no more, ladies			BOO
Mopper	Men	M	D-FS	BOS
Naginski	The buckle			
-----	The pasture	M	BF-EF	GSC
Nordoff	Serenade	H	CS-FS	AMP
-----	There shall be more joy	M	CS-FS	AMP
Olmstead	They sweet singing	HL	BF-EF	GSC
Parker	The south wind	LH	DF-GF	GAL
Price	Songs to the dark virgin	HL	BF-EF	GSC
Protheroe	Ah, love but a day	LMH	F-AF	GAM
-----	What is there hid in the heart of a rose?	ML		DIT
Rawls	The balloon man	L	A-FS	AMP
-----	Sail forth			
-----	The last song	MLH	E-AF	GSC
-----	Time for making songs	HM	CS-F	DIT
Rummel	Ecstasy	LMH	GF-AF	GSC
Rupp	Sweet nightingale			
Salter	The cry of Rachel	LH	C-AF	GSC
Saminsky	Mary Stuart's farewell to France			
Sargent	Manhattan joy ride	M	D-F	GSC
-----	River road			

(Sargent)	Stopping by woods	M	D-E	GSC
-----	Three a.m.	M	DF-E	GSC
Schuman	Orpheus with his lute	M	C-FS	GSC
Silberta	I met dame fate	L	BF-E	GSC
Spross	Will o' the wisp			JCH
Swanson	Pierrot	L	B-D	WTR
-----	The negro speaks of rivers	M		LEE
Thompson	Velvet shoes	M	C-E	ECS
Thomson	Dirge	M	D-F	GSC
Tureman	A winter sunset	L	BF-E	GSC
Tyson	Noon and night	LH	F-AF	GSC
-----	Sea moods	LH	E-AF	GSC
Warren	Heather	LH	FS-G	GSC
-----	Light the lamps up	HM	C-F	GSC
-----	Through my open window	HL	C-E	GSC
-----	We two	LH	E-A	GSC
Watts	Transformation	ML	AS-DS	GSC
-----	Wild tears	L	A-F	GSC
-----	Wings of night	LH	CS-G	GSC
Wolf	Weather forecast	H	EF-GS	GSC
Zimbalist	O take me to your breathing heart			

British Recital Songs

Contralto

Arne, T.	Come away death	M	C-AF	AUG
-----	Where the bee sucks	HM		†
-----	Why so pale and wan?			GSC
Bantock	Lament of Isis	L		AMP
-----	Silent strings	MH	F-G	BOO
Bax	I heard a piper piping	LH	D-G	CFI
Brewer	The fairy pipers	HML		BOH
Bridge	Love went a-riding	HL		BOS
-----	O that it were so	LMH	D-G	CHA
Brown	Shepherd thy demeanor vary			BOO
Clarke	The seal man	M		BOH
Dowland	Deare, if you change			BOO
-----	My thoughs are filled with hope			
-----	Sorrow, sorrow stay	M	D-D	BOS
-----	Woeful heart with grief oppressed			KEE
Dunhill	The cloths of heaven	LM	EF-G	STB
Edmunds	How should I my true love know?			

(Edmunds)	I know my love	HL	BF-EF	ROW
Elgar	The swimmer			BOO
-----	Where corals lie	HL		BOO
German	Charming Chloe	HML		NOV
Gibb	By a bier side			CUR
Gibbs	Five eyes	HL	D-D	BOS
Goossens	Melancholy	M		CHE
Green	I will lay me down in peace			
-----	Praised be the Lord	M	C-F	OXF
Head	A piper	HL		BOO
-----	Nocturne	HL		BOO
-----	Sweet chance that led my steps abroad	LM	C-F	BOH
-----	The ships of Arcady	ML	BF-EF	BOH
Hely-Hutchinson	Old mother Hubbard	HL	B-E	CFI
Henschel	Morning-hymn	MH	DS-GS	†
-----	There was an ancient king			ASC
Holst	Creation			GSC
-----	Hymn to the waters	M	B-FS	CHE
-----	Indra, God of storm and battle	M	B-F	CHE
-----	Speech	M	BF-F	CHE
-----	The heart worships	ML	BF-D	STB
Hook	Bright Phoebus	M	EF-F	GSC
Horn	I've been roaming	L	B-E	†
Hughes	O men from the fields	M	F-F	BOO
-----	The terrible robber men			
Ireland	Bed in summer			CUR
-----	Santa Chiara	ML	C-EF	AUG
Johnson	Care-charming sleep			
Morley	It was a lover and his lass	HM		DIT
Parry	Love is a bauble			NOV
-----	Why so pale and wan, fond lover	L		NOV
Peterkin	Advice to girls	H	CS-FS	CFI
Pilkington	Rest, sweet nymphs			STB
Purcell	Ah, how pleasant tis to love			AUG
-----	Bess of Bedlam			BOO
-----	Evening hymn	M	C-F	OXF
-----	Hark! how all things with one sound rejoice			NOV
-----	If music be the food of love	M	D-G	BOO
-----	Man is for woman made			
-----	Not all my torments			NOV
-----	Sweet, be no longer sad			NOV

133

(Purcell)	There's no swain on the plain	M	B-G	BAF
-----	Venus' song			AUG
Quilter	Blow, blow thou winter wind	HL	C-E	BOO
-----	Damask roses			BOO
-----	Love's philosophy	LMH	D-A	BOO
-----	Music and moonlight	L	C-EF	CUR
Rosseter	When Laura smiles	LM	D-E	STB
Rowley	Grieve not my heart			BOH
-----	The toll gate house			ROG
Sanderson	Quiet	ML	AF-EF	BOH
Scott	Lullaby	MML	BF-DF	GAL
Sharp	Whistle daughter, whistle			DIT
Shaw	Song of the Palanquin bearers	LH	E-F	CUR
Somervell	Shepherd's cradle song	HM		GSC
Stephenson	Ships that pass in the night	HML	DF-DF	BOO
Vaughn Williams	Boy Jonny	LH		BOH
-----	Four nights	L	AF-EF	OXF
-----	Linden Lea	HML	C-D	BOS
-----	Silent noon			GSC
-----	The new ghost			
-----	The water mill	L	C-D	OXF
Warlock	A prayer to St. Anthony of Padua	M	C-EF	CFI
-----	Consider	M	C-G	CFI
-----	In an arbour green	H	D-G	CFI
-----	Peterisms	H		CHE
-----	Rest, sweet nymphs	M	F-F	CFI
-----	Sleep			OXF
-----	The birds			

French Recital Songs

Contralto

Aubert	Vieille chanson espagnole			DUR
Bax	Femmes battex vos marys			
-----	Me suis en danse			
Bemberg	Chant hindou	HML	A-EF	†
Berlioz	La captive	HL		GSC
Bizet	Adieu de l'hôtesse arabe	H	BF-G	†
-----	Aubade			
-----	La sirène			
-----	Ma vie a son secret	L	AF-F	CHU
Caplet	La ronde	M		DUR

134

Chaminade	Chant slave			GSC
Chausson	Le colibri Violin or cello	M	F-GF	BOS
-----	Le temps des lilas	MH	D-GS	†
Debussy	Ballade des femmes de Paris			DUR
-----	Ballade que fait Villon à la requeste de sa mère			DUR
-----	Beau soir	LH	C-FS	†
-----	Chevaux de bois	H	C-G	†
-----	Je tremble en voyant ton visage			DUR
-----	La chevelure	M	CF-FS	†
-----	La flûte de Pan		B-B	†
-----	La mer est plus belle	HL		INT
-----	Le faune			DUR
-----	Mandoline	HM	BF-F	†
Duparc	Au pays où se fait la guerre			SAL
-----	Chanson triste	MH	FS-AF	†
-----	Lamento	ML	EF-EF	†
-----	Le manoir de Rosamunde	HL	B-F	BOS
-----	L'invitation au voyage	HM	E-F	†
-----	Phidylé	MH	EF-AF	BOS
Dupont	Mandoline			DUR
Fauré	Après un rêve	HM	C-F	†
-----	Automne	MH	D-FS	GSC
-----	Clair de lune	MH	C-G	†
-----	Fleur jetée	HM	BF-FS	†
-----	Le parfum impérissable	LH	GF-GF	
-----	Les berceaux	LMH	BF-G	†
-----	Nocturne	H	F-A	MAR
-----	Prison	LH		†
-----	Rencontre	H	EF-AF	†
-----	Toujours	LH	F-AF	†
Ferrari	Le miroir	M	E-F	GSC
Fontenailles	Souffrance			
Fourdrain	Carnaval	M	C-F	RIC
-----	Chevauchée cosaque	H	D-G	RIC
-----	Impression basque	M		RIC
Franck	La procession	LH	E-GS	†
-----	Le mariage des roses	M	E-FS	BOS
Georges	La pluie	HL		INT
Gounod	Au rossignol	LMH	D-G	CHO
Hahn	D'une prison	L	BF-EF	HEU
-----	L'heure exquise	M	DF-F	†
-----	Les cygnes			HEU
-----	Mai			HEU
-----	Offrande	M	D-D	†

135

(Hahn)	Paysage	MH	EF-G	HEU
Holmès	L'heure de pourpre			HEU
Honegger	Chanson (Ronsard) Flute and string quartet			SEN
-----	Les cloches			SEN
-----	Oh my love take my hand			SEN
-----	Psalm 130 (Mimaamaquim)			SAL
Hue	J'ai pleuré rêve	HL	D-E	BOS
Indy	Lied maritime	LH	B-G	†
Koechlin	L'hiver	H	E-G	†
Lalo	Chant breton	M	E-E	HAM
Martini	Plaisir d'amour	M	BF-EF	GSC
Massenet	Rose de mai			
Paladilhe	Lamento provinçal	M	CS-FS	HOM
-----	Psyché	HM	BF-F	GSC
Pessard	L'adieu du matin	ML	BF-D	GSC
Pierné	Le moulin	ML	C-E	BOS
Poldowski	Dansons la gigue	M	ÈF-G	MAR
-----	L'heure exquise	LMH	DF-AF	CHE
-----	Spleen	M	D-F	CHE
Poulenc	A sa guitare	M	D-FS	DUR
-----	Avant le cinéma	M		ROU
-----	Hôtel			AMP
-----	Le tombeau			HEU
-----	Priez pour paix	ML		ROU
-----	Voyage à Paris			AMP
Ravel	Chanson française			
-----	Kaddisch	H	C-G	DUR
-----	Nicolette	L	B-FS	ELK
-----	Tout gai!	MH	EF-F	
-----	Vocalise en forme de habanera	MH	BF-G	MAR
Rhené-Baton	Il pleut des pétales de fleurs	M	CS-E	DUR
Rosenthal	Grammaire			
-----	Le marabout			ESC
Saint-Saëns	L'attente			DUR
-----	La cloche	LH	DF-AF	†
Tremisot	Novembre			ENO
Vidal	Ariette	LH	F-A	GSC
Widor	Je ne veux pas autre chose	HL	C-EF	HAM

German Recital Songs

Contralto

Ahle	Bruenstiges Verlangen	M	E-E	GSC

Bach, C.P.E.	Suscepit Israel			
Bach, J.S.	Bist due bei mir	HML	A-EF	†
-----	Komm, suesser Tod	MH	C-G	†
-----	Kommt, Seelen, dieser Tag			
-----	Liebster Herr Jesu			BRH
Bach, P.E.	Bitten			
Beethoven	An die Geliebte	M	E-E	†
-----	Bitten			†
-----	Busslied			†
-----	Das Geheimnis			
-----	Die Ehre Gottes	HL	AF-EF	†
-----	Die Liebe des Naechsten			
-----	Die Trommel geruehret			†
-----	Faithfu' Johnie			
-----	God is my song			
-----	Ich liebe dich	HL	BF-DF	†
-----	Vom Tode	L	A-EF	GSC
-----	Wonne der Wehmut			†
Brahms	Ach, wende diesen Blick			†
-----	Am Sonntag Morgen	L	CS-FS	CFI
-----	An die Nachtigall	H	DS-G	†
-----	An eine Aeolsharfe	H	EF-AF	†
-----	Auf dem Kirchhofe	HL	BF-EF	†
-----	Botschaft	HL	D-F	†
-----	Bratschenlieder			†
-----	Dein blaues Auge	MH	BF-G	†
-----	Der Kranz			†
-----	Der Schmied	HL	EF-EF	†
-----	Der Tod, das ist die kuehle Nacht	L	AF-F	†
-----	Die Mainacht	HL	BF-FF	†
-----	Die Schnur, die Perl an Perle			†
-----	Ein Wanderer	LH	E-AF	†
-----	Feldeinsamkeit	HL	C-EF	†
-----	Gestillte Sehnsucht Viola and piano			†
-----	Immer leiser wird mein Schlummer	LH	DF-A	†
-----	In Waldeseinsamkeit	H	ES-G	†
-----	Juchhe!			†
-----	Komm bald	HM	CS-F	†
-----	Kommt dir manchmal in den Sinn	H	DS-GS	†
-----	Liebestreu	ML	C-F	†
-----	Maedchenlied	HL		†
-----	Meine Liebe ist gruen	MLH	ES-A	†
-----	Mit vierzig Jahren	HL	FS-D	CFI
-----	Muss es eine Trennung geben?	LH	FS-FS	†

137

(Brahms)	Nachtigall	MHL	BF-FS	†
-----	Nicht mehr zu dir zu gehen			†
-----	O kuehler Wald	MH	A-F	†
-----	O liebliche Wangen	MLH	E-G	†
-----	O wuesst' ich doch den Weg zurueck	H	E-FS	†
-----	Roeslein drei			†
-----	Sapphische Ode	HML		†
-----	Schwermut			†
-----	Sehnsucht	H	EF-AF	†
-----	Sonntag	H	D-G	†
-----	Spanisches Lied			†
-----	Staendchen	HL	BF-E	†
-----	Steig' auf, geliebter Schatten	HL	BF-EF	†
-----	Trueue Liebe	LMH	DS-E	†
-----	Vergebliches Staendchen	LMH		†
-----	Verzagen	MH	CS-FS	†
-----	Von ewiger Liebe	LMH	B-AF	†
-----	Wehe, so willst du mich wieder			†
-----	Wie die Wolke			†
-----	Wiegenlied			
-----	Wie Melodien zieht es	HL	A-E	†
-----	Willst du, dass ich geh'?	L	C-G	†
-----	Wir wandelten	LH	EF-GF	GSC
-----	Wisst ihr wann			†
Buxtehude	Lord save me			
Cornelius	Komm wir wandeln	H	FS-GS	SC
Franz	Er ist gekommen	HL	EF-F	†
-----	Es ragt ins Meer der Runenstein	HL	G-F	†
-----	For music	ML	C-D	†
-----	Im Fruhling	HL		GSC
-----	Im Herbst	HM	A-F	†
-----	Mutter, o sing mich zur Ruh	HL	E-G	†
-----	Sterne mit den gold'nen Fuesschen	HL	DS-E	†
Grosz	Rondel			
Handel	Begruessung			
-----	Dank sei Dir, Herr	M	CS-E	†
Haydn	Das Leben ist ein Traum			GSC
-----	Die Seejungfer			
-----	Ein kleines Haus			
-----	My mother bids me bind my hair	M	E-E	†
-----	Schaeferlied			

(Haydn)	She never told her love	HL	B-D	DIT
-----	The spirit's song	M	B-GF	†
-----	The wanderer			
Himmel	Die Sendung			SIM
Jensen	Wie so bleich			
Liszt	Am Rhein			
-----	Die Lorelei	LH	BF-BF	†
-----	Freudvoll und leidvoll			DUR
Loewe	Der heilige Franziskus	L	A-E	SC
-----	Die Uhr	HML	AF-EF	†
-----	Edward	HL	F-E	†
-----	Maedchen sind wie der Wind			SC
-----	Walpurgisnacht	H	G-G	SC
Mahler	Das Irdische Leben	HL	A-F	INT
-----	Der Schildwache Nachtlied	L	A-G	†
-----	Des Antonius von Padua Fischpredigt	HL	GF-F	†
-----	Ging heut Morgen uebers Feld	M	A-FS	INT
-----	Ich bin der Welt abbanden gekommen	HL		INT
-----	Ich hab' ein gluehend Messer	M	BF-GF	WEI
-----	Liebst du um Schoenheit	HL		INT
-----	Wer hat dies Liedlein erdacht?	HL	BF-E	INT
-----	Wo die schoenen Trompeten blasen	HL	GF-F	INT
Marx	Der Denker			
-----	Italienisches Wiegenlied			
-----	Venetianisches Wiegenlied			AMP
Mendelssohn	And'res Maienlied			AUG
-----	Schlafloser Augen Leuchte			AUG
Mozart	Als Luise die Briefe			GSC
-----	Die Alte			
-----	Warnung	HM	C-D	
-----	Wiegenlied	MH	C-G	†
Ott	Leichte Wahl			
Pfitzner	Der Einsame			BOO
-----	Im tiefen Wald verborgen			
-----	Nachts			BOO
Raff	Keine Sorg' um den Weg			
Reger	Am Bruennele			
-----	Das Dorf			AMP
-----	Mit Rosen bestreut			UNI
-----	Morgengesang			PET
-----	Volkslied			AMP
-----	Waldeinsamkeit	HML	A-D	BOS

Reichardt	Rhapsodie			MOS
Schoenberg	Song of the wood dove			AMP
Schubert	Am Bach, im Fruehling			PET
-----	An die Leier	LM	BF-F	†
-----	An Schwager Kronos	HL	G-E	†
-----	Auf dem Wasser zu singen	MH	EF-GF	†
-----	Auf der Bruecke	HL		†
-----	Aufenthalt	HLM	A-F	GSC
-----	Aufloesung	LH	D-A	†
-----	Aus Heliopolis			PET
-----	Ave Maria	LMH	F-F	†
-----	Dem Unendlichen	L	A-GF	†
-----	Der Atlas	HL	BF-F	†
-----	Der Doppelgaenger	HL	G-D	†
-----	Der Erlkoenig	HML	A-E	†
-----	Der Geistertanz	L	G-EF	†
-----	Der Juengling an der Quelle	LH	E-A	†
-----	Der Juengling auf dem Huegel	L	G-F	†
-----	Der Juengling und das Tod	M	DF-FF	†
-----	Der Koenig in Thule	L	F-F	PET
-----	Der Leiermann	ML	C-D	†
-----	Der Lindenbaum	HL	A-D	†
-----	Der Musensohn	LH	FS-G	†
-----	Der Neugierige	HL	CS-EF	†
-----	Der stuermische Morgen	HL		
-----	Der Tod und das Maedchen	HL	A-EF	†
-----	Der Wanderer	HML	FS-D	†
-----	Der Wanderer an den Mond	LM	D-F	PET
-----	Der Wegweiser	L	D-EF	†
-----	Der Zwerg	M	A-GF	PET
-----	Des Maedchens Klage	LH	C-E	†
-----	Die Allmacht	HML	G-E	GSC
-----	Die boese Farbe	HL	CS-F	†
-----	Die Forelle	MLH	EF-GF	†
-----	Die Hoffnung	HM	E-E	†
-----	Die junge Nonne	LH	C-GF	†
-----	Die Kraehe	HL	A-E	†
-----	Die liebe Farbe			
-----	Die Liebe hat gelogen	LM	G-F	†
-----	Die Maenner sind mechant			PET
-----	Die Nebensonnen	HL	F-D	†
-----	Die Post	HML	BF-EF	†
-----	Die Unterscheidung	LH	D-G	†
-----	Du bist die Ruh	LMH	EF-AF	†
-----	Du liebst mich nicht	LH	E-FS	†
-----	Ellens zweiter Gesang			PET
-----	Erstarrung	HL	D-F	†
-----	Fahrt zum Hades	HL	G-DF	PET

140

(Schubert)	Fischerweise	L	C-D	†
-----	Fragment aus dem Aeschylus			PET
-----	Fruehlingstraum	HL	C-D	†
-----	Gott im Fruehling			PET
-----	Gretchen am Spinnrade	H	F-A	†
-----	Gruppe aus dem Tartarus	L	CS-EF	†
-----	Heidenroeslein			
-----	Im Abendrot	HL	C-D	†
-----	Im Freien	HL	C-F	†
-----	In der Ferne	HL		GSC
-----	Iphigenia			PET
-----	Irrlicht			
-----	Lachen und Weinen	HL	C-EF	†
-----	Liebesbotschaft	H	E-G	†
-----	Lied der Mignon	HL		†
-----	Litanei	HLM	C-EF	†
-----	Meeresstille	HL	B-D	†
-----	Nachtgesang			PET
-----	Nacht und Traeume	HL	C-DF	†
-----	Rastlose Liebe	M	B-F	†
-----	Romanze aus Rosamunde			PET
-----	Schaefers Klagelied	HL	BF-D	†
-----	Seligkeit			
-----	Staendchen			
-----	Suleika I	LH	DS-G	†
-----	Thekla	HL	B-E	PET
-----	Ungeduld	HML		†
-----	Verklaerung			PET
-----	Wanderers Nachtlied 1	HL		†
-----	Wehmuth	HL	B-D	†
-----	Widerschein			PET
-----	Wohin?	HL	B-E	†
Schuetz	Aus dem 119th Psalm			
-----	O clap your hands			
Schumann, C.	Liebst du um Schoenheit			
Schumann, R.	Abends am Strande			
-----	Alte Laute	HL	DF-DF	†
-----	An den Sonnenschein	HL	A-D	†
-----	Auf das Trinkglas eines verstorbenen Freundes			
-----	Aus den Hebraeischen Gesaengen			
-----	Der Himmel hat eine Traene geweint			
-----	Der Nussbaum	LMH	D-FS	†
-----	Die Kartenlegerin			
-----	Die Lotusblume	HLM	BF-F	†
-----	Die Soldatenbraut	HL	AF-EF	†
-----	Die Tochter Jephthas	HL	A-E	

141

(Schumann)	Du bist wie eine Blume	HM	F-EF	†
-----	Du Ring an meinem Finger	HL	C-F	†
-----	Er, der Herrlichste von Allen	HL	A-EF	†
-----	Fruehlingsfahrt	HL	B-E	†
-----	Fruehlingsnacht	L	CS-E	†
-----	Heiss' mich nicht reden			
-----	Hoch, hoch sind die Berge			
-----	Im Walde	HL	A-D	†
-----	Im Westen	HL		†
-----	Kaeuzlein			
-----	Lied der Suleika			
-----	Lust der Sturmnacht			
-----	Mit Myrthen und Rosen	HL	A-D	DIT
-----	Mondnacht	M	E-FS	†
-----	O ihr Herren, o ihr Werthen	LH		†
-----	Schoene Wiege meiner Leiden	HL	C-EF	†
-----	Seit ich ihn gesehen	HL	DF-DF	†
-----	Talismane			
-----	Waldesgespraech	HL	A-FS	†
-----	Wehmut			†
-----	Wer machte dich so krank?			
-----	Widmung	HL	BF-F	†
Strauss	Allerseelen	HL	AS-E	†
-----	Befreit			HSC
-----	Caecilie	MH	E-B	†
-----	Die Georgine	LH	B-A	†
-----	Die Nacht	HL		†
-----	Freundliche Vision	HL	C-F	†
-----	Fruehlingsfeier			
-----	Geduld	LH	C-G	
-----	Heimliche Aufforderung	HL	B-E	†
-----	Im Spaetboot			
-----	In goldener Fuelle			†
-----	Liebeshymnus			†
-----	Maria ging hinaus			
-----	Mit deinen blauen Augen	LH	C-GS	†
-----	Morgen	HML	E-F	GSC
-----	Ruhe meine Seele			†
-----	Traum durch die Daemmerung	HML	BF-EF	†
-----	Wiegenliedchen			†
-----	Winterliebe			†
-----	Zueignung	HL	CS-FS	†
Trunk	Das Hemd			
-----	Fruehlingssonne			

(Trunk)	Suleika			
Wagner	Der Engel	LH	CS-G	†
-----	Schmerzen	HL		†
-----	Traeume	HL		†
Wolf	Agnes	HL		†
-----	Alle gingen, Herz, zu Ruh	HL	C-EF	†
-----	Als ich auf dem Euphrat schiffte			†
-----	An eine Aeolsharfe			†
-----	Auf einer Wanderung	HL		†
-----	Bedeckt mich mit Blumen	HL	B-D	†
-----	Bescheidene Liebe	MH	D-G	
-----	Cophtisches Lied I			†
-----	Dank des Paria			PET
-----	Das verlassene Maegdlein	HL	D-EF	†
-----	Die ihr schwebet	HL	EF-EF	INT
-----	Die Sproede			†
-----	Die Zigeunerin			†
-----	Dies zu deuten			PET
-----	Epiphanias	HL	B-D	†
-----	Er ist's	H	D-G	†
-----	Fussreise	HL	D-E	†
-----	Gebet	HL		†
-----	Geh' Geliebter, geh' jetzt			PET
-----	Gesang Weylas	HL	DF-F	†
-----	Hatt ich irgend wohl Bedenken			PET
-----	Ich hab' in Penna	LH		†
-----	Im Fruehling	HL	BF-F	†
-----	In dem Schatten meiner Locken	M	C-EF	†
-----	In der Fruehe	HL	C-C	†
-----	Kennst du das Land			†
-----	Klinge, klinge, mein Pandero	HL	CF-EF	†
-----	Mausfallen Spruechlein	HL	BF-E	†
-----	Mignon	LH		†
-----	Nachtzauber	HL	B-E	†
-----	Nimmersatte Liebe	LH	CF-AF	†
-----	Nun lass uns Frieden schliessen	HL		†
-----	Nun wandre, Maria	HL	EF-D	†
-----	Nur wer die Sehnsucht kennt			†
-----	Rat einer Alten			PET
-----	Ueber Nacht	LH	D-G	†
-----	Um Mitternacht	HL	G-EF	†
-----	Verborgenheit	HL	B-E	†
-----	Wenn du zu den Blumen gehst	HL	B-EF	†

(Wolf)	Wie glaenzt der helle Mond			†
-----	Zur Ruh', zur Ruh'	HL	A-GF	†
Wolff	Alle Dinge haben Sprache	M	BF-GF	†
-----	Die Heisse schwuele Sommernacht			HMP
-----	Ein solcher ist mein Freund	M	DS-F	†
-----	Ewig			
-----	Ich bin eine Harfe			HMP
-----	Maerchen	M	D-E	†
-----	Reim			
-----	Seidenschuh' ueber Leisten von Gold			
-----	Sommernacht			
-----	Wie Melodien aus reiner Sphaere hoer' ich			

Italian Recital Songs

Contralto

Arditi	Leggiero, invisibile			
Benati	Credi nell' alma mia			
Bononcini	Deh, più a me non v'ascondete	LH	EF-F	†
Caccini	Amarilli, mia bella	ML	C-D	†
Caldara	Come raggio di sol	HL	D-F	†
-----	Mirti, faggi			PET
-----	Sebben crudele	HML	E-DS	†
-----	Selve amiche, ombrose piante	HM	E-E	†
Carissimi	A morire!	ML	C-D	
-----	Vittoria, mio core	HLM	B-E	†
Cavalli	Beato chi può (Serse)			HEU
-----	Donzelle fuggite	HL	C-EF	†
Cesti	Ah, quanto è vero (Il Pomo d'Oro)	HL	F-F	DIT
-----	Che angoscia, che affanno (Il Pomo d'Oro)	HL	C-DF	DIT
-----	E dove t'aggiri (I' Pomo d'Oro)	HM	D-EF	DIT
-----	Intorno all'idol mio (Orontea)	MH	D-F	†
Cherubini	Ahi, che forse ai miei di (Demofonte)			RIC
Cimara	Fiocca la neve	H	G-G	GSC
-----	Stornellata marinara	HM		RIC
Cimarosa	Bel nume che adoro			RIC

De Luca	Non posso disperar	HL	C-E	GSC
Donaudy	Quando ti rivedrò			RIC
Durante	Danza, danza fanciulla gentile	HM	BF-F	†
-----	Vergin, tutta amor	LM	C-EF	†
Falconieri	Non più d'amore	HL	C-D	DIT
-----	Nudo arciero	HL	AF-AF	DIT
-----	O bellissimi capelli	HL	B-D	†
Frescobaldi	Se l'aura spira	HL	C-EF	DIT
Gagliano	Dormi, amore	HL	CS-E	DIT
Gasparini	Caro laccio, dolce nodo	M	EF-EF	GSC
Giordani	Caro mio ben	HML	B-D	†
Giordano	E l'Aprile che torna a me	H		RIC
Gluck	Spiagge amate (Paride ed Elena)			†
Handel	Ah! mio cor (Alcina)			†
-----	Ah! spietato (Amadigi)			
-----	Ben io sento l'ingrata spietata furio (Atalanta)	L	B-D	CFI
-----	Care selve (Atalanta)	MH	FS-A	†
-----	Ch'io mai vi possa (Siroe)			CFI
-----	Con rauco mormorio (Rodelinda)			
-----	Dove sei, amato bene (Rodelinda)	L	BF-EF	†
-----	Empio dirò tu sei (Julius Caesar)			
-----	Furibondo spira (Partenope)			KIS
-----	La speranza è giunto in porto (Ottone)			
-----	Lascia ch'io pianga (Rinaldo)			
-----	Notte cara (Floridante)			
-----	Ombra mai fu (Serse)	HM	BF-EF	†
-----	Piangero la (Julius Caesar)			CFI
-----	Rendi'l sereno al ciglio (Sosarme)	LH	EF-F	†
-----	Si, tra i ceppi (Berenice)	L	B-D	†
-----	Stille amare (Tolomeo)			MUP
-----	Tutta raccolta (Scipione)			CFI
-----	Un cenno leggia dretto (Serse)			
-----	V'adoro pupille (Julius Caesar)			BOO
-----	Verdi prati (Alcina)			
-----	Vieni o figlio caro e mi consola (Ottone)			CFI
Legrenzi	Che fiero costume	HML	C-D	†
Leoni	A little china figure	HM	DF-EF	GSC

Lotti	Pur dicesti, o bocca bella	LMH	E-FS	GSC
Malipiero	Inno a Maria Nostra Donna	H		CHE
Marcello	Il mio bel foco	LMH	C-G	†
-----	Non m'è grave morir per amore	L	C-E	GSC
Monteverdi	Illustatevi o cieli			
Paisiello	Chi vuol la zingarella	L	C-F	GSC
Pergolesi	Confusa, smarrita			GSC
-----	Il nocch'ier nella Tempesta (Salustia)			
-----	Per queste amore lagrime (Salustia)			
-----	Se tu m'ami	LMH	C-G	GSC
Peri	Funeste piaggie (Euridice)			GSC
-----	Invocazione di Orfeo (Euridice)	HL	E-CS	DIT
Provenzale	Deh, rendetemi	ML	D-D	DIT
Recli	Anda			
-----	Nenia popolare			
Respighi	E se un giorno tornasse	M		RIC
-----	Il tramonto			RIC
-----	Io sono la madre	L		RIC
-----	Nebbie			†
-----	Pioggia			BON
-----	Scherzo			BON
Rontani	Or ch'io non segno più	HL	CS-E	DIT
-----	Se bel rio	ML	D-C	GSC
Rosa	Selve, voi che le speranze	MH	D-G	DIT
-----	Star vicino	HL	D-E	†
-----	Vado ben spesso	ML	C-EF	†
Rossi	Ah, rendimi (Mitrane)	L	GS-FS	GSC
Rossini	La danza	MH	E-A	†
Sadero	Amuri, Amuri	M		CHE
Santoliquido	I canti della sera			RIC
Sarti	Lungi dal caro bene (Armide)	HL	G-D	GSC
Scarlatti, A.	Chi vuole innamorarsi	HL	D-EF	DIT
-----	La fortuna			BOS
-----	O cessate di piagarmi	HL	DS-E	†
-----	Rugiadose odorose (Il Pirro e Demetrio)	HL	D-E	DIT
-----	Se Florindo è fedele	LM	EF-EF	GSC
-----	Sento nel core	M	E-F	†
Scarlatti, D.	Consolati e spara amante	L	BF-E	GSC
-----	Qual farfalletta			
Secchi	Lungi dal caro bene	HL	A-FS	DIT
Stradella	Col mio sangue	HL	E-F	DIT

	comprenderei (Il Floridoro)			
(Stradella)	Per pietà (Il Floridoro)	HM	D-F	DIT
-----	Se nel ben			CFI
Strozzi	Amor dormiglione	HL	B-E	DIT
Torelli	Tu lo sai	HL	BF-F	†
Vivaldi	Un certo no so che	HL	BF-EF	†
Wolf-Ferrari	Rispetto			HSC

Russian Recital Songs
Contralto

Arensky	Valse	H	DF-GF	GSC
Borodin	A dissonance	MH	E-F	†
-----	Requiem of love			
Gliere	Ah, twine no blossoms	HM	CS-F	DIT
Gretchaninoff	Freedom			
-----	Hushed the song of the nightingale	MH	E-G	DIT
-----	In exile			
-----	Lullaby			
-----	Over the steppe	LM	C-G	GSC
-----	Rosy reflections			
-----	The snowdrop	HM	BF-F	DIT
-----	Wounded birch	HL	B-EF	†
Mednikoff	The hills of Gruzia	H	DS-A	LAC
Medtner	The angel			
-----	Waltz			
Mussorgsky	After the battle			GSC
-----	Death the commander			
-----	Fairy tales			
-----	Hopak	HM	CS-FS	GSC
-----	Gathering mushrooms			INT
-----	In the corner			GSC
-----	On the Dnieper			GSC
-----	Peasant cradle song	M		GSC
-----	Serenade			BES
-----	Sphinx			BRH
-----	The banks of the Don			GSC
-----	The classic			BRH
-----	The forgotten one			
-----	The magpie and the gypsy dancer			GSC
-----	The orphan girl			GSC
Rachmaninoff	Child, lovely blossom			
-----	Fate	L		BOO
-----	Floods of spring	HL		DIT
-----	In the silence of night	LH	D-A	GSC
-----	Lilacs	LH	EF-G	†
-----	Oh, no, I pray do not depart	H		DIT

(Rachmaninoff)	O thou billowy harvest field	HL	CS-E	GSC
-----	Solitude			
-----	The island	LH	DF-F	†
-----	The raising of Lazarus			BRH
-----	'Tis time	L		BOO
Stravinsky	Song of the dew			JUR
-----	The cloister (La novice)			DIT
Tchaikovsky	Complaint of the bride			
-----	He loved me so dear	HL		GSC
-----	Speak not, O beloved			
-----	Why	HL		†

Scandinavian Recital Songs

Contralto

Grieg	A dream			†
-----	A swan			†
-----	Autumnal gale	HL	A-F	CFI
-----	By the brook			GSC
-----	Digtervise	L	A-EF	HAN
-----	Eros	LM	C-F	†
-----	Good morning			†
-----	Henrik Wergeland			PET
-----	Hjemkomst	M	B-F	HAN
-----	Hunter's song	L	DS-E	GSC
-----	I love thee	HML	E-F	†
-----	In the boat	LM	D-ES	†
-----	Jeg lever et liv i laengsel	L	BF-E	HAN
-----	Love			PET
-----	Poesien			
-----	Rock, O wave			
-----	Spillemand			
-----	Spring rain			PET
-----	Springtide	M		DIT
-----	The first meeting			PET
-----	The return			
-----	There screamed a bird			PET
-----	Turisten	M	CS-F	HAN
-----	Vandring i skoven	M	D-FS	HAN
-----	Verse for an album			
-----	With a primrose	H	DF-GF	GSC
-----	With a water lily	HM	CS-EF	†
Heise	Arnes sang			
Jonsson	Under haeggarna			
Kilpinen	Die Fusswaschung			
-----	En vårmelodi			

(Kilpinen)	Ring, ring			
Lasson, P.	Were I the flaming sun	HL	DF-G	GSC
Lindberg	Hur skall man bruden klaeda?			
Lundvik	Sov i sommarsus			
Nordquist	Kunde jag dikta en visa			
Palmgren	Autumn	HL		BOS
Peterson-				
Berger	Aftonstaemming			
-----	Swedish folk song			
-----	Titania			
Rangstroem	En gammal Danstrym			
-----	Night			
-----	Pan			
-----	Tragedie			
Sibelius	Astray			AMP
-----	Black roses	M	A-ES	AMP
-----	But my bird is long in homing			
-----	Come away death			AMP
-----	Coming of spring			HAN
-----	Diamonds on the March snow			
-----	Die Liebelle			
-----	Driftwood			AMP
-----	From the north	H	DS-G	GSC
-----	In the field a maiden sings			
-----	O wert thou here			AMP
-----	Reeds, reeds rustle			
-----	Slow as the colors			
-----	Speedwell			
-----	Spring is fleeting			DIT
-----	The first kiss	M		AMP
-----	The question			
-----	The tryst	M		AMP
-----	Was it a dream			BRH
Sinding	I hear the gull			JCH
Sjoegren	Jeg giver mit digt			
Vehanen	The girl the boys all love			

Spanish Recital Songs

Contralto

Berger	No jardín			
Falla	Canción del amor dolido			CHE
-----	Chanson du feu follet	L	B-B	CHE
Granados	Andalusia			
-----	Elegie eterna			
Grever	Rataplán	HL	BF-D	GSC

Guastavino	Cita			
-----	La rose y la sauce			RIC
Nin	Canción gallega			ESC
-----	El vito			ESC
-----	Paño murciano			ESC
Obradors	Cantos populares			
-----	Coplas de curro dulce			
-----	Del cabello mas sutil			RIC
-----	Dos cantares populares			
-----	El majo celoso			
-----	El tumba y le			
-----	El vito			
-----	La guitarra sin primo			
-----	La mi sola laureola			
Ravel	Chanson espagnole			DUR
Sandoval	Chafrinita			
-----	Madrigal	HL	A-E	GSC
Tavares	Funeral of King Naga			
Turina	Farruca	M	A-F	UME
-----	Rima	H	A-A	AMP

Miscellaneous Recital Songs

Contralto

Bach-Gounod	Ave Maria			
Bartok	Tears of autumn	M	C-F	GSC
Berger	Lonely people			
Binder	Emathay			
-----	Hineh mahtov			
-----	Shir shomrim			
Bizet	Agnus Dei	HLM	C-AF	
Bruckner	Ave Maria			AMP
Chajes	Adarim			TRA
-----	By the rivers of Babylon			
-----	Old Jerusalem			
Dessau	Al sefat jam kinareth			
Dvořák	By the waters of Babylon			AMP
-----	Clouds and darkness			
-----	God is my shepherd			AMP
-----	Hear my prayer, O Lord			AMP
-----	I will life mine eyes			AMP
-----	I will sing new songs of gladness	HL		
-----	Lord, Thou art my refuge and shield			AMP
-----	Sing ye a joyful song			AMP

(Dvořák)	Songs my mother taught me	HM	E-E	
-----	Turn Thee to me			AMP
Fisher	Eili, eili	LMH	E-G	DIT
Franck	Panis angelicus	LM		
Hasse	Salve Regina			BRH
Lotti	Miserere			
Luzzi	Ave Maria	HL	BF-EF	GSC
Mignone	A sombre			
-----	Janaina			
Mozart	Alleluia	LMH	F-C	
Ravel	Mayerke mein suhn			RAV
Sakelariou	Pentozalis			
Schwadren	Wetov li			
Stakianaki	Duru duru			
Villa-Lobos	Nhapope			
Weiner	Der shelem zecher			

British Songs and Arias
For Opening Recitals

Contralto

Handel	Art thou troubled (Rodelinda)	M	F-F	GSC
-----	Let me wander not unseen (L'Allegro)	M	D-G	†
-----	Lord, to Thee each night and day (Theodora)	L	C-E	†
-----	The land of dreams			
Purcell	Ah, how pleasant 'tis to love			AUG
-----	Evening hymn	M	C-F	OXF
-----	If music be the food of love	M	D-G	BOO
-----	Not all my torments			NOV
-----	There's not a swain on the plain	M	B-G	BAF
-----	When I am laid in earth (Dido and Aeneas)	LH	C-G	†

German Songs for Opening Recitals

Contralto

Bach, J.S.	Bist du bei mir	HML	A-EF	†
Beethoven	God is my song			

151

(Beethoven)	Ich liebe dich	HL	BF-DF	†
Brahms	Ein Wanderer	LH	E-AF	†
-----	Nachtigall	MHL	BF-FS	†
-----	Verzagen	MH	CS-FS	†
Buxtehude	Singet dem Herrn			
	Violin and piano			
Handel	Begruessung			
Haydn	She never told her love	HL	B-D	DIT
Schubert	Gott im Fruehling			PET
-----	Liebesbotschaft	H	E-G	†
-----	Verklaerung			PET
Schuetz	Bringt her dem Herren			
Schumann	Mit Myrthen und Rosen	HL	A-D	†
Wolf	Ueber Nacht	LH	D-G	†

Italian Songs and Arias
For Opening Recitals

Contralto

Benati	Credi nell' alma mia			
Bononcini	Deh, più a me non	LH	EF-F	†
	v'ascondete			
Caccini	Amarilli, mia bella	ML	C-D	†
Caldara	Sebben crudele	HML	E-DS	†
Carissimi	Vittoria, mio core	HLM	B-E	†
Cavalli	Beato chi può (Serse)			HEU
-----	Donzelle fuggite	HL	C-EF	†
Cesti	Ah, quanto è vero	HL	F-F	DIT
	(Il Pomo d'Oro)			
-----	Che angoscia, che affanno	HL	C-DF	DIT
	(Il Pomo d'Oro)			
-----	E dove t'aggiri			DIT
	(Il Pomo d'Oro)			
Cherubini	Ahi, che forse ai miei di			RIC
	(Demofonte)			
Cimara	Stornellata marinara	HM		RIC
Donaudy	Quando ti rivedrò			RIC
Durante	Vergin, tutta amor	LM	C-EF	†
Falconieri	O bellissimi capelli	HL	B-D	†
Gluck	Spiagge amate			†
	(Paride ed Elena)			
Handel	Ah! mio cor (Alcina)			†
-----	Ah! spietato (Amadigi)			
-----	Care selve (Atalanta)	MH	FS-A	BOO
-----	Ch'io mai vi possa (Siroe)			†
-----	Dove sei, amato bene	L	BF-EF	†
	(Rodelinda)			

152

(Handel)	Furibondo spira			KIS
	(Partenope)			
-----	Lascia ch'io pianga	HM	EF-F	†
	(Rinaldo)			
-----	Notte cara (Floridante)			
-----	Ombra mai fu (Serse)	HM	BF-EF	†
-----	Piangero la sorte mia			CFI
	(Julius Caesar)			
-----	Rendi'l sereno al ciglio	LH	EF-F	†
	(Sosarme)			
-----	Si, tra i ceppi (Berenice)	L	B-D	†
-----	Tutta raccolta (Scipione)			CFI
-----	V'adoro pupille			BOO
	(Julius Caesar)			
Lotti	Pur dicesti, o bocca	LMH	E-FS	GSC
	bella			
Marcello	Il mio bel foco	LMH	C-G	†
Paisiello	Chi vuol la zingarella	L	C-F	GSC
Pergolesi	Salve Regina			
-----	Se tu m'ami	LMH	C-G	GSC
Peri	Invocazione di Orfeo	HL	E-CS	DIT
	(Euridice)			
Rosa	Star vicino	HL	D-E	RIC
-----	Vado ben spesso	ML	C-EF	†
Sarti	Lungi dal caro bene	HL	G-D	GSC
	(Armide)			
Scarlatti, A.	Sento nel core	M	E-F	†
Stradella	Per pietà (Il Floridoro)	HM	D-F	DIT
-----	Se nel ben			CFI
Vivaldi	Un certo no so che	HL	BF-EF	

American Songs For Closing Recitals

Contralto

Barber	I hear an army	LH	D-AF	GSC
-----	Sure on this shining night	MH	D-G	GSC
Carpenter	Light, my light	M	C-G	GSC
-----	Serenade	LH	CS-A	GSC
Castelnuovo-				
Tedesco	New York			
Charles	When I have sung my songs	HM	BF-EF	GSC
Dougherty	Portrait	HM	BF-G	GSC
Duke	On a March day	M	B-GF	BOH
Enders	Russian picnic	HM	C-G	GSC
Giannini	Sing to my heart a song	H	D-B	ELV
Guion	When you go			
Hageman	Miranda	HL		GAL

Horsman	The bird of the wilderness	LMH	DF-BF	GSC
Ilgenfritz	As we part			SCH
Kingsford	Command	HLM	EF-G	GSC
La Forge	Hills	HL		RIC
-----	Into the light	HL		RIC
-----	Song of the open	MH	EF-AF	DIT
Malotte	Upstream	M	C-F	GSC
Mana-Zucca	Rachem Trumpet	HML		C HA
Rogers	Sail forth			
-----	The last song	MLH	E-AF	GSC
-----	Time for making songs	HM	CS-F	DIT
Rummel	Ecstasy	LMH	GF-AF	GSC
Salter	The cry of Rachel	LH	C-AF	GSC
Silberta	I met dame fate	L	BF-E	GSC
Speaks	Morning	HML	BF-D	GSC
Swanson	Pierrot	L	B-D	WTR
Tyson	Sea moods	LH	E-AF	GSC
Warren	Heather	LH	FS-G	GSC
-----	We two	LH	E-A	GSC

(See also Negro Spirituals and Folk Songs.)

Miscellaneous Songs for Closing Recitals

Contralto

Binder	Emathay			
-----	Hineh mahtov			
Bizet	Adieu de l'hôtesse arabe	H	BF-G	†
Brahms	Juchhe!			†
-----	Meine liebe ist Gruen	MLH	ES-A	†
-----	Willst du, dass ich geh'?	L	C-G	†
Bridge	Love went a-riding	HL		BOS
Britten	Oliver Cromwell			BOH
Debussy	Chevaux de bois	H	C-G	†
Elgar	The swimmer			BOO
Falla	Jota	LH		AMP
-----	Polo	HL		AMP
Grever	Rataplán	HL	BF-D	GSC
Grieg	By the brook			GSC
-----	Digtervise	L	A-EF	HAN
-----	Good morning			†
-----	Hunter's song	L	DS-E	GSC
-----	Jeg lever et liv i laengsel	L	BF-E	HAN
Head	A piper	HL		BOO

Hely- Hutchinson	Old mother Hubbard	HL	B-E	CFI
Henschel	Morning-hymn	MH	DS-GS	DIT
Holst	Speech	M	BF-F	CHE
Korngold	Much ado about nothing			
Lasson	Were I the flaming sun	HL	DF-G	GSC
Mussorgsky	The forgotten one			
Nin	El vito			ESC
Obradors	Coplas de curro dulce			
-----	El tumba y le			
-----	El vito			
Quilter	Blow, blow thou winter wind	HL	C-E	BOO
-----	Love's philosophy	LMH	D-A	BOO
-----	Over the mountains			BOS
Rachmaninoff	Floods of spring	HL		DIT
-----	Oh, no, I pray do not depart	H		DIT
Respighi	Pioggia			BON
Schubert	Aufloesung	LH	D-A	†
-----	Die Forelle	MLH	EF-GF	†
Shaw	Romance			
Sibelius	The tryst	M		AMP
-----	Was it a dream?			BRH
Turina	Farruca	M	A-F	UME
Warlock	Yarmouth Fair	HL	B-E	CFI
Wolf	Er ist's	H	D-G	†

Atmospheric Songs

Contralto

Barber	Sleep now	MH	EF-AF	GSC
Brahms	Steig' auf, geliebter Schatten	HL	BF-EF	†
Burleigh	Sometimes I feel like a motherless child	HML		RIC
Carpenter	Go, lovely rose	M	DF-EF	GSC
-----	Odalisque	M	EF-EF	GSC
-----	Slumber song	ML	BF-F	GSC
-----	The day is no more	M	GS-DS	GSC
-----	The green river	M	B-E	GSC
-----	When I bring to you colour'd toys	LM	CS-FS	GSC
Charles	Clouds	HML	C-EF	GSC
-----	When I have sung my songs	HM	BF-EF	GSC
Cimara	Fiocca la neve	H	G-G	GSC
Dello Joio	New born	M	C-D	CFI

155

Dougherty	Loveliest of trees	HM	C-E	BOH
Duke	Loveliest of trees	L	C-D	GSC
Dunhill	The cloths of heaven	LM	EF-G	STB
Elgar	Sea pictures	L	A-A	BOO
Elmore & Reed	Come all ye who weary	L	C-D	JFI
Ferrari	Le miroir	M	E-F	GSC
Ferrata	Night and the curtains drawn			JFI
Franz	Sterne mit den gold'nen Fuesschen	HL	DS-E	†
Ganz	A memory	HM	B-D	GSC
Grieg	A dream			†
-----	A swan			†
-----	In the boat	LM	D-ES	†
-----	Spring rain			PET
Griffes	Night on ways unknown has fallen	L	GS-F	GSC
Hageman	Do not go, my love	HL	B-EF	GSC
Hahn	D'une prison	L	BF-EF	HEU
-----	L'heure exquise	M	DF-F	†
-----	Paysage	MH	EF-G	HEU
Harris	Fog	M	D-F	CFI
Haydn	She never told her love	HL	B-D	DIT
Holst	The heart worships	ML	BF-D	STB
Hovaness	How I adore thee	M		WHB
Hughes	O men from the fields	M	F-F	BOO
Lynn	Gently little Jesus	L	BF-BF	DIT
-----	The magic night of Christmas	M	D-D	DIT
MacGimsey	Sweet little Jesus boy	ML	D-D	CFI
Niles	I wonder as I wander	HL	BF-D	GSC
-----	Jesus, Jesus rest your head	HL	A-D	GSC
Paladilhe	Psyché	HM	BF-F	GSC
Poldowski	L'heure exquise	LMH	DF-AF	CHE
Rachmaninoff	Lilacs	LH	EF-G	†
Reger	The Virgin's slumber song	MMH	G-G	†
Sanderson	Quiet	ML	AF-EF	BOH
Schubert	Der Tod und das Maedchen	HL	A-EF	†
-----	Nacht und Traeume	HL	C-DF	†
Schumann	Der Nussbaum	LMH	D-FS	†
-----	Im Walde	HL	A-D	†
Sibelius	Reeds, reeds rustle			
Strauss	Die Nacht	HL		†
-----	Traum durch die Daemmerung	HML	BF-EF	†
Tureman	A winter sunset	L	BF-E	GSC

Tyson	Noon and night	LH	F-AF	GSC
Vaughan				
Williams	Four nights	L	AF-EF	OXF
-----	Silent noon			GSC
Warlock	Sleep			OXF
Watts	Wings of night	LH	CS-G	GSC
Wolf	In dem Schatten meiner Locken	M	C-EF	†
-----	Verborgenheit	HL	B-E	†

American Dramatic Songs

Contralto

Barber	I hear an army	LH	D-AF	GSC
Beach	Ah, love but a day			ASC
Campbell-				
Tipton	The crying of water	LH	FS-GS	GSC
Carpenter	Light, my light	M	C-G	GSC
-----	Slumber song	ML	BF-F	GSC
-----	The green river	M	B-E	GSC
-----	To one unknown	M	A-DS	GSC
Duke	Calvary	L	G-F	CFI
-----	On a March day	M	B-GF	BOH
-----	Wild swans	H	D-A	MER
Elwell	Renouncement	M	G-G	GSC
Enders	Russian picnic	HM	C-G	GSC
Giannini	Sing to my heart a song	H	D-B	ELV
Griffes	Evening song	H	DS-GS	GSC
-----	We'll to the woods and gather May	M	D-F	GSC
Guion	Wild geese	M	D-F	CFI
Hageman	Do not go, my love	HL	B-EF	GSC
-----	Music I heard with you	MH	E-A	GAL
Horsman	The bird of the wilderness	LMH	DF-BF	GSC
Johnson	Roll Jerd'n roll	M	EF-F	GSC
La Forge	Song of the open	MH	EF-AF	DIT
Protheroe	Ah, love but a day	LMH	F-AF	GAM
Rogers	The last song	MLH	E-AF	GSC
-----	Time for making songs	HM	CS-F	DIT
Salter	The cry of Rachel	LH	C-AF	GSC
Speaks	Morning	HML	BF-D	GSC
Tyson	Sea moods	LH	E-AF	GSC
Warren	We two	LH	E-A	GSC

British Dramatic Songs and Arias

Contralto

Bridge	O that it were so	LMH	D-G	CHA
Clarke	The seal man	M		BOH
Del Riego	Homing	HML	BF-E	CHA
Elgar	Sea pictures	L	A-A	BOO
-----	The swimmer			BOO
Head	Nocturne	HL		BOO
Henschel	Morning-hymn	MH	DS-GS	†
Parry	Love is a bauble			NOV
Purcell	When I am laid in earth	LH	C-G	†
	(Dido and Aeneas)			
Quilter	Blow, blow thou winter	HL	C-E	BOO
	wind			
Ronald	Prelude	HML	B-D	ENO
Sullivan	The lost chord	HL	C-F	GSC

French Dramatic Songs and Arias

Contralto

Bemberg	Du Christ avec ardeur	M	DF-AF	†
	(La Mort de Jeanne d'Arc			
Bizet	Habanera (Carmen)	HM	D-F	†
Debussy	Chevaux de bois	H	C-G	†
Duparc	Au pays où se fait la			SAL
	guerre			
-----	Le manoir de Rosamunde	HL	B-F	BOS
-----	Phidylé	MH	EF-AF	BOS
Fauré	Automne	MH	D-FS	GSC
-----	Fleur jetée	HM	BF-FS	†
-----	Prison	LH		†
-----	Toujours	LH	F-AF	†
Gounod	O ma lyre immortelle	M	C-G	†
	(Sappho)			
Hahn	D'une prison	L	BF-EF	HEU
-----	Offrande	M	D-D	†
Halévy	Humble fille des champs			GSC
	(Charles VI)			
Honegger	Les cloches			SEN
Hue	J'ai pleuré en rêve	HL	D-E	BOS
Indy	Lied maritime	LH	B-G	†
Lesuer	Hélas sans m'entendre			CHE
	(Ossian ou les Bardes)			
Massenet	Werther! qui m'aurait dit			HEU
	(Air de lettres) (Werther)			

Meyerbeer	Ah! mon fils (Le Prophéte)	M	B-AS	†
Paladilhe	Lamento provincal	M	CS-FS	HOM
Poldowski	Dansons la gigue	M	EF-G	MAR
-----	L'heure exquise	LMH	DF-AF	CHE
Rhené-Baton	Il pleut des pétales de fleurs	M	CS-E	DUR
Saint-Saëns	Amour, viens aider (Samson et Dalila)	HM	AF-G	†
-----	L'attente			DUR

German Dramatic Songs and Arias

Contralto

Brahms	Ach, wende diessen Blick			†
-----	Am Sonntag Morgen	L	CS-FS	†
-----	Nich mehr zu dir zu gehen			†
-----	Treue Liebe	LMH	DS-E	†
-----	Von ewiger Liebe	LMH	B-AF	†
Franz	Im Herbst	HM	A-F	†
Liszt	Die Lorelei	LH	BF-BF	†
-----	Freudvoll und leidvoll			DUR
Loewe	Edward	HL	F-E	†
-----	Walpurgisnacht	H	G-G	SC
Mahler	Das Irdische Leben	HL	A-F	INT
-----	Ich hab' ein gluehend Messer	M	BF-GF	WEI
Schubert	An Schwager Kronos	HL	G-E	†
-----	Aufenthalt	HLM	A-F	†
-----	Dem Unendlichen	L	A-GF	†
-----	Der Atlas	HL	BF-F	†
-----	Der Doppelgaenger	HL	G-D	†
-----	Der Erlkoenig	HML	A-E	†
-----	Der Lindenbaum	HL	A-D	†
-----	Der Tod und das Maedchen	HL	A-EF	†
-----	Der Zwerg	M	A-GF	PET
-----	Die Allmacht	HML	G-E	†
-----	Die junge Nonne	LH	C-GF	†
-----	Die Kraehe	HL	A-E	GSC
-----	Die Liebe hat gelogen	LM	G-F	†
-----	Du liebst mich nicht	LH	E-FS	†
-----	Erstarrung	HL	D-F	†
-----	Fahrt zum Hades	HL	G-DF	PET
-----	Fragment aus dem Aeschylus			PET

(Schubert)	Fruehlingstraum	HL	C-D	†
-----	Gruppe aus dem Tartarus	L	CS-EF	†
-----	In der Ferne	HL		†
-----	Schaefers Klagelied	HL	BF-D	†
Schumann	Fruehlingsfahrt	HL	B-E	†
-----	Heiss' mich nicht reden			
-----	Mit Myrthen und Rosen	HL	A-D	†
-----	Schoene Wiege meiner Leiden	HL	C-EF	†
-----	Talismane			
-----	Waldesgespraech	HL	A-FS	†
Strauss	Caecilie	MH	E-B	†
-----	Ruhe meine Seele			†
-----	Zueignung	HL	CS-FS	†
Wagner	Schmerzen	HL		†
-----	So ist es denn aus mit den ewigen Goettern (Die Walkuere)			GSC
-----	Weiche, Wotan! (Das Rheingold)			GSC
Wolf	Alle gingen, Herz, zu Ruh	HL	C-EF	†
-----	Die ihr schwebet	HL	EF-EF	INT
-----	Epiphanias	HL	B-D	†
-----	Geh' Geliebter, geh' jetzt			PET
-----	Nachtzauber	HL	B-E	†
-----	Ueber Nacht	LH	D-G	†
-----	Zur Ruh', zur Ruh'	HL	A-GF	†

Italian Dramatic Songs and Arias

Contralto

Donizetti	O mio Fernando (La Favorita)	M	B-A	†
Durante	Vergin, tutta amor	LM	C-EF	†
Giordano	Temer? perche? (Andrea Chenier)			BRO
Pergolesi	Confusa, smarrita			GSC
Ponchielli	Voce di donna (La Gioconda)	HM	A-G	GSC
Respighi	Io sono la madre	L		RIC
-----	Nebbie			†
Verdi	Re dell' abisso (Un Ballo in Maschera)			RIC
-----	Stride la vampa (Il Trovatore)	M	B-G	†

160

Miscellaneous Dramatic Songs and Arias

Contralto

Borodin	A dissonance	MH	E-F	†
Dvořák	By the waters of Babylon			AMP
-----	Hear my prayer, O Lord			AMP
Gliere	Ah, twine no blossoms	HM	CS-F	DIT
Granados	La maja dolorosa	M		INT
Gretchaninoff	Over the steppe	LM	C-G	GSC
-----	Wounded birch	HL	B-EF	†
Grieg	A dream			†
-----	A swan			†
-----	Autumnal gale	HL	A-F	CFI
-----	Digtervise	L	A-EF	HAN
-----	Eros	LM	C-F	†
-----	Henrik Wergeland			PET
-----	Hjemkomst	M	B-F	HAN
-----	In the boat	LM	D-ES	†
-----	Jeg lever et liv i laengsel	L	BF-E	HAN
-----	Poesien			
-----	Verse for an album			
Mussorgsky	After the battle			GSC
-----	Divination by water (Khovantchina)	L	GS-FS	GSC
-----	Hopak	HM	CS-FS	GSC
-----	Martha's song (Khovantchina)	ML		GSC
-----	On the Dnieper			GSC
-----	The orphan girl			GSC
Rachmaninoff	Christ is risen	LM	D-F	GAL
-----	Floods of spring	HL		DIT
-----	Oh, no, I pray do not depart	HL		DIT
-----	O thou billowy harvest field	HL	CS-E	GSC
-----	To the children	MH	F-G	DIT
Sibelius	Black roses	M	A-ES	AMP
-----	The tryst	M		AMP
-----	Was it a dream?			BRH
Stravinsky	Song of the dew			JUR
-----	The cloister (La novice)			DIT
Tchaikovsky	Adieu forêts (Jeanne d'Arc)	HM	BF-FS	GSC
-----	Complaint of the bride			
-----	None but the lonely heart	HLM	C-F	DIT
-----	Pauline's romance (Pique Dame)	M	BF-AF	GSC

161

(Tchaikovsky)	Why	HL		†
Turina	Rima	H	A-A	AMP

Humorous Songs

Contralto

Arne, T.	Why so pale and wan			GSC
Bernstein	I hate music	H	C-A	WIT
Brahms	Der Kranz			†
-----	Vergebliches Staendchen	LHM	E-FS	†
Britten	Oliver Cromwell			BOH
Carpenter	Don't ceare	M	C-D	GSC
-----	If	M	D-E	GSC
-----	To a young gentleman	M	C-F	GSC
Davis	Deaf old woman			GAL
Debussy	Ballade des femmes de Paris			DUR
Dougherty	Love in the dictionary	M	C-G	GSC
Enders	Russian picnic	HM	C-G	GSC
Gibbs	Five eyes	HL	D-D	BOS
Grieg	My Johann	HL	BF-EF	GSC
Hadley	My shadow			ASC
Hely- Hutchinson	Old mother Hubbard	HL	B-E	CFI
Johnston	Because I were shy	L	B-E	CRA
Lehmann	The cuckoo	HH	D-B	BOH
Mahler	Des Antonius von Padua Fischpredigt	HL	GF-F	†
-----	Wer hat dies Liedlein erdacht?	HL	BF-E	INT
Mozart	Die Alte			
-----	Warnung	HM	C-D	
Nordoff	Serenade	H	CS-FS	AMP
-----	There shall be more joy	M	CS-FS	AMP
Paisiello	Chi vuol la zingarella	L	C-F	GSC
Parry	Love is a bauble			NOV
Rawls	The balloon man	L	A-FS	AMP
Reger	Waldeinsamkeit	HML	A-D	BOS
Reichardt	Rhapsodie			MOS
Rich	American lullaby	LH	C-F	GSC
Rontani	Or ch'io non segno più	HL	CS-E	DIT
Rosenthal	Le marabout			ESC
Scarlatti, A.	Chi vuole innamorarsi	HL	D-EF	DIT
Schubert	Die Maenner sind mechant			PET
-----	Heidenroeslein			
Spross	Will o' the wisp			JCH
Wolf	Weather forecast	H	EF-GS	GSC

162

(Wolf)	Epiphanias	HL	B-D	†
-----	Ich hab' in Penna	LH		†
-----	Nimmersatte Liebe	LH	CF-AF	†

American Folk Songs (Arr.)
Contralto

Bacon	Adam and Eve	M	B-D	CFI
Bartholomew	Dearest Billie	M	E-E	GSC
Brockway	Barbara Allen			GRA
-----	Frog went-a-courting			GRA
-----	Sourwood mountain			GRA
Copland	At the river			
-----	Ching-a-ring chaw			
-----	The golden willow tree			
-----	The little horses			
-----	Zion's walls			
Davis	Deaf old woman			GAL
-----	He's gone away	M	C-E	GAL
Hughes	Birds' courting song			GSC
Matteson	The blue eyed boy			GSC
Niles	Down in the valley			GSC
-----	Go 'way from my window	MH	C-G	GSC
-----	I wonder as I wander	HL	BF-D	GSC
-----	Jesus, Jesus rest your head	HL	A-D	GSC
-----	Sing we the Virgin Mary			
Schindler	Mother dearest	M	A-G	GSC
Shaw	He's gone away	M	C-E	DIT

British Folk Songs (Arr.)
Contralto

Britten	Little Sir William			BOH
-----	O can ye sew cushions			BOH
-----	Oliver Cromwell			BOH
-----	The ash grove			BOH
-----	The Bonny Earl O' Moray			BOH
-----	The plough boy			BOH
-----	The Sally gardens			BOH
-----	The trees they grow so high			BOH
Clayton	O men from the fields	M	C-F	GAL
Gatty	Bendemeer's stream	LMH		BOO
Harty	The lowlands of Holland			OXF
Hopekirk	Coming through the rye			DIT
-----	Loch Lomond			DIT
Hughes	Down by the Sally gardens			BOO
-----	I know my love			BOO
-----	The lover's curse			BOO
Johnston	Because I were shy	L	B-E	CRA

163

Kennedy-Fraser	A fairy's love song			BOO
-----	An Eriskay love lilt			BOO
-----	Kishmul's galley			BOO
-----	Land of heart's desire			BOO
-----	The mull fisher's love song			BOO
Kreisler	Loch Lomond			
Lawson	Turn ye to me	M	B-E	GSC
Liddle	Friar John			
Page	The foggy dew			DIT
-----	The harp that once through Tara's halls			DIT
Quilter	Barbara Allen			BOO
-----	Over the mountains			BOS
-----	Ye banks and braes	M	DF-EF	BOH
Reid	Turn ye to me			BOO
Vaughan Williams	King William	L	D-D	OXF
-----	Lullaby of the Madonna	L	BF-D	GRA
-----	Rolling in the dew			OXF
Warlock	Willow, willow			OXF
-----	Yarmouth Fair	HL	B-E	CFI
Welsh	All through the night			
Wilson	Come let's be merry			BOO

Miscellaneous Folk Songs (Arr.)

Contralto

Bakaleinikoff	Pozhalieh (Russian Gypsy Air)			
Brahms	In stiller Nacht			†
Dvořák	Gypsy Songs	LH	D-A	AMP
Falla	Asturiana	HL		AMP
-----	El paño moruno	HL		AMP
-----	Jota	LH		AMP
-----	Nana	HL		AMP
-----	Polo	HL		AMP
-----	Seguidilla murciana	HL		AMP
Lefkowitz	Korobooshka (Russian gypsy air)			
Liddle	An old French carol	LM	F-F	BOO
Obradors	Con amores a mi madre			RIC
Poniridis	Lullaby			
Ravel	Chanson espagnole	LH	D-BF	DUR
-----	Cinq mélodies populaires grecques			CUR
Respighi	Three Armenian folk songs			
Sfakianaki	Duru duru			
Vehanen	Tuku, tuku lampaitani			GAL

164

Weckerlin	O ma tendre musette	LM	A-E	GSC
-----	Menuet d'Exaudet	H	D-G	GSC
-----	Venez, agreable printemps	M	C-F	

Negro Spirituals

Contralto

Boatner	Oh, what a beautiful city!	HL	D-E	GSC
-----	On mah journey	LH	EF-EF	RIC
-----	Trampin' (Tryin' to make heaven my home)	L	D-F	ELK
Brown	Dere's no hidin' place down dere			CFI
-----	Every time I feel de spirit	L		AMP
-----	Hammer song	L	A-C	AMP
-----	Hear de lam's a cryin'			SC
--,--	Sometimes I feel like a motherless child	L		AMP
Burleigh	Balm in Gilead	HL		RIC
-----	De gospel train	HL		RIC
-----	Deep river	HML		RIC
-----	Go down, Moses	HL		RIC
-----	Hard trials	M		RIC
-----	Heav'n Heav'n	HL		RIC
-----	I don't feel no-ways tired	M		RIC
-----	Joshua fit de battle ob Jericho	LH	DS-E	RIC
-----	Nobody knows de trouble I've seen	HL		RIC
-----	Oh, Peter, go ring-a-dem bells			RIC
-----	Ride on, King Jesus	H		RIC
-----	Sinner, please doan let dis harves' pass	M		RIC
-----	Sometimes I feel like a motherless child	HML		RIC
-----	Swing low, sweet chariot	HL		RIC
-----	Were you there?	HML		RIC
-----	Wide river			
Dawson	Talk about a chile that do love Jesus			
Dett	A man goin' roun'			
-----	Sit down servant			GSC
Fisher	Little wheel a-turnin' in my heart			

165

Hayes	I can't stay away			
Johnson	At the feet of Jesus	L		
-----	City called Heaven			ROB
-----	Crucifixion			
-----	Dere's no hidin' place down dere			
-----	Fix me, Jesus	L	BF-DF	GSC
-----	Hold on			ROB
-----	Honor, honor	HM	C-E	CFI
-----	My good Lord done been here	HM	BF-F	CFI
-----	Nobody knows the trouble I see			
-----	Ride on, King Jesus			CFI
-----	Roll, Jerd'n roll	M	EF-F	GSC
-----	Take my mother home	M	BF-EF	CFI
-----	Witness	HM	D-F	CFI
Kerby- Forrest	Glory ina mah soul			
-----	He's got the whole world in his hands	M	G-E	MLS
Lawrence	Let us break bread together	HML	BF-EF	MCR
MacGimsey	If he change my name			
-----	Sweet little Jesus boy	ML	D-D	CFI
McFeeters	Redeemed	L	BF-F	MLS
Payne	Crucifixion	L	C-C	GSC
Price	My soul's been anchored in the Lord			GAM
Ryder	He ain't coming here to die no more			
-----	Let us break bread together	LH	D-G	JFI
Saunders	The Lord's Prayer	L	BF-C	BOH

American Songs Employing Agility

Contralto

Buzzi-Peccia	Under the greenwood tree	LMH		DIT
Charles	Let my song fill your heart	LH		GSC
Curran	Ho! Mr. Piper	LH	D-G	GSC
Griffes	We'll to the woods and gather May	M	D-F	GSC
Hageman	Miranda	HL		GAL
Hopkinson	O'er the hills	LH	C-G	†
Nordoff	There shall be more joy	M	CS-FS	AMP

Speaks	In May time	HL	D-E	JCH

British Songs and Arias
Employing Agility

Contralto

Arne, T.	Where the bee sucks	HM		†
German	Charming Chloe	HML		NOV
Handel	Hence, Iris, hence away (Semele)	L		NOV
-----	In the battle, fame pursuing (Deborah)	L	A-D	†
-----	Lord, to Thee each night and day (Theodora)	L	C-E	†
-----	O thou that tellest good tidings to Zion (The Messiah)	L	A-C	†
Hely-Hutchinson	Old mother Hubbard	HL	B-E	CFI
Hook	Bright Phoebus	M	EF-F	GSC
Morley	It was a lover and his lass	HM		DIT
Parry	Love is a bauble			NOV
Purcell	From rosy bow'rs (Don Quixote)			AUG
-----	Hark! how all things with one sound rejoice			NOV
-----	Nymphs and shepherds (The Libertine)	HM	C-F	†
Quilter	Love's philosophy	LMH	D-A	BOO
Wilson	Come let's be merry			BOO

French Songs and Arias
Employing Agility

Contralto

Berlioz	La captive	HL		GSC
Bizet	Adieu de l'hôtesse arabe			†
-----	Ouvre ton coeur	MH	DS-GS	†
Campra	Charmant papillon (Les Fêtes Venitiennes)	MH	D-G	GSC
Chausson	Le colibri			BOS
Falla	Polo	HL		AMP
Ferrari	Le jardin d'amour	LM	EF-F	GSC
Georges	La pluie	HL		INT

Massé	Chanson du tigre (Paul et Virginie)			
Meyerbeer	Nobles seigneurs, salut! (Les Huguenots)			†
-----	O pretres de Baal (Le Prophète)			BRO
Vidal	Ariette	LH	F-A	GSC

German Songs and Arias
Employing Agility

Contralto

Bach, J.S.	From the bondage (St. John Passion)	L	BF-EF	†
-----	Gelobet sei der Herr (Cantata 129) Oboe d'amore			AUG
-----	Hochgelobter Gottessohn (Cantata 6) English horn or viola or violin			NOV
-----	In Jesu Demut (Cantata 151) Oboe d'amore or violin			AUG
-----	It is finished (St. John Passion)	L	B-D	†
-----	Mein glaeubiges Herze (Cantata 68)	HML		†
Brahms	Botschaft	HL	D-F	†
-----	O liebliche Wangen	MLH	E-G	†
Haydn	My mother bids me bind my hair	M	E-E	†
Mahler	Des Antonius von Padua Fischpredigt	HL	GF-F	†
-----	Wer hat dies Liedlein erdacht?	HL	BF-E	INT
Schubert	Irrlicht			
-----	Ungeduld	HML		†
Schumann	Fruehlingsnacht	L	CS-E	†
-----	Waldesgespraech	HL	A-FS	†
Wolf	Die Zigeunerin			†

Italian Songs and Arias
Employing Agility

Contralto

Arditi	Leggiero, invisible			
Carissimi	Vittoria, mio core	HLM	B-E	†

168

Donizetti	Il segreto per esser felici (Lucrezia Borgia)	M	C-G	†
Durante	Danza, danza fanciulla gentile	HM	BF-F	†
Handel	Ben io sento l'ingrata spietata furio (Atalanta)	L	B-D	CFI
-----	Ch'io mai vi possa (Siroe)			†
-----	Furibondo spira (Partenope)			KIS
-----	Si, tra i ceppi (Berenice)	L	B-D	†
Lotti	Pur dicesti, o bocca bella	LMH	E-FS	GSC
Rossini	Bel raggio lusinghier (Semiramide)	H	CS-A	GSC
-----	La danza	MH	E-A	†
-----	Non più mesta (La Cenerentola)	M	A-B	GSC
Sadero	Amuri, Amuri	M		CHE
Scarlatti, A.	Rugiadose odorose (Il Pirro e Demetrio)	HL	D-E	DIT
-----	Se Florindo è fedele	LM	EF-EF	GSC
Scarlatti, D.	Consolati e spara amante	L	BF-E	GSC
-----	Qual farfalletta			
Vivaldi	Un certo no so che	HL	BF-EF	†

Miscellaneous Songs and Arias
Employing Agility

Contralto

Bach, J.S.	Qui sedes ad dexteram Patris (Mass in B Minor) Oboe d'amore			†
Falla	Canción del amor dolido			CHE
-----	Chanson du feu follet	L	B-B	CHE
-----	Nana	HL		AMP
-----	Seguidilla murciana	HL		AMP
Grieg	Good morning			†
Mozart	Alleluja	LMH	F-C	†
-----	Laudamus Te (C Minor Mass)			PET
Pergolesi	Fac ut portem (Stabat Mater)			DES
Stravinsky	The cloister (La novice)			DIT
Turina	Farruca	M	A-F	UME

American Songs Employing
Crescendo and Diminuendo

Contralto

Bacon	A clear midnight			NEM
Barber	Sleep now	MH	EF-AF	GSC
Beach	Ah, love but a day			ASC
Cadman	From the land of the sky-blue water			WHI
Campbell-Tipton	The crying of water	LH	FS-GS	GSC
Carpenter	Go, lovely rose	M	DF-EF	GSC
-----	Odalisque	M	EF-EF	GSC
-----	The day is no more	M	GS-DS	GSC
-----	The sleep that flits on baby's eyes	M	B-FS	GSC
-----	Watercolors	M	C-F	GSC
-----	When I bring to you colour'd toys	LM	CS-FS	GSC
Charles	Clouds	HML	C-EF	GSC
Duke	Loveliest of trees	L	C-D	GSC
Engel	Sea shell	M	EF-EF	GSC
Fairchild	A memory			BOS
La Forge	Hills	HL		RIC
Naginski	The pasture	M	BF-EF	GSC
Niles	I wonder as I wander	HL	BF-D	GSC
-----	Jesus, Jesus rest your head	HL	A-D	GSC
Nordoff	Serenade	H	CS-FS	AMP
Rogers	At parting	LH	CS-FS	GSC
Thompson	Velvet shoes	M	C-E	ECS
Watts	Wings of night	LH	CS-G	GSC

British Songs and Arias Employing
Crescendo and Diminuendo

Contralto

Goossens	Melancholy	M		CHE
Handel	Art thou troubled (Rodelinda)	M	F-F	GSC
-----	He shall feed His flock (The Messiah)	L	C-D	†
-----	He was despised (The Messiah)	L	B-D	†
-----	Let me wander not unseen (L'Allegro)	M	D-G	†

Head	The ships of Arcady	ML	BF-EF	BOH
Horn	I've been roaming	L	B-E	†
Ireland	Bed in summer			CUR
Purcell	I attempt from love's sickness to fly (The Indian Queen)	MH	CS-E	†
Shaw	Song of the Palanquin bearers	LH	E-F	CUF
Warlock	Rest, sweet nymphs	M	F-F	CFI

French Songs and Arias Employing Crescendo and Diminuendo

Contralto

Debussy	C'est l'extase	LH	CS-A	†
-----	La flûte de Pan		B-B	†
-----	Voici que le printemps	LH	CS-G	BOS
Duparc	Chanson triste	MH	FS-AF	†
-----	L'invitation au voyage	HM	E-F	†
-----	Phidylé	MH	EF-AF	BOS
Fauré	Au bord de l'eau	HL	C-F	†
-----	Clair de lune	MH	C-G	†
-----	Green	HL	CS-GF	†
Koechlin	L'hiver	H	E-G	†
Liszt	S'il est un charmant gazon	HL		†
Martini	Plaisir d'amour	M	BF-EF	GSC
Meyerbeer	Nobles Seigneurs, salut! (Les Huguenots)	LH	C-C	†
Paladilhe	Psyché	HM	BF-F	GSC

German Songs and Arias Employing Crescendo and Diminuendo

Contralto

Bach, J.S.	Ach, lege das Sodom (Cantata 48) Oboe or violin			
-----	Ich sehe schon im Geist (Cantata 43) 2 Oboes and continuo			NOV
-----	Schlafe, mein Liebster (Christmas Oratorio)			
Brahms	Komm bald	HM	CS-F	†
-----	Sonntag	H	D-G	†
-----	Spanisches Lied			†
-----	Therese	HL	B-D	†
-----	Wie Melodien zieht es	HL	A-E	†

171

Franz	Sterne mit den gold'nen Fuesschen	HL	DS-E	†
Reger	Mit Rosen bestreut			UNI
-----	Waldeinsamkeit	HML	A-D	BOS
Schubert	Auf dem Wasser zu singen	MH	EF-GF	†
-----	Der Juengling auf dem Huegel	L	G-F	†
-----	Der Musensohn	LH	FS-G	†
-----	Der Wanderer	HML	FS-D	†
-----	Der Wanderer an den Mond	LM	D-F	PET
-----	Fruehlingstraum	HL	C-D	†
-----	Gott im Fruehling			PET
-----	Gretchen am Spinnrade	H	F-A	†
-----	Hark! hark! the lark	LMH	F-G	GSC
-----	Lachen und Weinen	HL	C-EF	†
-----	Liebesbotschaft	H	E-G	†
-----	Nacht und Traeume	HL	C-DF	†
Schumann	Der Nussbaum	LMH	D-FS	†
-----	Die Soldatenbraut	HL	AF-EF	†
Strauss	Die Nacht	HL		†
Wolf	In dem Schatten meiner Locken	M	C-EF	†
-----	Mausfallen Spruechlein	HL	BF-E	†
-----	Nun lass uns Frieden schliessen	HL		†
-----	Nun wandre, Maria	HL	EF-D	†
-----	Wenn du zu den Blumen gehst	HL	B-EF	†
Wolff	Maerchen	M	D-E	†

Italian Songs and Arias Employing Crescendo and Diminuendo

Contralto

Caldara	Sebben crudele	HML	E-DS	†
-----	Selve amiche, ombrose piante	HM	E-E	†
Cesti	Intorno all' idol mio (Orontea)	MH	D-F	†
De Luca	Non posso disperar	HL	C-E	GSC
Falconieri	O bellissimi capelli	HL	B-D	†
Frescobaldi	Se l'aura spira	HL	C-EF	DIT
Handel	Ombra mai fu (Serse)	HM	BF-EF	†
Marcello	Non m'è grave morir per amore	L	C-E	GSC
Monteverdi	Lasciatemi morire (Arianna)	ML	D-D	†

172

Pergolesi	Se tu m'ami	LMH	C-G	GSC
Rontani	Se bel rio	ML	D-C	†
Rosa	Selve, voi che le speranze	MH	D-G	DIT
-----	Vado ben spesso	ML	C-EF	†
Scarlatti, A.	La fortuna			BOS
-----	Sento nel core	M	E-F	†

Miscellaneous Songs and Arias Employing
Crescendo and Diminuendo

Contralto

Gretchaninoff	The snowdrop	HM	BF-F	DIT
Grieg	In the boat	LM	D-ES	†
-----	Springtide	M		DIT
-----	With a water lily	HM	CS-EF	†
Mussorgsky	Oriental chant (Josua Navine Cantata)	ML	BF-E	GSC
-----	The banks of the Don			GSC
Rachmaninoff	Lilacs	LH	EF-G	†
-----	The island	LH	DF-F	†

American Songs and Arias Employing
Piano Singing

Contralto

Bacon	A clear midnight			NEM
Barber	Sleep now	MH	EF-AF	GSC
Campbell-Tipton	The crying of water	LH	FS-GS	GSC
Carpenter	Go, lovely rose	M	DF-EF	GSC
-----	May the maiden			DIT
-----	Odalisque	M	EF-EF	GSC
-----	On a screen	L	BF-DF	GSC
-----	The day is no more	M	GS-DS	GSC
-----	The green river	M	B-E	GSC
-----	The sleep that flits on baby's eyes	M	B-FS	GSC
-----	Watercolors	M	C-F	GSC
-----	When I bring to you colour'd toys	LM	CS-FS	GSC
Charles	Clouds	HML	C-EF	GSC
-----	When I have sung my songs	HM	BF-EF	GSC
Engel	Sea shell	M	EF-EF	GSC

Fairchild	A memory			BOS
Farwell	These saw visions			GAL
Foote	Tranquillity	HL	BF-E	ASC
Ganz	A memory	HM	B-D	GSC
Hageman	Do not go, my love	HL	B-EF	GSC
Ives	Evening			GSC
MacGimsey	Sweet little Jesus boy	ML	D-D	CFI
Manning	Shoes	M	EF-F	GSC
Menotti	Lullaby (The Consul)			GSC
Naginski	The pasture	M	BF-EF	GSC
Nevin	Mighty lak' a rose			JCH
Niles	I wonder as I wander	HL	BF-D	GSC
-----	Jesus, Jesus rest your head	HL	A-D	GSC
Nordoff	Serenade	H	CS-FS	AMP
Schuman	Orpheus with his lute	M	C-FS	GSC
Thompson	Velvet shoes	M	C-E	ECS
Watts	Wings of night	LH	CS-G	GSC

British Songs and Arias Employing
Piano Singing

Contralto

Bax	I heard a piper piping	LH	D-G	CFI
Dunhill	The cloths of heaven	LM	EF-G	STB
Elgar	Sea pictures	L	A-A	BOO
Handel	Let me wander not unseen L'Allegro	M	D-G	†
Head	Nocturne	HL		BOO
-----	The ships of Arcady	ML	BF-EF	BOH
Pilkington	Rest, sweet nymphs			STB
Sanderson	Quiet	ML	AF-EF	BOH
Scott	Lullaby	MML	BF-DF	GAL
Vaughan Williams	Silent noon			GSC

French Songs and Arias Employing
Piano Singing

Contralto

Debussy	La flûte de Pan		B-B	†
Fauré	Après un rêve	HM	C-F	†
-----	Clair de lune	MH	C-G	†
Ferrari	Le miroir	M	E-F	GSC
Franck	Le mariage des roses	M	E-FS	BOS

174

Gounod	Au rossignol	LMH	D-G	CHO
Hahn	D'une prison	L	BF-EF	HEU
-----	L'heure exquise	M	DF-F	†
-----	Offrande	M	D-D	†
-----	Paysage	MH	EF-G	HEU
Lully	Bois épais (Amadis)	ML	C-EF	†
Paladilhe	Psyché	HM	BF-F	GSC
Pessard	L'adieu du matin	ML	BF-D	GSC
Poldowski	L'heure exquise	LMH	DF-AF	CHE
Weckerlin	Menuet d'Exaudet	H	D-G	GSC
-----	O ma tendre musette	LM	A-E	GSC
Widor	Je ne veux pas autre chose	HL	C-EF	HAM

German Songs and Arias Employing
Piano Singing

Contralto

Bach, J.S.	Jesus schlaeft (Cantata 81)	L	A-D	GSC
Beethoven	Ich liebe dich	HL	BF-DF	†
Brahms	In Waldeseinsamkeit	H	ES-G	†
-----	Komm bald	HM	CS-F	†
-----	Sapphische Ode	HML		†
-----	Spanisches Lied			†
-----	Staendchen	HL	BF-E	†
-----	Steig' auf, geliebter Schatten	HL	BF-EF	†
Franz	Sterne mit den gold'nen Fuesschen	HL	DS-E	†
Mahler	Ich bin der Welt abbanden gekommen	HL		INT
-----	Liebst du um Schoenheit	HL		INT
-----	Wo die schoenen Trompeten blasen	HL	GF-F	INT
Mendelssohn	O rest in the Lord (Elijah)	L	B-D	†
Schubert	Auf dem Wasser zu singen	MH	EF-GF	†
-----	Ave Maria	LMH	F-F	†
-----	Der Tod und das Maedchen	HL	A-EF	†
-----	Der Wanderer an den Mond	LM	D-F	PET
-----	Du bist die Ruh	LMH	EF-AF	†
-----	Fruehlingstraum	HL	C-D	†
-----	Gott im Fruehling			PET

(Schubert)	Im Abendrot	HL	C-D	GSC
-----	Lachen und Weinen	HL	C-EF	†
-----	Liebesbotschaft	H	E-G	†
-----	Nacht und Traeume	HL	C-DF	†
Schumann	Der Nussbaum	LMH	D-FS	†
-----	Mondnacht	M	E-FS	†
Strauss	Allerseelen	HL	AS-E	†
-----	Die Nacht	HL		†
-----	Fruendliche Vision	HL	C-F	†
-----	Traum durch die Daemmerung	HML	BF-EF	†
-----	Wiegenliedchen			†
Wagner	Der Engel	LH	CS-G	†
Wolf	In dem Schatten meiner Locken	M	C-EF	†
-----	Mausfallen Spruechlein	HL	BF-E	†
-----	Nachtzauber	HL	B-E	†
-----	Schlafendes Jesuskind	HL	AS-F	†
-----	Verborgenheit	HL	B-E	†
-----	Wie glaenzt der helle Mond			†
Wolff	Ich bin eine Harfe			HMP
-----	Maerchen	M	D-E	†

Italian Songs and Arias Employing
Piano Singing

Contralto

Bononcini	Deh, più a me non v'ascondete	LH	EF-F	†
Cimara	Fiocca la neve	H	G-G	GSC
Frescobaldi	Se l'aura spira	HL	C-EF	DIT
Gagliano	Dormi, amore (La Flora)	HL	CS-E	DIT
Gluck	O del mio dolce ardor (Paride ed Elena)			
Handel	Care selve (Atalanta)	MH	FS-A	†
Monteverdi	Lasciatemi morire (Arianna)	ML	D-D	†
Paradies	M'ha preso alla sua ragna	M		GSC
Rontani	Se bel rio	ML	D-C	†
Secchi	Lungi dal caro bene	HL	A-FS	DIT

176

Miscellaneous Songs Employing
Piano Singing

Contralto

Arensky	Valse	H	DF–GF	GSC
Dvořák	God is my shepherd			AMP
-----	I will lift mine eyes			AMP
-----	Songs my mother taught me	HM	E–E	†
Gretchaninoff	Hushed the song of the nightingale	MH	E–G	DIT
Grieg	A dream			†
-----	A swan			†
-----	In the boat	LM	D–ES	†
Mednikoff	The hills of Gruzia	H	DS–A	LAC
Rachmaninoff	In the silence of night	LH	D–A	GSC
Sibelius	The tryst	M		AMP

American Songs Employing
Rapid Enunciation

Contralto

Boatner	Oh, what a beautiful city!	HL	D–E	GSC
Burleigh	Joshua fit de battle ob Jericho	LH	DS–E	RIC
Carpenter	Don't ceare	M	C–D	GSC
-----	The cock shall crow	M	B–E	GSC
Hadley	My shadow			ASC
Hageman	Miranda	HL		GAL
Manning	Shoes	M	EF–F	GSC
Spross	Will o' the wisp			JCH

British Songs Employing
Rapid Enunciation

Contralto

Brewer	The fairy pipers	HML		BOH
Britten	Oliver Cromwell			BOH
Elgar	Sea pictures	L	A–A	BOO
German	Charming Chloe	HML		NOV
Gibbs	Five eyes	HL	D–D	BOS
Head	A piper	HL		BOO
Molloy	The Kerry dance	LH	C–G	GSC

177

Morley	It was a lover and his lass	HM		DIT
Purcell	There's not a swain on the plain	M	B-G	BAF
Vaughan Williams	The water mill	L	C-D	OXF

French Songs and Arias Employing Rapid Enunciation

Contralto

Bizet	Habanera (Carmen)	HM	D-F	†
Caplet	La ronde	M		DUR
Debussy	Ballade des femmes de Paris			DUR
-----	Chevaux de bois	H	C-G	†
-----	La flûte de Pan		B-B	†
-----	Mandoline	HM	BF-F	†
Fauré	Toujours	LH	F-AF	†
Fourdrain	Carnaval	M	C-F	RIC
Pessard	L'adieu du matin	ML	BF-D	GSC
Poldowski	Dansons la gigue	M	EF-G	MAR
Ravel	Nicolette	L	B-FS	ELK
Saint-Saëns	L'attente			DUR

German Songs Employing Rapid Enunciation

Contralto

Brahms	Juchhe!			†
-----	Meine Liebe ist gruen	MLH	ES-A	†
-----	O liebliche Wangen	MLH	E-G	†
-----	Staendchen	HL	BF-E	†
-----	Vergebliches Staendchen	LHM	E-FS	†
Loewe	Walpurgisnacht	H	G-G	SC
Mozart	Warnung	HM	C-D	
Schubert	Die Forelle	MLH	EF-GF	†
-----	Die Post	HML	BF-EF	†
-----	Erstarrung	HL	D-F	†
-----	Fischerweise	L	C-D	†
-----	Ungeduld	HML		†
-----	Wohin?	HL	B-E	†
Schumann	Die Kartenlegerin			
Wolf	Ich hab' in Penna	LH		†

178

Italian Songs and Arias Employing
Rapid Enunciation

Contralto

Carissimi	Vittoria, mio core	HLM	B-E	†
Cavalli	Donzelle fuggite	HL	C-EF	†
Donizetti	Il segreto per esser felici (Lucrezia Borgia)	M	C-G	†
Durante	Danza, danza fanciulla gentile	HM	BF-F	†
Falconieri	Non più d'amore	HL	C-D	DIT
-----	Nudo arciero	HL	AF-AF	DIT
Handel	Ch'io mai vi possa (Siroe)			†
Legrenzi	Che fiero costume	HML	C-D	†
Paisiello	Chi vuol la zingarella	L	C-F	GSC
Rontani	Or ch'io non segno più	HL	CS-E	DIT
Rossini	La danza	MH	E-A	†
Scarlatti, A.	Chi vuole innamorarsi	HL	D-EF	DIT

Miscellaneous Songs Employing
Rapid Enunciation

Contralto

Falla	Canción del amor dolido			CHE
-----	Chanson du feu follet	L	B-B	CHE
-----	Seguidilla murciana	HL		AMP
Grieg	Digtervise	L	A-EF	HAN
-----	In the boat	LM	D-ES	†
-----	My Johann	HL	BF-EF	GSC
-----	With a water lily			†
Mussorgsky	The magpie and the gypsy dancer			GSC

American Songs Employing
Sustained Singing

Contralto

Barber	A nun takes the veil	MH	G-G	GSC
-----	Sure on this shining night	MH	D-G	GSC
Burleigh	Deep river	HML		RIC
-----	Sometimes I feel like a motherless child	HML		RIC
-----	Were you there?	HML		RIC

179

Carpenter	Highway men	M	C-F	GSC
-----	Slumber song	ML	BF-F	GSC
-----	The player queen	M	BF-EF	GSC
-----	To one unknown	M	A-DS	GSC
Dello Joio	New born	M	C-D	CFI
Edwards	By the bend of the river	HML	C-E	GSC
-----	Into the night	HML	C-DF	GSC
Foster, S.C.	Ah, may the red rose live always!			GSC
Griffes	By a lonely forest pathway	HML	A-EF	GSC
-----	Evening song	H	DS-GS	GSC
Hageman	Music I heard with you	MH	E-A	GAL
Harris	Fog	M	D-F	CFI
Hawley	Ah, 'tis a dream	L	G-C	JCH
Hindemith	The wildflower's song	MH	E-G	AMP
Horsman	The bird of the wilderness	LMH	DF-BF	GSC
Metcalf	At nightfall	HML	C-DF	ASC
Moore	Sigh no more, ladies			BOO
Scott	Think on me	HML	D-EF	GAL
Tyson	Noon and night	LH	F-AF	GSC
Watts	Transformation	ML	AS-DS	GSC

British Songs and Arias Employing Sustained Singing

Contralto

Bantock	Silent strings	MH	F-G	BOO
Bridge	O that it were so	LMH	D-G	CHA
Britten	The Sally gardens			BOH
Del Riego	Homing	HML	BF-E	CHA
Dowland	Sorrow, sorrow stay	M	D-D	BOS
-----	Woeful heart with grief oppressed			KEE
Dunhill	To the Queen of Heaven	M	C-G	GSC
Handel	Thou shalt bring them in (Israel in Egypt)	L	B-D	†
-----	Vouchsafe, O Lord (Dettingen Te Deum)	HM		ELV
Henschel	Morning-hymn	MH	DS-GS	†
-----	There was an ancient king			ASC
Holst	The heart worships	ML	BF-D	STB
Purcell	If music be the food of love	M	D-G	BOO
-----	Sweet, be no longer sad			NOV

(Purcell)	When I am laid in earth (Dido and Aeneas)	LH	C-G	†
Ronald	Prelude	HML	B-D	ENO
Sullivan	The lost chord	HL	C-F	GSC
Vaughan Williams	Four nights	L	AF-EF	OXF
-----	Linden-Lea	HML	C-D	BOS
Warlock	Sleep			OXF
Welsh	All through the night			

French Songs and Arias Employing Sustained Singing

Contralto

Bemberg	Chant hindou	HML	A-EF	†
-----	Du Christ avec ardeur (La Mort de Jeanne d'Arc)	M	DF-AF	†
Berlioz	La captive	HL		GSC
Bizet	Adieu de l'hôtesse arabe	H	BF-G	†
-----	Ma vie a son secret	L	AF-F	CHU
Chaminade	Chant slave			GSC
Chausson	Le colibri Violin or cello	M	F-GF	BOS
-----	Le temps des lilas	MH	D-GS	†
Debussy	Ballade que fait Villon à la requeste de sa mère			DUR
-----	Beau soir	LH	C-FS	†
-----	Je tremble en voyant ton visage			DUR
-----	La chevelure	M	CF-FS	†
Duparc	Au pays où se fait la guerre			SAL
-----	Lamento	ML	EF-EF	†
Fauré	Automne	MH	D-FS	GSC
-----	Le parfum impérissable	LH	GF-GF	
-----	Les berceaux	LMH	BF-G	†
-----	Nocturne	H	F-A	MAR
-----	Prison	LH		†
-----	Rencontre	H	EF-AF	†
Gluck	Divinités du Styx (Alceste)	MH	DF-AF	†
-----	Je n'ai jamais chéri la vie (Alceste)	L	A-F	GSC
Gounod	O ma lyre immortelle (Sappho)	M	C-G	†
Honegger	Chanson (Ronsard) Flute and string quartet			SEN

(Honegger)	Oh my love take my hand			SEN
Hue	J'ai pleuré en rêve	HL	D-E	BOS
Indy	Lied maritime	LH	B-G	†
Lalo	Chant breton	M	E-E	HAM
Leroux	Le nil	LH	E-A	†
Massenet	Elégie	LM	C-GF	GSC
Meyerbeer	Ah! mon fils	M	B-AS	†
	(Le Prophète)			
Paladilhe	Lamento provincal	M	CS-FS	HOM
Poulenc	A sa guitare	M	D-FS	DUR
Ravel	Kaddisch	H	C-G	DUR
-----	Vocalise en forme de	MH	BF-G	MAR
	habanera			
Rhene-Baton	Il pleut des pétales de	M	CS-E	DUR
	fleurs			
Saint-Saëns	Amour, viens aider	HM	AF-G	†
	(Samson et Dalila)			
-----	La cloche	LH	DF-AF	†
-----	Mon coeur s'ouvre à	HLM	BF-GF	†
	ta voix (Samson et Dalila)			
-----	Printemps qui commence	M	B-E	†
	(Samson et Dalila)			
Weckerlin	Venez, agréable printemps	M	C-F	

German Songs and Arias Employing
Sustained Singing

Contralto

Ahle	Bruenstiges Verlangen	M	E-E	GSC
Bach, J.S.	Ach Herr! was ist ein			AUG
	Menschenkind (Cantata 110)			
	Oboe d'amore			
-----	Ach, schlaefrige Seele			AUG
	(Cantata 115)			
-----	Bist du bei mir	HML	A-EF	†
-----	Geist und Seele wird			
	verwirret (Cantata 35)			
-----	Schlage doch, gewuenschte			RIC
	Stunde (Cantata 53)			
-----	Weh der Seele			BRO
	(Cantata 102) Oboe			
Beethoven	Das Geheimnis			
-----	Die Ehre Gottes	HL	AF-EF	†
-----	Faithfu' Johnie			
-----	Vom Tode	L	A-EF	GSC
-----	Wonne der Wehmut			†
Bohm	Calm as the night	HML	A-EF	†

182

Brahms	An die Nachtigall	H	DS-G	†
-----	An eine Aeolsharfe	H	EF-AF	†
-----	Auf dem Kirchhofe	HL	BF-EF	†
-----	Dein blaues Auge	MH	BF-G	†
-----	Der Tod, das ist die kuehle Nacht	L	AF-F	†
-----	Die Mainacht	HL	BF-FF	†
-----	Feldeinsamkeit	HL	C-EF	†
-----	Immer leiser wird mein Schlummer	LH	DF-A	GSC
-----	Liebestreu	ML	C-F	†
-----	Mit vierzig Jahren	HL	FS-D	†
-----	Muss es eine Trennung geben?	LH	FS-FS	†
-----	Nachtigall	MHL	BF-FS	†
-----	O kuehler Wald	MH	A-F	†
-----	O wuesst' ich doch den Weg zurueck	H	E-FS	†
-----	Schwermut			†
-----	Treue Liebe	LMH	DS-E	†
-----	Verzagen	MH	CS-FS	†
-----	Wir wandelten	LH	EF-GF	†
Bruch	Penelope's sorrow (Odysseus)			SIM
Cornelius	Komm, wir wandeln	H	FS-GS	SC
Franz	Es ragt ins Meer der Runenstein	HL	G-F	†
-----	Im Herbst	HM	A-F	†
-----	Mutter, o sing mich zur Ruh	HL	E-G	†
Haydn	She never told her love	HL	B-D	DIT
Himmel	Die Sendung			SIM
Jensen	Wie so bleich			
Liszt	Freudvoll und leidvoll			DUR
Loewe	Der heilige Franziskus	L	A-E	SC
Mendelssohn	But the Lord is mindful of His own (Saint Paul)	L	A-D	†
-----	Woe unto them who forsake him (Elijah)	L	B-E	GSC
Mozart	Wiegenlied	MH	G-G	†
Schoenberg	Song of the wood dove			AMP
Schubert	Am Bach im Fruehling			PET
-----	An die Leier	LM	BF-F	†
-----	An die Musik	HL	A-DS	†
-----	Der Doppelgaenger	HL	G-D	†
-----	Der Leiermann	ML	C-D	†
-----	Der Lindenbaum	HL	A-D	†
-----	Der Neugierige	HL	CS-EF	†
-----	Der Wegweiser	L	D-EF	†

(Schubert)	Des Maedchens Klage	LH	C-E	†
-----	Die Allmacht	HML	G-E	†
-----	Die Kraehe	HL	A-E	†
-----	Die Liebe hat gelogen	LM	G-F	†
-----	Die Maenner sind mechant			PET
-----	Die Nebensonnen	HL	F-D	†
-----	Du liebst mich nicht	LH	E-FS	†
-----	In der Ferne	HL		†
-----	Litanei	HLM	C-EF	†
-----	Nachtgesang			PET
-----	Schaefers Klagelied	HL	BF-D	†
-----	Thekla	HL	B-E	PET
-----	Wanderers Nachtlied 1	HL		†
-----	Wehmuth	HL	B-D	†
Schuetz	Aus dem 119th Psalm			
Schumann	An den Sonnenschein	HL	A-D	†
-----	Aus den Hebraeischen Gesaengen			
-----	Der Himmel hat eine Traene geweint			
-----	Die Lotusblume	HLM	BF-F	†
-----	Du bist wie eine Blume	HM	F-EF	†
-----	Du Ring an meinem Finger	HL	C-F	†
-----	Hoch, hoch sind die Berge			
-----	Im Westen	HL		†
-----	Lied der Suleika			
-----	Mit Myrthen und Rosen	HL	A-D	†
-----	Seit ich ihn gesehen	HL	DF-DF	†
-----	Wehmut			†
-----	Wer machte dich so krank?			
Strauss	Befreit			HSC
-----	Im Spaetboot			
-----	Liebeshymnus			†
-----	Mit deinen blauen Augen	LH	C-GS	†
-----	Morgen	HML	E-F	†
-----	Ruhe meine Seele			†
Wagner	Schmerzen	HL		GSC
-----	Traeume	HL		†
Wolf	Agnes	HL		†
-----	Alle gingen, Herz, zu Ruh	HL	C-EF	†
-----	An eine Aeolsharfe			†
-----	Bedeckt mich mit Blumen	HL	B-D	†
-----	Das verlassene Maegdlein	HL	D-EF	†
-----	Gebet	HL		†
-----	Gesang Weylas	HL	DF-F	†
-----	Im Fruehling	HL	BF-F	†
-----	In der Fruehe	HL	C-C	†

(Wolf)	Um Mitternacht	HL	G-EF	†
-----	Zur Ruh', zur Ruh'	HL	A-GF	†
Wolff	Alle Dinge haben Sprache	M	BF-GF	†
-----	Ewig			

Italian Songs and Arias Employing Sustained Singing

Contralto

Bellini	Scombra è la sacra selva (Norma)			RIC
Caccini	Amarilli, mia bella	ML	C-D	†
Caldara	Come raggio di sol	HL	D-F	†
Cavalli	Beato chi può (Serse)			HEU
Cesti	Che angoscia, che affanno (Il Pomo d'Oro)	HL	C-DF	DIT
-----	E dove t'aggiri (Il Pomo d'Oro)			DIT
Cherubini	Ahi, che forse ai miei di (Demofonte)			RIC
Cimara	Stornellata marinara	HM		RIC
Cimarosa	Bel nume che adoro			RIC
Donaudy	Quando ti rivedrò			RIC
Donizetti	O mio Fernando (La Favorita)	M	B-A	†
Durante	Vergin, tutta amor	LM	C-EF	†
Giordano	O grandi occhi lucenti (Fedora)			BRO
Gluck	Che farò senza Euridice (Orphée)	ML	BF-F	†
-----	Spiagge amate (Paride ed Elena)			†
Handel	Dove sei, amato bene (Rodelinda)	L	BF-EF	†
-----	Lascia ch'io pianga (Rinaldo)	HM	EF-F	DIT
-----	Rend'l sereno al ciglio (Sosarme)	LH	EF-F	†
-----	Stille amare (Tolomeo)			MUP
-----	Tutta raccolta (Scipione)			CFI
-----	V'adoro pupille (Julius Caesar)			BOO
-----	Verdi prati (Alcina)			†
L-----	Vieni o figlio caro e mi consola (Ottone)			†
Monteverdi	Tu se' morta (Orfeo)	M	C-E	GSC
Peri	Funeste piaggie (Euridice)			GSC

(Peri)	Invocazione di Orfeo (Euridice)	HL	E-CS	DIT
Ponchielli	Voce di donna (La Gioconda)	HM	A-G	GSC
Respighi	Io sono la madre	L		RIC
-----	Nebbie			†
Rosa	Star vicino	HL	D-E	†
Scarlatti, A.	O cessate di piagarmi	HL	DS-E	†
Stradella	Col mio sangue comprenderei (Il Floridoro)	HL	E-F	DIT
-----	Per pietà (Il Floridoro)	HM	D-F	DIT
-----	Se nel ben			CFI
Torelli	Tu lo sai	HL	BF-F	†
Verdi	Re dell' abisso (Un Ballo in Maschera)			RIC

Miscellaneous Songs and Arias
Employing Sustained Singing

Contralto

Bach-Gounod	Ave Maria			†
Borodin	A dissonance	MH	E-F	†
Dvořák	By the waters of Babylon			AMP
-----	Hear my prayer, O Lord			AMP
-----	Inflammatus et accensus (Stabat Mater)	L	A-EF	NOV
-----	Lord, thou art my refuge and shield			AMP
-----	Turn Thee to me			AMP
Gliere	Ah, twine no blossoms	HM	CS-F	DIT
Granados	La maja dolorosa	M		INT
Gretchaninoff	Over the steppe	LM	C-G	GSC
-----	Wounded birch	HL	B-EF	†
Grieg	I love thee	HML	E-F	†
Hasse	Salve regina			BRH
Mussorgsky	Martha's song (Khovantchina)	ML		GSC
-----	On the Dnieper			GSC
-----	Sphinx			BRH
Rachmaninoff	Christ is risen	LM	D-F	GAL
-----	O thou billowy harvest field	HL	CS-E	GSC
-----	To the children	MH	F-G	DIT
Sibelius	Black roses	M	A-ES	AMP
-----	From the north	H	DS-G	GSC
-----	The first kiss	M		AMP
-----	Was it a dream			BRH

Sinding	I hear the gull			JCH
Tchaikovsky	Complaint of the bride			
-----	None but the lonely heart	HLM	C-F	DIT
-----	Pauline's romance (Pique Dame)	M	BF-AF	GSC
-----	Why	HL		†

American Songs Employing Spirited Singing

Contralto

Barber	I hear an army	LH	D-AF	GSC
Boatner	Oh, what a beautiful city!	HL	D-E	GSC
Burleigh	Joshua fit de battle ob Jericho	LH	DS-E	RIC
Carpenter	Don't ceare	M	C-D	GSC
-----	If	M	D-E	GSC
-----	Light, my light	M	C-G	GSC
-----	Serenade	LH	CS-A	GSC
-----	The cock shall crow	M	B-E	GSC
-----	To a young gentleman	M	C-F	GSC
Duke	On a March day	M	B-GF	BOH
Enders	Russian picnic	HM	C-G	GSC
Giannini	Sing to my heart a song	H	D-B	ELV
Griffes	We'll to the woods and gather May	M	D-F	GSC
Guion	Wild geese	M	D-F	CFI
Hadley	My shadow			ASC
Hageman	Miranda	HL		GAL
Johnson	Roll Jerd'n roll	M	EF-F	GSC
La Forge	Song of the open	MH	EF-AF	DIT
Nordoff	There shall be more joy	M	CS-FS	AMP
Rawls	The balloon man	L	A-FS	AMP
Rogers	The last song	MLH	E-AF	GSC
Rummel	Ecstasy	LMH	GF-AF	GSC
Salter	The cry of Rachel	LH	C-AF	GSC
Speaks	Morning	HML	BF-D	GSC
Spross	Will o' the wisp			JCH
Weaver	Moon-marketing	LMH	E-G	GSC

British Songs and Arias Employing
Spirited Singing

Contralto

Arne, T.	Why so pale and wan?			GSC
Brewer	The fairy pipers	HML		BOH
Bridge	Love went a-riding	HL		BOS
Elgar	The swimmer			BOO
German	Charming Chloe	HML		NOV
Gibbs	Five eyes	HL	D-D	BOS
Handel	Hence, Iris, hence away (Semele)	L		NOV
-----	Lord, to thee each night and day (Theodora)	L	C-E	†
Head	A piper	HL		BOO
Hook	Bright Phoebus	M	EF-F	GSC
Johnston	Because I were shy	L	B-E	CRA
Lehmann	The cuckoo	HH	D-B	BOH
Molloy	The Kerry dance	LH	C-G	GSC
Morley	It was a lover and his lass	HM		DIT
Parry	Love is a bauble			NOV
Purcell	Hark! how all things with one sound rejoice			NOV
-----	Nymphs and shepherds (The Libertine)	HM	C-F	†
-----	There's not a swain on the plain	M	B-G	BAF
Quilter	Blow, blow thou winter wind	HL	C-E	BOO
-----	Love's philosophy	LMH	D-A	BOO
Rowley	The toll gate house			ROG
Warlock	Consider	M	C-G	CFI
-----	In an arbour green	H	D-G	CFI

French Songs and Arias Employing
Spirited Singing

Contralto

Bizet	Habanera (Carmen)	HM	D-F	†
-----	Ouvre ton coeur	MH	DS-GS	†
Caplet	La ronde	M		DUR
Debussy	Ballade des femmes de Paris			DUR
-----	Chevaux de bois	H	C-G	†
-----	La mer est plus belle	HL		†

				DUR
(Debussy)	Le faune			†
-----	Mandoline	HM	BF-F	
Duparc	Le manoir de Rosamunde	HL	B-F	BOS
Dupont	Mandoline			DUR
Fauré	Fleur jetée	HM	BF-FS	†
-----	Toujours	LH	F-AF	†
Georges	La pluie	HL		INT
Gluck	Amours, sors pour jamais (Armide)			PET
Honegger	Les cloches			SEN
Pierné	Le moulin	ML	C-E	BOS
Poldowski	Dansons la gigue	M	EF-G	MAR
Ravel	Chanson espagnole	LH	D-BF	DUR
-----	Nicolette	L	B-FS	ELK
Saint-Saëns	L'attente			DUR
Vidal	Ariette	LH	F-A	GSC

German Songs Employing Spirited Singing

Contralto

Bach, J.S.	Mein glaeubiges Herze (Cantata 68)	HML		†
Beethoven	An die Geliebte	M	E-E	†
-----	Busslied			†
-----	Die Trommel geruehret			†
Brahms	Botschaft	HL	D-F	†
-----	Der Schmied	HL	EF-EF	†
-----	Juchhe!			†
-----	Meine Liebe ist gruen	MLH	ES-A	†
-----	O liebliche Wangen	MLH	E-G	†
-----	Sehnsucht	H	EF-AF	†
-----	Vergebliches Staendchen	LHM	E-FS	†
Franz	Er ist gekommen	HL	EF-F	†
Loewe	Maedchen sind wie der Wind			SC
-----	Walpurgisnacht	H	G-G	SC
Mahler	Das Irdische Leben	HL	A-F	INT
-----	Ging heut Morgen uebers Feld	M	A-FS	INT
-----	Ich hab' ein gluehend Messer	M	BF-GF	WEI
-----	Wer hat dies Liedlein erdacht?	HL	BF-E	INT
Schubert	Aufenthalt	HLM	A-F	†
-----	Die Forelle	MLH	EF-GF	†
-----	Die Post	HML	BF-EF	†

(Schubert)	Ellens zweiter Gesang			PET
-----	Erstarrung	HL	D-F	†
-----	Fischerweise	L	C-D	†
-----	Heidenroeslein			
-----	Rastlose Liebe	M	B-F	†
-----	Suleika I	LH	DS-G	†
-----	Wohin?	HL	B-E	†
Schumann	Er, der Herrlichste von Allen	HL	A-EF	†
-----	Fruehlingsnacht	L	CS-E	†
-----	Im Walde	HL	A-D	†
-----	Schoene Wiege meiner Leiden	HL	C-EF	†
-----	Waldesgespraech	HL	A-FS	†
-----	Widmung	HL	BF-F	†
Strauss	Caecilie	MH	E-B	†
-----	Heimliche Aufforderung	HL	B-E	†
-----	Zueignung	HL	CS-FS	†
Wolf	Auf einer Wanderung	HL		†
-----	Die ihr schwebet	HL	EF-EF	†
-----	Die Zigeunerin			†
-----	Er ist's	H	D-G	†
-----	Fussreise	HL	D-E	†
-----	Geh' Geliebter, geh' jetzt			PET
-----	Ich hab' in Penna	LH		†
-----	Klinge, klinge, mein Pandero	HL	CF-EF	†
-----	Nimmersatte Liebe	LH	CF-AF	DIT

Italian Songs and Arias Employing Spirited Singing

Contralto

Carissimi	Vittoria, mio core	HLM	B-E	†
Cavalli	Donzelle fuggite	HL	C-EF	†
Donizetti	Il segreto per esser felici (Lucrezia Borgia)	M	C-G	†
Durante	Danza, danza fanciulla gentile	HM	BF-F	†
Falconieri	Non più d'amore	HL	C-D	DIT
-----	Nudo arciero	HL	AF-AF	DIT
Giordano	Temer? perche? (Andrea Chenier)			BRO
Handel	Ch'io mai vi possa (Siroe)			†
-----	Furibondo spira (Partenope)			KIS

190

				CFI
(Handel)	Piangero la sorte mia (Julius Caesar)			
-----	Si, tra i ceppi (Berenice)	L	B-D	†
Legrenzi	Che fiero costume	HML	C-D	†
Leoncavallo	Mattinata	MLH	C-AF	†
Marcello	Il mio bel foco	LMH	C-G	†
Paisiello	Chi vuol la zingarella	L	C-F	GSC
Pergolesi	Confusa, smarrita			GSC
Respighi	Pioggia			BON
-----	Scherzo			BON
Rontani	Or ch'io non segno più	HL	CS-E	DIT
Rossi	Ah, rendimi (Mitrane)	L	GS-FS	GSC
Rossini	Bel raggio lusinghier (Semiramide)	H	CS-A	GSC
Scarlatti, A.	Chi vuole innamorarsi	HL	D-EF	DIT
-----	Se Florindo è fedele	LM	EF-EF	GSC
Scarlatti, D.	Consolati e spara amante	L	BF-E	GSC
-----	Qual farfalletta			

Miscellaneous Songs and Arias Employing
Spirited Singing

Contralto

Dvořák	I will sing new songs of gladness	HL		†
-----	Sing ye a joyful song			AMP
Falla	Canción del amor dolido			CHE
-----	Chansón du feu follet	L	B-B	CHE
-----	El paño moruno	HL		AMP
-----	Seguidilla murciana	HL		AMP
-----	Siete canciones	HL		AMP
Grieg	Good morning			†
-----	Hunter's song	L	DS-E	GSC
-----	Jeg lever et liv i laengsel	L	BF-E	HAN
-----	My Johann	HL	BF-EF	GSC
-----	Poesien			
-----	Turisten	M	CS-F	HAN
Mozart	Alleluja	LMH	F-C	†
Mussorgsky	Hopak	HM	CS-FS	GSC
-----	In the corner			INT
-----	The magpie and the gypsy dancer			GSC
Rachmaninoff	Floods of spring	HL		DIT
-----	Oh, no, I pray do not depart	H		DIT
Stravinsky	The cloister (La novice)			DIT

191

Turina	Farruca	M	A-F	UME
-----	Rima	H	A-A	AMP

Songs and Arias Employing Staccato

Contralto

Arne, T.	Where the bee sucks	HM		†
Fourdrain	Carnaval	M	C-F	RIC
Haydn	My mother bids me bind my hair	M	E-E	
Rossini	Non più mesta (La Cenerentola)	M	A-B	GSC
Scarlatti, A.	Rugiadose odorose (Il Pirro e Demetrio)	HL	D-E	DIT
Schubert	Der Juengling an der Quelle	LH	E-A	†

American and British Songs of Popular Appeal

Contralto

Beach	Ah, love but a day			ASC
Besley	The second minuet	HL		BOO
Brahe	Bless this house	HML	A-EF	BOO
Cadman	From the land of the sky-blue water			WHI
-----	The moon drops low	HL		ASC
Charles	When I have sung my songs	HM	BF-EF	GSC
Del Riego	Homing	HML	BF-E	CHA
Dougherty	Love in the dictionary	M	C-G	GSC
Edwards	By the bend of the river	HML	C-E	GSC
-----	Into the night	HML	C-DF	GSC
Enders	Russian picnic	HM	C-G	GSC
Foster	The Americans come	MH	F-BF	JFI
Fox	The hills of home	HML	BF-DF	CFI
Friml	L'amour, toujours l'amour			HAR
German	Who'll buy my lavender	HML		BOO
Giannini	Sing to my heart a song	H	D-B	ELV
Griffes	We'll to the woods and gather May	M	D-F	GSC
Hely-Hutchinson	Old mother Hubbard	HL	B-E	CFI
Henschel	Morning-hymn	MH	DS-GS	†
La Forge	Song of the open	MH	EF-AF	DIT

Lehmann	The cuckoo	HH	D-B	BOH
Manning	Shoes	M	EF-F	GSC
Molloy	The Kerry Dance	LH	C-G	GSC
Nevin	Mighty lak' a rose			JCH
Rich	American lullaby	LH	C-F	GSC
Rogers	At parting	LH	CS-FS	GSC
Romberg	Faithfully yours			HAR
Ronald	Prelude	HML	B-D	ENO
Scott	Think on me	HML	D-EF	GAL
Speaks	Morning	HML	BF-D	GSC
Spross	Will o' the wisp			JCH
Strelezki	Dreams	LMH	B-A	GSC
Sullivan	The lost chord	HL	C-F	GSC
Tyson	Noon and night	LH	F-AF	GSC
Weatherly	Danny boy	LMH		BOO
Weaver	Moon-marketing	LMH	E-G	GSC
Wilson	O sing a new song			
Wood	A brown bird singing	HLM	FS-G	CHA

(See also Humorous Songs, Negro Spirituals,
Folk Songs, Operetta Songs and Opera Arias.)

Miscellaneous Songs of Popular Appeal

Contralto

Bach-Gounod	Ave Maria			†
Berger	They all dance the Samba	M	A-FS	GSC
Bizet	Agnus Dei	HLM	C-AF	†
-----	Ouvre ton coeur	MH	DS-GS	†
Bohm	Calm as the night	HML	A-EF	†
Cavalli	Donzelle fuggite	HL	C-EF	†
Dvořák	Songs my mother taught me	HM	E-E	†
Grieg	A dream			†
-----	I love thee	HML	E-F	†
-----	My Johann	HL	BF-EF	GSC
Korngold	Much ado about nothing			
Leoncavallo	Mattinata	MLH	C-AF	†
Leroux	Le nil Cello or violin	LH	E-A	†
Massenet	Elégie	LM	C-GF	GSC
Mozart	Alleluja	LMH	F-C	†
Ponce	Estrellita	LH		†
Rachmaninoff	To the children	MH	F-G	DIT
Reichardt	In the time of roses			†
Rossini	La danza	MH	E-A	†
Sadero	Amuri, Amuri	M		CHE
Schubert	An die Musik	HL	A-DS	†

(Schubert)	Ave Maria	LMH	F-F	GSC
-----	Hark! hark! the lark	LMH	F-G	†
-----	Staendchen			
Schumann	Widmung	HL	BF-F	†
Sieczynski	Vienna, city of my dreams			HAR
Strauss, R.	Zueignung	HL	CS-FS	†
Tchaikovsky	None but the lonely heart	HLM	C-F	DIT
Velazquez	Bésame mucho	M	CS-D	SOU

(See also Humorous Songs, Negro Spirituals,
Folk Songs, Operetta Songs and Opera Arias.)

Arias From British Operas

Contralto

Britten	Flower song			BOH
	(Rape of Lucretia)			
Purcell	Celia has a thousand charms			
	(The Rival Sisters)			
-----	From rosy bow'rs			AUG
	(Don Quixote)			
-----	I attempt from love's sickness	MH	CS-E	†
	to fly (The Indian Queen)			
-----	Nymphs and shepherds	HM	C-F	†
	(The Libertine)			
-----	Retired from any mortal's			NOV
	sight (King Richard II)			
-----	When I am laid in earth	LH	C-G	†
	(Dido and Aeneas)			

Arias From French Operas

Contralto

Bizet	Card Scene (Carmen)			†
-----	Habanera (Carmen)	HM	D-F	†
Campra	Charmant papillon	MH	D-G	GSC
	(Les Fêtes Venitiennes)			
Gluck	Amours, sors pour jamais			PET
	(Armide)			
-----	Divinités du Styx	MH	DF-AF	†
	(Alceste)			
-----	Je n'ai jamais chéri la	L	A-F	GSC
	vie (Alceste)			
Gounod	O ma lyre immortelle	M	C-G	†
	(Sappho)			

(Gounod)	Si le bonheur (Faust)			†
Halévy	Humble fille des champs (Charles VI)			GSC
Lesueur	Hélas sans m'entendre (Ossian ou les Bardes)			CHE
Lully	Bois épais (Amadis)	ML	C-EF	†
-----	J'ai perdu la beauté (Persée)			
-----	Je porte l'épouvante (Persée)			
Massé	Chanson du tigre (Paul et Virginie)			
Massenet	Ne me refuse pas (Hérodiade)			HEU
-----	Va! laisse couler mes larmes (Werther)			
-----	Werther! qui m'aurait dit (Air de lettres) (Werther)			
Meyerbeer	Ah! mon fils (Le Prophète)	M	B-AS	†
-----	Nobles seigneurs, salut! (Les Huguenots)	LH	C-C	GSC
-----	O prêtres de Baal (Le Prophète)			BRO
Saint-Saëns	Amour, viens aider (Samson et Dalila)	HM	AF-G	†
-----	Mon coeur s'ouvre à ta voix (Samson et Dalila)	HLM	BF-GF	†
-----	Printemps qui commence (Samson et Dalila)	M	B-E	†

Arias From German Operas

Contralto

Bruch	Penelope's sorrow (Odysseus)			SIM
Wagner	Gerechtiger Gott (Rienzi)	H	C-A	PET
-----	Hoere mit Sinn (Goetterdaemmerung)			
-----	So ist es denn aus mit den ewigen Goettern (Die Walkuere)			GSC
-----	Weiche, wotan! (Das Rheingold)			GSC
Weber	Hier dicht am Quell (Euryanthe)			PET

Arias From Italian Operas

Contralto

Bellini	Scombra è la sacra selva (Norma)			RIC
Boito	Padre nostro (Nerone)			
Cilea	Acerba volutta (Adriana Lecouvreur)			SON
-----	O vagabonda stella d'oriente (Adriana Lecouvreur)			AMP
Donizetti	Deh, non voler (Anna Bolena)			
-----	Il segreto per esser felici (Lucrezia Borgia)	M	C-G	†
-----	O mio Fernando (La Favorita)	M	B-A	†
Giordano	O grandi occhi lucenti (Fedora)			BRO
-----	Temer? perche? (Andrea Chenier)			BRO
Gluck	Che farò senza Euridice (Orphée)	ML	BF-F	†
Monteverdi	Lasciatemi morire (Arianna)	ML	D-D	†
-----	Oblivian soave (L'Incoronazione di Poppea)			HEU
-----	Tu se morta (Orfeo)	M	C-E	GSC
Ponchielli	Voce di donna (La Gioconda)	HM	A-G	GSC
Rossini	Ah quel giorno (Semiramide)			
-----	Bel raggio lusinghier (Semiramide)	H	CS-A	GSC
-----	Non più mesta (La Cenerentola)	M	A-B	GSC
-----	Re dell' abisso (Un Ballo in Maschera)			RIC
-----	Stride la vampa (Il Trovatore)	M	B-G	†

Miscellaneous Opera Arias

Contralto

Cadman	Song of the Robin Woman (Shanewis)	MH	CS-GS	MOR
Kodaly	Czardas (Hary Janos)			
Menotti	Lullaby (The Consul)			GSC
-----	The black swan (The Medium)	M	D-G	GSC

Mussorgsky	Divination by water (Khovantchina)	L	GS-FS	GSC
-----	Martha's song (Khovantchina)	ML		GSC
-----	Song of Khivria (The Fair at Sorotchinsk)			GSC
Tchaikovsky	Adieu forêts (Jeanne d'Arc)	HM	BF-FS	GSC
-----	Pauline's romance (Pique Dame)	M	BF-AF	GSC

Arias from Oratorios and Latin Works
Contralto

Bach, J. S.	Agnus Dei (Mass in B Minor) Violin			†
-----	Esurientes implevit bonis (Magnificat in D Major)			†
-----	Et exultavit spiritus meus (Magnificat in D)			
-----	From the bondage (St. John Passion)	L	BF-EF	†
-----	It is finished (St. John Passion)	L	B-D	†
-----	Prepare thyself Zion (Christmas Oratorio)			
-----	Qui sedes ad dexteram Patris (Mass in B Minor) Oboe d'amore			†
Bemberg	Du Christ avec ardeur (La Mort de Jeanne d'Arc)	M	DF-AF	†
Bennett	O Lord, thou has searched (Woman of Samaria)			
Dvořák	Inflammatus et accensus (Stabat Mater)	L	A-EF	NOV
Gaul	Thou art the guide (Ten Virgins)			
Handel	Daughter of Zion (Brocke's Passion)			
-----	Father, whose blessing (Ode from St. Cecelia's Day)			
-----	Hence, Iris, hence away (Semele)	L		NOV
-----	Heroes, when with glory burning (Joshua)			
-----	He shall feed His flock (The Messiah)	L	C-D	GSC

(Handel)	He was despised (The Messiah)	L	B-D	†
-----	In the battle, fame pursuing (Deborah)	L	A-D	†
-----	Let me wander not unseen (L'Allegro)	M	D-G	†
-----	Lord, to thee each night and day (Theodora)	L	C-E	†
-----	O Lord whose mercies numberless (Saul)			
-----	O thou that tellest good tidings to Zion (The Messiah)	L	A-C	†
-----	Peaceful rest (Hercules)			
-----	Return, O God of hosts (Samson)	L	B-E	GSC
-----	Thou shalt bring them in (Israel in Egypt)	L	B-D	†
-----	What though I trace each herb and flower (Solomon)		CS-E	†
-----	Where shall I fly? (Hercules)			†
Mendelssohn	But the Lord is mindful of His own (Saint Paul)	L	A-D	†
-----	O rest in the Lord (Elijah)	L	B-D	†
-----	Woe unto them who forsake (Elijah)	L	B-E	†
Mozart	Laudamus Te (C Minor Mass)			PET
Parker	Gens duce splendida (Hora Novissima)			NOV
Pergolesi	Fac ut portem (Stabat Mater)			DES
Rossini	Fac ut portem (Stabat Mater)	L	B-G	DIT
Saint-Saëns	Expectans Dominum (Christmas Oratorio)			GSC
-----	Patiently (Christmas Oratorio)			
Sullivan	God shall wipe away all tears (The Light of the World)	L	B-E	GSC
-----	Love not the world (The Prodigal Son)	L		GSC
Verdi	Liber scriptus (The Requiem)			GSC

Cantata Arias

Contralto

Bach, J.S.	Ach, bleibe doch, mein liebstes Leben (Cantata 11) Violin		NOV

(Bach, J.S.)	Ach, es bleibt in meiner Liebe (Cantata 77) Trumpet	
-----	Ach Herr! was ist ein Menschenkind (Cantata 110) Oboe d'amore	AUG
-----	Ach, lege das Sodom (Cantata 48) Oboe or violin	
-----	Ach, schlaefrige Seele (Cantata 115)	AUG
-----	Ach, unaussprechlich ist die Not (Cantata 116) Oboe d'amore	NOV
-----	Betoerte Welt (Cantata 94) Flute	
-----	Christen muessen auf der Erden (Cantata 44) Oboe	
-----	Christi Glieder ach bedenket (Cantata 132) Violin	
-----	Die Obrigkeit ist Gottes Gabe (Cantata 119) Flute or Violin	NOV
-----	Ein ungefaerbt Gemuete (Cantata 24) Violin or viola	
-----	Ermuntert euch (Cantata 176) Oboe	BRO
-----	Es kommt ein Tag, so das Verborgne richtet (Cantata 136) Oboe d'amore	
-----	Gelobet sei der Herr (Cantata 129) Oboe d'amore	AUG
-----	Ich sehe schon im Geist (Cantata 43) 2 Oboes and continuo	NOV
-----	Ich traue seiner Gnaden (Cantata 97) Violin	PET
-----	Ich will doch wohl Rosen brechen (Cantata 86) Violin	
-----	In Jesu Demut (Cantata 151) Oboe d'amore or violin	
-----	Kein Arzt ist ausser Dir zu finden (Cantata 103) Violin or flute	
-----	Koennen nicht die roten Wangen (Cantata 205) Oboe d'amore	
-----	Kreuz und Krone (Cantata 12) Oboe	NOV
-----	Leget euch dem Heiland unter (Cantata 182) Flute or violin	BRO
-----	Mein glaeubiges Herze HML (Cantata 68)	†

(Bach, J.S.)	Schaeme dich, o Seele, nicht (Cantata 147) Oboe d'amore			
-----	Was Gott tut, das ist wohlgethan (Cantata 100, verse 5) Oboe d'amore			AUG
-----	Weh der Seele (Cantata 102) Oboe			BRO
-----	Willkommen! will ich sagen (Cantata 27) English horn			NOV
Bruch	Andromache's lament (Achilles)			
Gaul	Eye hath not seen (The Holy City)	ML	B-D	GSC
Handel	Dell bell' idolo mio (Cantata 2)			
-----	Vouchsafe, O Lord (Dettingen Te Deum)	HM		ELV
Mussorgsky	Oriental chant (Josua Navine Cantata)	ML	BF-E	GSC
Tunder	Wachet auf, ruft uns die Stimme (Tunder's Cantata)			BAR

Operetta, Musical Comedy
or Show Songs

Contralto

Coward	If love were all (Bitter Sweet)			HAR
De Koven	Oh promise me	HML	C-D	†
Friml	Huguette Waltz (The Vagabond King)			FAM
-----	Totem tom-tom (Rose Marie)			HAR
Herbert	I can't do that sum (Babes in Toyland)			WIT
-----	Moonbeams (The Red Mill)			WIT
-----	'Neath the southern moon (Naughty Marietta)			
Kern	Can't help lovin' dat man (Show Boat)	L	BF-EF	HAR
-----	Smoke gets in your eyes (Roberta)			HAR
Kreisler	Stars in my eyes (The King Steps Out)			CHA
Luders	The tale of the seashell (The Prince of Pilsen)			WIT

Porter	Begin the Beguine (Jubilee)	L	BF-F	HAR
-----	I've got you under my skin (Born to Dance)			CHA
-----	Night and day (Gay Divorcee)	M	BF-EF	HAR
-----	So in love (Kiss Me Kate)			CHA
Rodgers	I could write a book (Pal Joey)			CHA
-----	I'm falling in love with love (South Pacific)			BRO
-----	I'm in love with a wonderful guy (South Pacific)			CHA
-----	It might as well be spring (State Fair)			CHA
-----	June is bustin' out all over (Carousel)			WIL
-----	So far (Allegro)			CHA
Romberg	Mother (My Maryland)			HAR
Schwartz	Something to remember you by (Three's a Crowd)			HAR
Sullivan	I'm called Little Buttercup (H. M. S. Pinafore)			GSC
Wickham	Time for love (Rosalind)			
Youmans	Through the years (Through the Years)	HML	A-F	MLR
Yvain	My man (Ziegfeld Follies)			FEI

Song Cycles (or groups of songs)

Contralto

Bantock	Sappho			
Berger	Three songs on poems of Langston Hughes			
Bernstein	I hate music	H	C-A	WIT
Brahms	Two songs for alto, viola and piano	L		AMP
-----	Zigeuner Lieder			
Carpenter	Gitanjali	M	B-G	GSC
-----	Watercolors	M	C-F	GSC
Cornelius	Six Christmas songs	HL		BOS
Dvořák	Biblical songs	HL		AMP
-----	Gypsy songs	LH	D-A	AMP
Elgar	Sea pictures	L	A-A	BOO
Falla	El amor brujo	M		BRO
-----	Siete canciones	HL		AMP
Granados	La maja dolorosa	M		INT
Grieg	Five poems of Otto Benson			HAN

Griffes	Five poems of ancient China and Japan	M	AS-EF	GSC
Honegger	Quatre chansons pour voix grave			SAL
Kilpinen	Lieder um den Tod	M		AMP
Mahler	Kindertotenlieder	L	G-GF	INT
Mussorgsky	Songs and dances of death			INT
Poulenc	Le bestiaire String quartet, flute, clarinet and bassoon	M		AMP
Ravel	Cinq mélodies populaires grecques			
-----	Quatre chants populaires	M		DUR
Santoliquido	Three poesie persiane			FOR
Schoenberg	Das Buch der haengenden Gaerten			AMP
Schubert	Gesaenge des Harfners 1, 2 and 3			PET
Schumann	Frauenliebe und Leben	HL		GSC
Still	Songs of separation			LEE
Tchaikovsky	Three songs after Tolstoi Op. 38, 1, 2 and 3			
Villa-Lobos	Serestas			
Woodford-Finden	Indian love lyrics			BOO

Solo Cantatas

Contralto

Bach, J.S.	Geist und Seele wird verwirret (Cantata 35)	
-----	Schlage doch, gewuenschte Stunde (Cantata 53)	RIC
-----	Widerstehe doch der Suende (Cantata 54) Strings and continuo	
Bassani	Cantata for one voice	
Pergolesi	Salve Regina	

See Solo Cantatas of Pergolesi, Handel and
Scarlatti, Kirchenkantaten of Buxtehude and
Symphoniae Sacrae of Schuetz.

Concert Arias

Contralto

Haydn	Ariadne auf Naxos (Concert Aria)			
Mozart	Ombra felice			INT

Christmas Songs

Contralto

Adam	O Holy night			†
Andrews	I heard the bells on Christmas day	L	A-E	GAL
Bach, J.S.	Prepare thyself Zion (Christmas Oratorio)			
-----	Schlafe, mein Liebster (Christmas Oratorio)			
-----	Von der Welt verlang ich nichts (Cantata 64) Oboe d'amore			
Bacon	Ancient Christmas carol			NEM
Baldwin	Little Lordeen	L	BF-EF	WIT
Bax	A Christmas carol	H	DF-A	CHE
Berlin	White Christmas (Holiday Inn)			BER
Brahms	Geistliches Wiegenlied Piano and viola			†
Branscombe	Hail ye time of holidays			
Bush	I saw a maiden fair	L	C-DF	GRA
Candlyn	The song of Mary	M	B-D	GRA
Coerne	A rhyme for Christmas-tide	L	CS-CS	DIT
De Koven	The white Christ	L	C-D	GSC
Dunhill	To the Queen of Heaven	M	C-G	GSC
Elmore and Reed	Come all ye who weary	L	C-C	JFI
Evans	The Virgin had a baby	L	C-EF	BOH
Grieg	Christmas song			AUG
Handel	O thou that tellest good tidings to Zion (The Messiah)	L	A-C	†
Harker	A child is born in Bethlehem	LH	D-G	GSC
Head	Slumber song of the Madonna	HL		BOO
Herbert	Toyland (Babes in Toyland)			WIT
Holmès	Noël d'Irlande	HL		DIT

Humperdinck	Weihnachten			
Ives	A Christmas carol			NEM
Liddle	An old French carol	LM		BOO
Lynn	Gently little Jesus	L	BF-BF	DIT
-----	The magic night of Christmas	M	D-D	DIT
Martin	The Holy Child	HML	G-G	ENO
McKinney	The Holy Mother sings	MH	AF-AF	JFI
Neidlinger	The manger cradle	L	EF-F	GSC
Niles	The cherry tree			GSC
Owen	Lute book lullaby	L	A-D	GRA
Prokoff	Christmas cradle song	LM	D-E	CHA
Reger	The Virgin's slumber song	MMH	G-G	†
Rodney	A dream of Bethlehem	MML	G-DF	ENO
Saint-Saëns	Expectans Dominum (Christmas Oratorio)			GSC
Taylor	Christmas folk song	L	BF-EF	GRA
Thiman	In the bleak midwinter	L	A-E	NOV
Warren	Christmas candle	HML	D-E	GSC
Wentzel	Lamkins Cello and piano			GRA
Wolf	Schlafendes Jesuskind	HL	AS-F	†
Yon	Gesu Bambino	HL	B-E	JFI

Easter Songs

Contralto

Bach, J.S.	Hochgelobter Gottessohn (Cantata 6) English horn or viola or violin			NOV
-----	Ich will nach dem Himmel zu (Cantata 146) Violin			BRO
-----	Jesus from the grave is risen	M	F-EF	CFI
-----	Zum reinen Wasser (Cantata 112) Oboe d'amore			NOV
Barnes	Easter	HM	D-EF	GSC
Cadman	Hail joyous morn	HL	BF-DF	WIL
Coleridge-Taylor	Easter morn	MH	DF-AF	BOO
Curran	Crucifixion			
Diack	All in the April evening	LMH	D-G	BOO
Duke	Calvary	L	G-F	CFI
Harker	As it began to dawn	ML	G-DF	GSC
La Forge	Before the Crucifix	HML	BF-EF	GSC
Mac Farlane	On wings of living light	MH	D-G	GSC

MacGimsey	I was there when they crucified my Lord	HL		CFI
O'Hara	There is no death	LMH	EF-AF	CHA
Parker	Come see the place	HL		GSC
Rachmaninoff	Christ is risen	LM	D-F	GAL
Schubert	Ave Maria	LMH	F-F	†
Turner	Hail your risen Lord	HL	C-D	GSC
Yon	O faithful Cross	HM	C-EF	JFI
-----	Our Paschal Joy	LH	AF-AF	JFI

Patriotic Songs

Contralto

Bone and Fenton	Prayer for a waiting world	L		CFI
Bowles	An American hero	M	E-E	AXE
Chadwick	He maketh wars to cease	ML		ASC
Dungan	Eternal life	HL		PRE
Foster, F.	The Americans come	MH	F-BF	JFI
Lester	Greater love hath no man	LH	B-E	CFI
O'Hara	There is no death	LMH	EF-AF	CHA
Steffe	Battle hymn of the Republic			
Ward-Stephens	Phantom legions	MHH	EF-BF	CHA

Sacred Songs

Contralto

Bach, J.S.	Draw near to me	HML		GSC
Beethoven	The worship of God in nature			
Bitgood	Be still and know that I am God	ML		GRA
-----	The greatest of these is love	M		GRA
Bizet	O Lord be merciful	HL		GSC
Bone and Fenton	First Psalm	LM	DF-F	CFI
-----	They word is a lamp	LH	C-F	ROW
Brown	What are these which are arrayed	HLM	C-F	ASC
Buck	Fear not ye, O Israel	HLM		GSC
-----	Until God's day	L	BF-EF	GSC

Campbell-Tipton	I will give thanks unto the Lord	LMH	DF-AF	GSC
Candlyn	God that madest earth and heaven	M	C-F	GRA
Chadwick	A ballad of trees and the Master	HML	A-F	DIT
Charles	Incline Thine ear	HL	BF-D	GSC
Clokey	God is in everything	LH	D-G	JFI
Davis	Be ye kind, one to another	L		GAL
-----	Let not your heart be troubled	HML		WOO
Dickinson	Roads	L		GRA
Dvořák	By the waters of Babylon			AMP
-----	God is my shepherd			AMP
-----	Hear my prayer, O Lord			AMP
-----	I will life mine eyes			AMP
-----	Sing ye a joyful song			AMP
-----	Turn Thee to me			AMP
Edmunds	Praise we the Lord	HL	D-D	ROW
Goodhall	The mountain	M	D-E	GAL
Gounod	O Divine Redeemer	LMH	C-G	GSC
Green	Praised be the Lord	M	C-F	OXF
Guion	Prayer	HL		GSC
-----	The cross bearer	HM	B-DS	GSC
Handel	Thanks be to Thee	M	CS-E	†
Henschel	Morning-hymn	MH	DS-GS	†
Holst	The heart worships	ML	BF-D	STB
Kountz	What shall I ask?	L		GAL
La Forge	They that trust in the Lord	HL	BF-EF	GAL
-----	What shall I render unto the Lord?	HL	C-D	GSC
Lederer	Psalm 104	L	A-E	CFI
Liddle	How lovely are Thy dwellings	HML		BOS
MacDermid	In my Father's house are many mansions	HML		FRS
MacGimsey	Think on these things	LM	BF-EF	CFI
Malotte	The Lord's prayer			
-----	The twenty-third Psalm	HLM	C-F	GSC
McGill	Thine eternal peace	HL	A-CS	GSC
Mendelssohn	But the Lord is mindful of His own (Saint Paul)	L	A-D	†
-----	O rest in the Lord (Elijah)	L	B-D	†
-----	Woe unto them who forsake him (Elijah)	L	B-E	†

O'Connor and				
Morris	Fill thou my life, O Lord	L	BF-EF	CFI
O'Hara	Art thou the Christ?	HML	A-D	GSC
Rogers	Out of the depths	HL		ASC
Sanderson	Green pastures	HL	BF-EF	BOO
Schubert	The Omnipotent			
-----	To the Infinite			
Scott	Consider the lilies	HL	C-E	GSC
-----	Ride on, ride on	HML		FLA
Speaks	Thou wilt keep him in	HML		GSC
	perfect peace			
Stickles	Saith the Lord	LH	D-F	CHA
Sullivan	Love not the world	L		GSC
	(The Prodigal Son)			
Tchaikovsky	Lord, Almighty God	M		GRA
	(Moscow Cantata)			
Thompson	My Master hath a garden	M		ECS
Voris	Song of mothers	LH	D-FS	GRA
Watts	Intreat me not to leave	L	A-F	GSC
	thee			
Weaver	Build Thee more stately	M	C-E	GAL
	mansions			
Wolf	Gebet	HL		†

Wedding Songs

Contralto

Beethoven	Ich liebe dich	HL	BF-DF	†
Bond	I love you truly			BOS
De Koven	Oh promise me	HML	C-D	†
	(Robin Hood)			
Franck	O Lord most Holy	LM	A-FS	BOS
Grieg	I love thee	HML	E-F	†
Lippe	How do I love thee?			BOS
Luzzi	Ave Maria	HL	BF-EF	GSC
Sacco	With this ring	M	F-F	BVC
Schubert	Du bist die Ruh	LMH	EF-AF	†
-----	Ungeduld	HML		†
Schumann	Du Ring an meinem	HL	C-F	†
	Finger			
-----	Widmung	HL	BF-F	†
Thiman	The God of love my	ML	A-D	NOV
	Shepherd is			
Youmans	Through the years	HML	A-F	MLR
	(Through the Years)			

Songs and Arias With Added
Accompanying Instrument

Contralto

Bach, J.S.	Ach, bleibe doch, mein liebstes Leben (Cantata 11) Violin	NOV
-----	Ach, es bleibt in meiner Liebe (Cantata 77) Trumpet	
-----	Ach Herr! was ist ein Menschenkind (Cantata 110) Oboe d'amore	AUG
-----	Ach, lege das Sodom (Cantata 48) Oboe or violin	
-----	Ach, unaussprechlich ist die Not (Cantata 116) Oboe d'amore	NOV
-----	Betoerte Welt (Cantata 94) Flute	
-----	Christen muessen auf der Erden (Cantata 44) Oboe	
-----	Christi Glieder, ach bedenket (Cantata 132) Violin	
-----	Die Obrigkeit ist Gottes Gabe (Cantata 119) Flute or violin	NOV
-----	Ein ungefaerbt Gemuete (Cantata 24) Violin or viola	
-----	Ermuntert euch (Cantata 176) Oboe	BRO
-----	Es kommt ein Tag so das Verborgne richtet (Cantata 136) Oboe d'amore	
-----	Gelobet sei der Herr (Cantata 129) Oboe d'amore	AUG
------	Hochgelobter Gottessohn (Cantata 6) English horn or viola or violin	NOV
-----	Ich will doch wohl Rosen brechen (Cantata 86) Violin	
-----	Ich will nach dem Himmel zu (Cantata 146) Violin	BRO
-----	In Jesu Demut (Cantata 151) Oboe d'amore or violin	AUG
-----	Jesus ist ein guter Hirt (Cantata 85) Violin or cello	RIC
-----	Kein Arzt ist ausser Dir zu finden (Cantata 103) Violin or flute	
-----	Kreuz und Krone (Cantata 12) Oboe	NOV

(Bach, J.S.)	Leget euch dem Heiland unter (Cantata 182) Flute or violin			BRO
-----	Schaeme dich, o Seele, nicht (Cantata 147) Oboe d'amore			
-----	Von der Welt verlang ich nichts Cantata 64) Oboe d'amore			
-----	Wat Gott tut, das ist wohlgethan (Cantata 100, verse 5) Obbe d'amore			AUG k
-----	Weh der Seele (Cantata 102) Oboe			BRO
-----	Widerstehe doch der Suende (Cantata 54) Strings and continuo			
-----	Willkommen! will ich sagen (Cantata 27) English horn			NOV
-----	Zum reinen Wasser (Cantata 112) Oboe d'amore			NOV
Barber	Dover Beach String quartet	M	BF-F	GSC
Brahms	Geistliches Wiegenlied Piano and viola			†
-----	Gestillte Sehnsucht Viola and piano			†
Buxtehude	Jubilate domino Viola di gamba and harpsichord			UGR
-----	Singet dem Herrn Violin and piano			
Chausson	Le colibri Violin or cello	M	F-GF	BOS
Honegger	Chanson (Ronsard) Flute and string quartet			SEN
Leroux	Le nil Cello or violin	LH	E-A	†
Mana-Zucca	Rachem Trumpet	HML		CHA
Poulenc	Le bestiaire String quartet, flute, clarinet and bassoon	M		AMP
Wentzel	Lamkins Cello and piano			GRA

209

American and British Songs of Limited Range

Mezzo Soprano or Contralto

Anderson	Song of Mary	M	D-E	WES
Balfe	Killarney	H	D-E	GSC
Barber	A Nun takes the veil	MH	G-G	GSC
-----	Monks and raisons	M	DF-E	GSC
-----	Rain has fallen	HM	D-E	GSC
Bartholomew	Dearest Billie	M	E-E	GSC
Bax	Oh dear what can the matter be	M	D-EF	CHE
Bloch	The vagabond	M	E-E	GSC
Boatner	Oh what a beautiful city	HL	D-E	GSC
-----	On mah journey	LH	EF-EF	RIC
Bowles	Cabin	ML	CS-CS	GSC
-----	Letter to Freddy	M	EF-EF	GSC
Branscombe	Across the blue Aegean	M	G-G	GAL
Burleigh	Joshua fit de battle ob Jericho	LH	DS-E	RIC
Carpenter	Don't ceare	M	C-D	GSC
-----	If	M	D-E	GSC
-----	Odalisque	M	EF-EF	GSC
Carter	Dust of snow	M	D-E	AMP
Clokey	The storke	M	C-D	JFI
De Koven	Oh promise me (Robin Hood)	HML	C-D	GSC
Dello Joio	Mill doors	M	D-E	CFI
-----	New born	M	C-D	CFI
Dougherty	Declaration of independence	L	C-C	GSC
-----	Sonatina	M	E-FS	GSC
Dowland	Awake sweet love	M	E-F	STB
-----	Come again, sweet love	M	D-E	STB
-----	Flow, my tears	M	D-E	STB
-----	Now, O now, I needs must part	M	D-D	DIT
-----	Sorrow, sorrow stay	M	D-D	BOS
Duke	Loveliest of trees	L	C-D	GSC
Gibbs	Five eyes	HL	D-D	BOS
Green	Salvation belongeth unto the Lord	M	F-EF	OXF
Guion	Mam'selle Marie	M	D-E	GSC
Hadley	My shadow	M	D-E	ASC
Hageman	Animal crackers	HL	C-D	GSC
Handel	Art thou troubled	M	F-F	GSC
-----	He shall feed His flock (The Messiah)	L	C-D	GSC

(Handel)	Love's a dear deceitful jewel	LH	F-F	RBR
Harris	Agatha Morley	M	C-D	CFI
Hindemith	Envoy	M	EF-F	AMP
-----	The whistling thief	M	E-F	AMP
Holst	The heart worships			
Hook	Bright Phoebus	M	EF-F	GSC
Howe	Berceuse	HM	FF-F	GSC
Hughes	Open the door softly	LMH	G-G	ENO
Johnson	Roll Jerd'n roll	M	EF-F	GSC
Kramer	Our lives together	HL	D-E	GAL
Mac Dowell	The Sea	HL	D-D	BRH
Mac Gimsey	Sweet little Jesus Boy	ML	D-D	CFI
-----	Trouble	ML	C-D	CFI
Manning	Shoes	M	EF-F	GSC
Metcalf	At nightfall	HML	C-DF	ASC
Milford	So sweet love seemed	HL	D-D	GRA
Naginski	Night song at Amalfi	M	D-EF	GSC
Payne	Crucifixion	L	C-C	GSC
Peterkin	The garden of bamboos	M	EF-F	OXF
Porter, Q.	Music when soft voices die	HM	D-C	MUP
Quilter	Drink to me only	LMH	GF-GF	BOH
-----	Ye banks and braes	M	DF-EF	BOO
Ronald	Love I have won you	HML	EF-EF	ENO
Rosseter	When Laura smiles	LM	D-E	STB
Rummel	Ecstasy	LMH	GF-AF	GSC
Sacco	Mexican serenade	HL	D-EF	BOS
Sargent	Double feature	M	C-D	DIT
-----	Stopping by woods	M	D-E	GSC
-----	Three a.m.	M	DF-E	GSC
Scott	Think on me	HML	D-EF	GAL
-----	Wailie wailie	M	D-E	DIT
Shaw	Song of the palanquin bearers	LH	E-F	CUR
Speaks	In May time	HL	D-E	JCH
Stephenson	Love is a sickness	HML	C-D	BOO
-----	Ships that pass in the night	HML	DF-DF	BOO
Vaughn Williams	King William	L	D-D	OXF
-----	Linden Lea	HML	C-D	BOS
-----	Robin Hood and the pedlar	M	D-E	OXF
-----	The water mill	L	C-D	OXF
Warlock	Have you seen but a white lily grow	M	E-F	OXF
-----	Rest sweet nymphs	M	F-F	CFI
-----	The night	M	D-E	OXF

French Songs of Limited Range

Mezzo Soprano or Contralto

David	Charmant oiseau (La Perle du Bresil)	M	D-E	GSC
Duparc	Lamento	M	EF-EF	BOS
-----	L'invitation au voyage	HM	E-F	O
Fauré	Adieu	MH	F-F	MAR
-----	Arpege	MH	E-FS	HAM
-----	Dans les ruines d'une abbaye	M	E-FS	GSC
-----	La fée aux chansons	LH	F-F	HAM
-----	Le parfum imperissable	LH	GF-GF	
-----	Mandoline	HL	F-E	GSC
-----	Serenade Toscane	MH	G-AF	HAM
-----	Spleen	H	E-FS	MAR
Ferrari	Le jardin d'amour	LM	EF-F	GSC
Franck	Le mariage des roses	M	E-FS	BOS
-----	Lied	LH	FS-FS	
Hue	J'ai pleuré en rêve	HL	D-E	BOS
Lalo	Chant Breton	M	E-E	HAM
Lully	Au clair de la lune	M	E-D	CFI
Massenet	Crepuscule	M	D-E	GSC
Poldowski	Effet de neige	M	EF-F	CHE
Poulenc	Reine des mouettes	M	EF-F	SAL
Saint Saens	Mai	H	G-FS	DUR
Weckerlin	Aminte	M	C-D	GSC

German Songs of Limited Range

Mezzo Soprano or Contralto

Ahle	Bruenstiges Verlangen	M	E-E	GSC
Beethoven	An die Geliebte	M	E-E	AUG
-----	Freudvoll und Leidvoll	M	DS-E	GSC
Brahms	Bei dir sind meine Gedanken	MH	E-FS	GSC
-----	Das Maedchen spricht	H	E-FS	CFI
-----	Der Schmied	HL	EF-EF	GSC
-----	Dort in den Weiden	LH	A-A	CFI
-----	Klage	LH	FS-FS	CFI
-----	Mein Maedel hat einen Rosenmund	M	F-F	GSC
-----	Mit vierzig Jahren	HL	FS-D	CFI
-----	Muss es eine Trennung geben	LH	FS-FS	CFI
-----	O wuesst ich doch dem Weg zurueck	H	E-FS	CFI

(Brahms)	Treue Liebe	LMH	DS-E	GSC
Franz	Er ist gekommen	HL	EF-F	DIT
-----	For music	ML	C-D	DIT
-----	Sterne mit den gold'nen Fuesschen	HL	DS-E	DIT
-----	Stille Sicherheit	M	E-F	GSC
Haydn	My mother bids me bind my hair	M	E-E	GSC
-----	She never told her love	M	D-EF	
Liszt	Die Lorelei	LH	BF-BF	CFI
Loewe	Walpurgisnacht	H	G-G	SC
Mendelssohn	An die Entfernte	M	F-F	
-----	Bei der Wiege	M	DF-EF	GSC
-----	Pagenlied	M	E-E	
-----	Schilflied	M	F-FS	
Mozart	Abendempfindung	M	E-F	
-----	Warnung	HM	C-D	
-----	Wiegenlied	MH	G-G	GSC
Reger	Des kindes Gebet	H	F-G	BOT
Schubert	An den Mond	HL	F-GF	GSC
-----	Auf dem Flusse	HL	F-E	GSC
-----	Der Koenig in Thule	L	F-F	PET
-----	Der Musensohn	LH	FS-G	DIT
-----	Der Schmetterling	LH	E-F	DIT
-----	Der Zwerg	M	A-GF	PET
-----	Die Hoffnung	HM	E-E	
-----	Die Rose	M	G-FS	PET
-----	Du liebst mich nicht	LH	E-FS	GSC
-----	Fruehlingsglaube Sehnsucht	M	EF-F	GSC
-----	Im Abendrot	HL	C-D	GSC
-----	Lob der Traenen	LM	F-F	GSC
-----	Nacht und Traeume	HL	C-DF	CFI
-----	Sei mir gegruesst	LH	G-G	GSC
-----	Seufzer	M	CS-D	BIR
-----	Wanderers Nachlied, 2	LH	F-F	GSC
Schumann	Alte Laute	HL	DF-DF	DIT
-----	Du bist wie eine Blume	HM	F-EF	GSC
-----	Erstes gruen	HL	D-D	GSC
-----	Marienwuermchen	HL	D-D	GSC
-----	Mondnacht	M	E-FS	GSC
-----	Seit ich ihn gesehen	HL	DF-DF	GSC
-----	Wenn ich in deine Augen seh	HL	EF-EF	GSC
Wolf	Morgenthau	M	C-C	PRE

Italian Songs of Limited Range

Mezzo Soprano or Contralto

Bononcini	Deh piu a me non v'ascondete	LH	EF-F	GSC
Caccini	Amarilli, mia bella	ML	C-D	GSC
Caldara	Sebben crudele	HML	E-DS	GSC
-----	Selve amiche, ombrose piante	HM	E-E	GSC
Carissimi	A morire	ML	C-D	
Cesti	Ah! quanto è vero (Il Pomo d'Oro)	HL	F-F	DIT
-----	Che angoscia che affanno (Il Pomo d'Oro)	HL	C-DF	DIT
Cimara	Fiocca la neve	LMH	G-G	GSC
Donaudy	O del mio amato ben	M	EF-F	RIC
Falconieri	Non più d'amore	HL	C-D	DIT
-----	Nude arciero	HL	AF-AF	DIT
Gasparini	Caro laccio dolce nodo	M	EF-EF	GSC
Handel	Cara sposa (Rinaldo)	M	CS-D	
-----	Rendi'l aereno al ciglio (Sosarme)	LH	EF-F	GSC
Legrenzi	Che fiero costume	HML	C-D	GSC
Lotti	Pur dicesti, o bocca bella	LMH	E-FS	GSC
Monteverdi	Lasciatomi morire	ML	D-D	DIT
Paradies	M'ha preso alla sua ragna	M	EF-F	GSC
Pergolesi	Nina	HL	CS-D	DIT
Provenzale	Deh rendetemi	ML	D-D	DIT
Rontani	Se bel rio	ML	D-C	GSC
Scarlatti, A.	Chi vuole innamorarsi	HL	D-EF	DIT
-----	O cessate di piagarmi	HL	DS-E	GSC
-----	Se Florindo è fedele	LM	EF-EF	GSC
Stradella	Col mio sangue comprenderei (Il Floridoro)	HL	E-F	DIT
Tosti	La Serenata	HLM	D-EF	GSC

Other Songs of Limited Range

Mezzo Soprano or Contralto

Alnaes	En morgen var din grav	M	CS-D	HAN
Bantock	Easter hymn	M	FS-F	CHE
Beethoven	A prayer	M	EF-F	BIR
Borodin	A dissonance	MH	E-F	GSC
Buck	The Virgin's lullaby	HL	B-CS	GSC

214

Bush	I saw a maiden fair	L	C-DF	GRA
Chopin	Lithuanian song	ML	C-C	GSC
Cui	The statue at Czarskoe Selo	HM	DF-EF	DIT
Dvořák	Songs my mother taught me	HM	E-E	GSC
Edmunds	Praise we the Lord	HL	D-D	ROW
Elmore-Reed	Come all ye who weary	L	C-C	JFI
Falla	Chanson du feu follet	L	B-B	CHE
Franck	O Lord most Holy	LM	A-FS	BOS
Goodhall	The mountain	M	D-E	GAL
Gounod	There is a green hill far away	LMH	E-F	GSC
Grandi-Clokey	O fair art thou	ML	BF-C	JFI
Grieg	Hunter's song	L	DS-E	GSC
-----	I love thee	HML	E-F	GSC
-----	In the boat	LM	D-ES	DIT
-----	The old mother	ML	D-D	DIT
-----	To Norway	M	E-F	DIT
Hinchliffe	Tranquillity	M	E-F	CFI
Jacob	Shepherd	M	E-FS	OXF
Lynn	Gently little Jesus	L	BF-BF	DIT
-----	The magic night of Christmas	M	D-D	DIT
Martin	The Holy Child	HML	G-G	ENO
Mussorgsky	Divination by water (Khovantchina)	L	GS-FS	GSC
Neidlinger	The manger cradle	L	EF-F	GSC
Niles	Our lovely lady singing	M	EF-F	GSC
O'Connor	Alleluia	ML	D-D	BOO
Prokoff	Christmas cradle	LM	D-E	CHA
Rachmaninoff	To the children	MH	F-G	DIT
Reger	The Virgin's slumber song	MH	G-G	DIT
Reimann	Joseph tender, Joseph mine	M	F-F	GRA
Schubert	They sang that night in Bethlehem	LMH	EF-EF	GSC
Scott	The first Easter morn	LH	F-G	GSC
Stevenson	Praise	M	F-F	CFI
Tchaikovsky	A legend	M	D-E	GSC
Turner	Hail your risen Lord	HL	C-D	GSC
Tuthill	Prayer for those at home	HL	C-D	BOH
Valverde	Clavelitos	MH	E-F	GSC
Vaughn Williams	And all in the morning	L	D-E	GAL
Warlock	The first mercy	M	F-F	BOO
Warren	Christmas candle	HML	D-E	GSC

Mezzo Soprano or Contralto

Balfe	This is they deed (Bohemian Girl)	A&BS	
Bellini	Mira o Norma (Norma)	S&A	RIC
Berlioz	Reine d'un jeune empire (Les Troyens)	M&A or S&A	
Cilea	Io son sua per l'amor (Adriana Lecouvreur)	S&A	SON
Debussy	Duo de la lettre (Pelleas et Melisande)	A&Br	DUR
Delibes	Sous le dome épais (Lakmé)	S&A	GSC
Donizetti	Ah! mio bene (La Favorita)	A&T	BRO
-----	Al bel destin (Linda di (Chamounix)	S&A	
-----	Mad Scene (Linda di Chamounix)	S&A	
-----	Quando le soglie paterne (La Favorita)	A&Bs	BRO
-----	Vieni, ah vien (La Favorita)	A&T	BRO
Gluck	Duet, Act Three (Orfeo ed Euridice)	S&A	DUR
Humperdinck	Abendsegen (Haensel und Gretel)	S&A	AMP
Lalo	En silence pourquoi souffrir? (Le Roi d'Ys)	S&A	HEU
Massenet	C'est le soir la brise pure (Le Roi de Lahore)	S&A	HEU
Meyerbeer	Pour garder a ton fils (Le Prophet)	S&A	
Mozart	Ah, perdona al primo affetto (La Clemenza di Tito)	S&A	ECS
Offenbach	Belle Nuit-Barcarolle (Tales of Hoffman)	S&A	GSC
Puccini	Tutti i fior (Madama Butterfly)	S&A	RIC
Rossini	Bell image (Semiramide)	A&Bs	
-----	Serbami ognor si fido (Semiramide)	S&A	
Strauss	Herr Cavalier (Der Rosenkavalier)	A&Bs	BOO
Tchaikovsky	Tis evening (Pique Dame)	S&A	GSC
Thomas	As-tu souffert? (Mignon)	A&Bs	HEU

Verdi	Ai nostri monti (Il Trovatore)	A&T	GSC
-----	Già i sacerdoti adunansi (Aida)	A&T	GSC
-----	Mal reggendo all'aspro assalto (Il Trovatere)	A&T	GSC
-----	Si la stanchezza (Il Trovatore)	A&T	CFI

Operetta Duets

Mezzo Soprano or Contralto

Berlin	It's a lovely day today (Call Me Madam)	A&Br	BER
-----	You're just in love (Call Me Madam)	A&Br	BER
Caryll	Wait till the cows come home (Jack o Lantern)	A&Br	CHA
Herbert	A kiss in the dark (Orange Blossoms)	A&Bs or A&Br	WIT
-----	Because you're you (The Red Mill)	A&Br A&T	WIT
-----	Gypsy love song (The Fortune Teller)	A&Bs or A&T	WIT
-----	In the isle of our dreams (The Red Mill)	A&Br	WIT
-----	Kiss me again (Mlle. Modiste)	A&T	WIT
-----	Moonbeams (The Red Mill)	A&T	WIT
-----	Thine Alone (Eileen)	A&T	WIT
-----	When you're away (The Only Girl)	A&T	
Heuberger	Im chambre separée (Der Opernball)	A&Bs	
Lehar	My little nest of heavenly blue (Frasquita)	A&Br	MAR
-----	Wenn zwei sich lieben (Der Rastelbinder)	A&T	WEI
Porter	In the still of the night (Rosalie)	A&B	CHA
Rodgers	You'll never walk alone (Carousel)	A&Br	CHA
Romberg	Deep in my heart dear (The Student Prince)	A&T	HAR
-----	Once upon a time	A&T	WIT

Youmans	Tea for two (No, No, Nanette)	S&A	HAR

Oratorio, Mass or Cantata Duets

Mezzo Soprano or Contralto

Bach, J. S.	Beruft Gett Selbst (Cantata 88)	S&A	
-----	Ten Ted (Cantata 4)	S&A	NOV
-----	Die Armut se Gott auf sich nimmt – with violin (Cantata 91)	S&A	
-----	Du wahrer Gott und David's Sohn -obbligati of 2 oboes (Cantata 23)	S&A	BRO
-----	Er kennt die rechten freunden Student violin or small choir (Cantata 93)	S&A	NOV
-----	Gedenk an Jesu bittern Tod – flute and english horn or violin and viola (Cantata 101)	S&A	
-----	Gottes Wert – English horn or viola (Cantata 167)	S&A	
-----	Herr du siehst – flute & oboe d'amore or 2 violins or violin, viola (Cantata 9)	S&A	
-----	Ich fuerchte Zwar des Grabes (Cantata 66)	A&T	
-----	Wenn des Kreuzes bitter- keiten – flute and oboe or 2 violins or violin and viola (Cantata 99)	S&A	
-----	Wenn Sorgen auf mich dringen – violin or oboe d'amore (Cantata 3)	S&A	
-----	Wir eilen – cello obbligato (Cantata 78)	S&A	BRO
Elgar	Doubt not Thy Father's care (The Light of Life)	S&A	NOV
Handel	O Fairest of ten thousand (Saul)	S&A	NOV
-----	O peerless maid (Joshua)	S&A	NOV
-----	Our limpid streams (Joshua)	S&A	NOV
-----	Smiling Freedom (Deborah)	S&A	NOV

(Handel)	Where do thy ardours (Deborah)	S&A	NOV
-----	These labours past	S&A	NOV
Mendelssohn	I waited for the Lord (Hymn of Praise)	S&A	GSC
Pergolesi	Quando corpus morietur (Stabat Mater)	S&A	ECS

British Song Duets

Mezzo Soprano or Contralto

Beethoven	Sweet Power of Song	S&A	ECS
-----	Where flowers were springing	S&A	ECS
Huhn	Be Thou exalted	A&Br	GSC
Keel	You spotted snakes	S&A	BOU
Lawes	The Angler's Song	S&A	ECS
Morley	Sweet Nymph	S&A	ECS
Purcell	Let us wander	S&A	AUG
-----	Lost is my quiet	S&A	AUG
-----	Shepherd leave decoying	S&A	AUG
-----	Sound the trumpet	S&A	AUG
-----	We the spirits of the air	S&A	
Ronald	Down in the forest	A&Br	BOH
-----	O lovely night	A&Br	ENO
Somervell	Under the greenwood tree	S&A	BOO
Thiman	Spring wind	S&A	BOO

French Song Duets

Mezzo Soprano or Contralto

Chausson	La nuit	S&A	HAM
Franck	L'ange gardien	S&A	
-----	O Lord most holy	S&A	BOS
-----	The Virgin by the manger	S&A	GSC
Paladilhe	Au bord de l'eau	S&A	HEU

German Song Duets

Mezzo Soprano or Contralto

Brahms	Am Strande	S&A	PET

(Brahms)	Der Jaeger und sein Liebchen	A&Br	PET
------	Die Beten der Liebe	S&A	PET
------	Die Meere	S&A	PET
------	Die Nonne und der Ritter	A&Br	PET
------	Die Schwestern	S&A	
------	Edward	A&T	
------	Es rauschet das Wasser	A&Br	
------	Four Duets for alto and baritone with piano, Op. 28	A&Br	PET
------	Four Duets for Soprano and Contralto	S&A	
------	Guter Rat	S&A	PET
------	Klaenge	S&A	
------	Klosterfraeulein	S&A	PET
------	Phaenomen	S&A	
------	Three duets for Soprano and Alto	S&A	
------	Vor der Tuer	A&Br	
------	Weg der Liebe, 1	S&A	PET
------	Weg der Liebe, 2	S&A	PET
Mendelssohn	Gruess	S&A	WOO
------	I would that my love	S&A	NOV
------	My bark is bound to the gale	S&A	
------	The Sabbath morn	S&A	NOV
Reger	Schnee	S&A	
Rubenstein	Meeresabend	S&A	PET
Schumann	Ich bin dein Baum	A&Bs	PET
------	Schoen Bluemelein	S&A	PET
------	Unter'm Fenster	S&A	

Italian Song Duets

Mezzo Soprano or Contralto

Clari	Cantando un di	S&A	ECS
------	Long live song	S&A	ECS
------	Sventurato son	S&A	ECS
Handel	Beato in ver chi puo	S&A	PET
------	Fronda leggiera e mobile	S&A	PET
------	No di voi nun vo fidarmi, 1	S&A	PET
------	No di voi non vo fidarmi, 2	S&A	PET
Legrenzi	Fierezza si vaga	S&A	
Lully	Bel tempo che vola	S&A	ECS
Monteverdi	Ohime dov'e il mio ben	S&A	
Rossi	Vo fuggir lontan da te two violins	S&A	PET

Steffani	Occhi perche piangete	S&A	

Mezzo Soprano or Contralto

Couperin	Venite exultemus domino - organ	S&A	
Mendelssohn	They have taken away my Lord	S&A	ECS
Rubinstein	Der Engel	S&A	PET
-----	Im heilischen Land	S&A	PET

Trios

Mezzo Soprano or Contralto

Handel	Disdainful of danger (Judas Maccabaeus)	T&A&Bs	NOV
Menotti	Trio (TheConsul)	S&A&Br	GSC
Offenbach	Tu ne chanteras plus (Tales of Hoffman)	S&Ms&B	GSC
Ponchielli	Figlia che reggi il tremulo piè (La Gioconda)	S&A&T	RIC
Saint-Saens	Je viens celebrer la victoire (Samson et Dalila)	A&T&Bs	DUR
Talbot	The joy of life (The Arcadians)	T&A&Br	CHA
Verdi	Della citta all occaso (Un Dallo in Maschera)	S&A&T	
-----	Vieni! o diletta (Aida)	S&A&T	

Contemporary Chamber Operas

Mezzo Soprano or Contralto

		(minutes)	
Barab	Game of Chance	35 2S, M, BS-BR	BOO
-----	Reba	40 T, S, C, BR	BOO
Bucci	The Dress	28 three	CHA
deBanfield	Lord Byron's love letter	70 2S, C, T	RIC
diGiovanni	Medea	60 S, C, T, BR, & cho.	SPA
Elkus	Tom Sawyer	60 S, C, BS	NOV
Floyd	Slow Dusk	38 S, M, T, BR	BOO
Haubiel	Sunday costs five pesos	35 S, C, &T	CMP

Johnson	A letter to Emily		S, M, BR, BS-BR	MER
Lochram	A letter to Emily	40	S, M, BAR, BS-BR	MER
Low	Rapunzel	40	S, C, BAR	SOU
Martin	The marriage	90	S, M, T, BAR	BOO
Mennini	The Rope	48	C, T, BAR, BS	BOO
Menotti	The Old Maid and the Thief	55	2S, M, BAR	RIC
Moore	Gallantry	35	BR, S, M, T (dancers opt.)	GSC
Petit	The Game of Love and Chance	25	S, M, BAR	MER
Phillips	Don't We All	30	four	
Ratner	The Necklace	40	S, M, BAR	MER
Siegmeister	Miranda and the Dark Young Man	60	S, M, BAR, BS-BAR	TEM
Stravinsky	Mavra	30	S, M, C, T	BOO

Standard Chamber Operas

Mezzo Soprano or Contralto

Bizet	Djamileh	60	M, T, BR speaker & cho.	PET
Cadman	The Willow Tree	55	S, C, T, BR	MER
Gluck	Orfeo ed Euridice	120	3S, M, Ch	GSC
Massenet	Portrait of Manon	45	S, M, T, BR, cho	MER
Mascagni	Zanetto	69	S, M or T	SON
Monteverdi	Orfeo	60	S, C, T, BS, sp	AMP
Mozart	Bastien and Bastienne	35	3	MAR
Offenbach	Marriage by lanternlight	35	2S, M, T	WIT
Pergolesi	Jealous Husband	100	S, M, T, BS	MER